IT'S
NOBODY'S
FAULT

IT'S NOBODY'S FAULT

New Hope and Help for
Difficult Children and Their Parents

HAROLD S. KOPLEWICZ, M.D.

TIMES 𝕋 BOOKS

RANDOM HOUSE

Library of Congress Cataloging-in-Publication Data

Koplewicz, Harold S.
It's nobody's fault : new hope and help for difficult children
and their parents / Harold S. Koplewicz.
p.   cm.
Includes Index.
ISBN 0-8129-2473-8
1. Child psychiatry—Popular works.   I. Title.
RJ499.34.K67   1996
618.92'89—dc20   95-39396

Book design by M. Kristen Bearse

To Linda,
a truly perceptive,
wise, and beautiful woman

Author's Note

THERE ARE DOZENS of stories in this book about people I have encountered during my many years of practicing psychiatry. I talk about many children and adolescents I've treated and parents I have counseled. On occasion I describe youngsters who have been cared for by my colleagues. The facts as I relate them here are accurate, but some of the details have been changed in an effort to keep the identities of all concerned private and confidential.

Acknowledgments

THE FIRST PERSON I want to thank is Kathleen Moloney, whose skills as an interviewer and writer helped make this book possible.

My thanks go also to my agent, Wendy Lipkind. I have thought about writing a book for years; Wendy persuaded me that there's no time like the present. Fortunately my editor, Betsy Rapoport, had the same idea. Her enthusiasm and her words of encouragement have been much appreciated.

My colleagues in the Division of Child and Adolescent Psychiatry at Schneider Children's Hospital were exceptional in their generosity and their understanding during all phases of this project. Many of them shared their wisdom and their experiences during the information-gathering period and offered valuable suggestions and honest appraisals as the book progressed. I am especially grateful to Joe Blader, Ph.D., Robert H. Dicker, M.D., Carmel Foley, M.D., David J. Ganeles, M.D., Stanley M. Hertz, M.D., Emily Klass, Ph.D., Michael H. Kronig, M.D., Marc W. Reitman, M.D., Mary V. Solanto, Ph.D., and Neil M. Smoke, D.O. I am thankful also to Howard Abikoff, Ph.D., Carmen Alonso, M.D., Keith Ditkowsky, M.D., Anita Gurian, Ph.D., Glenn S. Hirsch, M.D., Vivian Kafantaris, M.D., and Richard Morrissey, Ph.D., for sharing their experiences. Rona Novick, Ph.D., and Richard Gallagher, Ph.D., were especially helpful in making the principles of behavioral therapy understandable.

Other colleagues made significant contributions as well. Michael Maloney, M.D., Katherine Halmi, M.D., and David Herzog, M.D., shared their considerable expertise on eating disorders. Steven Suomi, Ph.D., chief of the Laboratory of Comparative Ethology at the National Institutes of Health, let me observe firsthand the work he is doing on animal behavior and temperament and was a gracious host. Bennett

Leventhal, M.D., was enormously generous with his knowledge of brain chemistry, and he, too, made suggestions about the work in progress. Many friends and family members were supportive and understanding during this project, especially Dominick Abel, Virginia Anthony, Ken Burrows, Michael Carlisle, Gabrielle Carlson, M.D., Gail Furman, Ph.D., Erica Jong, Edith Koplewicz, Stanley Kutcher, M.D., Owen Lewis, M.D., Reina Marin, Ph.D., Brian Novick, M.D., Sally Peterson, Ph.D., Al Ravitz, M.D., Peter Ross, Michael Strober, Ph.D., and Jamie Talan. I am deeply grateful to Margery Rosen for her generous and indispensable advice and support. Judith Schumer merits special thanks for helping with the title.

Jackie Eichhorn, my secretary in the office, did a great job of juggling my schedule so that I could find time for this project. Special thanks go to my assistant, Vera Connolly, who always makes my professional life run smoothly. The extra mile that she went, especially in putting together the charts and the "Resources and Support Groups" section at the back of the book, is much appreciated.

The heart of *It's Nobody's Fault* is, I believe, the stories of the children I've encountered over the years. I would not have been able to do those stories justice without the candid contributions of many of the parents of those kids. I am grateful to the many mothers and fathers who agreed to be interviewed and gave so generously of their time, especially Karen Chapnick, Brooke Garber Neidich, Sherry Laniado, Nancy Morris, and Bernard Rosenblum.

Long before there was any thought of a book I was helped more than I can say by Donald Klein, M.D., and Rachel G. Klein, Ph.D., my mentors and good friends. It was they who set me on this path. I thank them both for their advice, their encouragement, and their inspiration.

Somewhere in the pages of *It's Nobody's Fault* I say that one of the most important things a child can do is choose the right parents. I made the best possible choice with mine. Roma and Joseph Koplewicz are remarkable people, and I thank them for everything.

Finally, on the home front I received indispensable wisdom and moral support from my wife, Linda Sirow. Some of my best insights about children come, directly and indirectly, from my three wonderful sons, Joshua, Adam, and Sam. I could not have done it—any of it—without my family.

Contents

Afterword
251

APPENDIX ONE
A Definition of Terms

253

APPENDIX TWO
Resources and Support Groups

259

APPENDIX THREE
Psychopharmacology at a Glance

267

Index
295

Introduction

THE FIRST TIME I knew I wanted to be a doctor I was about four years old, sitting in the office of my pediatrician over on Eastern Parkway in Brooklyn. If I close my eyes, I can still see his face and his friendly Norman Rockwell office, with the big brown leather furniture and a bowlful of lollipops on the desk. I wanted to grow up to be just like him.

It wasn't until I was in medical school that I settled on psychiatry. I was working in a psychiatric community clinic headed by a man whose conviction and passion were so strong that he excited everyone around him. He was the first person I knew who took a "team" approach to treating mental illness. He talked about how medicine worked for certain disorders and psychotherapy worked for other disorders and how sometimes what was needed was a little bit of both. I was intrigued.

Then, in 1980, I read a book that changed my life. This book, *Diagnosis and Drug Treatment of Psychiatric Disorders: Adults and Children*, opened my eyes as nothing else had to the importance of diagnosis in the treatment of mental illness. What I read also made it quite clear that the role of medication in that treatment was indispensable. It sealed my fate.

Just about the time I became a child and adolescent psychiatrist, I also became a father for the first time, so I discovered for myself how it feels to be a parent. I understand what it's like to want the best for a child and how frustrating it is not to be able to make the world perfect for a son or daughter. I also know that the last place on earth a parent wants to be with a child is a doctor's office. I've heard parents describe the feeling they get when they find out that something is wrong with their child—"a sinking feeling in the pit of my stomach," they say—and I know what they mean. Parents have told me that there is a special pain attached to receiving unwelcome news from a child psychiatrist, and I can appreciate those feelings as well. Most parents don't need an excuse to feel anxious or guilty about their children. Hearing that a child has psychological problems automatically pushes many mothers and fathers into guilt overdrive.

Over the years I've read many studies about genetics, but now that I'm the father of three, I've learned something firsthand. My wife and I have three sons, and while the boys are remarkably similar in some ways—they look very much alike, for instance—they couldn't be more different in others. One is left-handed, and the other two lead with their right hands. They have very different social skills, anxiety levels, and abilities when it comes to sports, art, and learning. Their temperaments are not at all alike. The genes of their parents combined to make a baby three times, and each time the results were different. In these pages I call this phenomenon *DNA Roulette.* By the time you have come to the end of this book, I hope you'll have a full understanding of what DNA Roulette means.

There are other terms you'll see often in *It's Nobody's Fault.* One of the most important is *no-fault brain disorder,* by which I mean that the disorders examined here—attention deficit hyperactivity disorder, separation anxiety disorder, depression, social phobia, Tourette syndrome, and all the others—exist not because of what a child's parents do but because of how his brain works, the brain that he was born with. As I'll explain, a child's brain disorder is not his parents' fault. It's nobody's fault.

However, finding the right treatment is a parent's responsibility. Parents don't make their children sick, but it is their job to do everything possible to see that their kids get better. The good news is that there is much that can be done to do just that, much more today than even a decade ago. Most of the advances in the treatment of no-fault brain disorders have come in psychopharmacology, the use of medication to treat the symptoms of a no-fault brain disorder. *Medication*—there's another word you'll be seeing often in this book. Another is *drugs,* a word that stops a lot of parents cold. Many, perhaps even most, of the mothers and fathers who bring their kids to my office have a problem with the idea that their child might have to take drugs to treat a disorder, for a period of months or even years. They worry about side effects and fear that they'll somehow "lose" their child if he's under the influence of medication. What I hope I make clear in this book is that the role of medication in treating no-fault brain disorders is incredibly important. The side effects of *not* taking drugs to treat a serious problem can often be more harmful than those associated with taking the medicine.

One of my first patients as a psychiatric resident was Ned, a boy I don't think I'll ever forget. He was about nine years old when his mother brought him to see me. He had been having a terrible time in school; his performance was poor, and his teacher was complaining about his behavior. He didn't have much of a social life either. None of the other kids in the class wanted to play with him, and their parents didn't like having him around.

After making a diagnosis of attention deficit hyperactivity disorder, I prescribed medication for Ned (a small dose of Ritalin twice a day) and saw him once a month for nearly a year. We talked about what was going on in his life—his parents were going through a particularly unpleasant divorce—and worked on improving his social skills and self-esteem. After the year was up I saw him only every few months, to monitor his progress. His improvement was remarkable in every way. His grades were terrific, he had lots of friends, and his parents said it was a joy to be with the "new Ned."

A few years after I first saw Ned, he invited me to his elementary school graduation. He was getting a class prize for the best science project, and he wanted me to hear his acceptance speech. Ned said that his mother was having a party at the house afterward, and he wanted me to be there too. I told him that I would really like to be there, but I had a few questions.

"Where do you think I should sit?" I asked him.

"Well, if you sit with my mom or my dad, the other one will be jealous," he answered. "Maybe you could sit with my friends' parents."

"Okay. And how should I introduce myself?" I asked.

This question was clearly harder than the first one.

"We can tell people you're my veterinarian," the boy ventured.

"But you don't have any pets," I said.

"I'll say I used to have a bird with a wing that was broken. But then you fixed it, and it flew away."

I told him that I didn't think that making up a story was a good idea, and he agreed to think about it.

Graduation day came, and I stood at the back of the room and listened to Ned's speech. I wasn't able to go the family party, so after the ceremony Ned took me over to meet his grandparents. "This is Dr. Koplewicz," he said. "He's my . . . my friend." True to his word, the youngster had come up with a description of our relationship without making anything up. After meeting the family I stayed for a while, watching as Ned, clutching his award, talked animatedly to his friends and family.

When *I* think about my role in Ned's life, or in the lives of any of the children I care for, the image I always come back to is roadblocks, impediments on the path that keep these kids from getting where they want and need to go. It's my job to help them climb over those road-blocks or push them out of the way. I say to them, "Look, there's a way of getting from here to there. I'm going to show you how." I give them the tools they need to clear the path. Along the way I try to reassure the parents of these troubled kids and give them hope.

That's what I've tried to do in this book as well. I hope that parents and other readers will come away with new hope for their difficult, troubled children and will be inspired to do everything in their means to get their children the help they need in order to lead happy, fulfilling lives.

Living with
a Child's
Brain Disorder

The four chapters of Part One focus on what a no-fault brain disorder is and how it affects—directly and indirectly—the lives of children, their parents, their teachers, their friends, and the rest of the world. This section also explores the role of the health professional in the treatment of children's brain disorders.

CHAPTER 1

It's Nobody's Fault

It's a typical day in early October. The school year has started, so I'm seeing quite a few new patients. The first child I talk to is William, age seven, who starts my day off with a real bang. William's motor just won't quit. He doesn't sit or even perch. He walks around my office, touching everything as he goes. At one point he sits behind my desk and spins in my chair. William's nickname at home is "The Magician," because he's always making things disappear. "He can lose his homework walking from the kitchen to the bedroom," his mother tells me.

After William comes Margot, nine years old and as quiet and sad as William is animated. Her parents tell me that Margot has trouble sleeping. For the last two months she's been getting up every night and crawling into bed with Mom and Dad. They give her warm milk, rub her back, and put her back in her own bed, but a short time later there she is again. Sometimes they find her asleep on the floor of their bedroom in the morning. When her parents leave my office so that I can speak to the little girl alone, Margot starts to cry. I tell her that Mom and Dad are waiting right down the hall. She begs me to let them stay just outside the door.

I see a lot of good-looking children in my line of work, but my next patient, 11-year-old Kenny, with his dark skin, dimples, and huge hazel eyes, would stand out in any crowd. Kenny has come to see me because his parents are worried that he might hurt himself. According to his mother and father, Kenny has always been conscientious and hard-working, giving "110 percent" to everything he does. His grades are excellent, he's a better than average athlete, and he has plenty of friends. Until recently he seemed fine. A few months ago, however, he turned cranky and irritable. One night not too long ago he became more upset than his parents had ever seen him; he said that he wished he were dead and locked the door to his room. He's been complaining of headaches almost every day.

"She's driving us crazy," said Delia's mother within seconds of crossing the threshold of my office in the midafternoon. Delia, 10 years old, didn't *look* as if she could drive anyone crazy. She had a winning smile and a delightful personality. But she's been making demands at home that her parents can no longer meet. The ritual that she insists on at bedtime is the worst, her parents say. Every night she says, "I love you, Mom" and "I love you, Dad," and her parents have to say, "I love you too, Delia" right back. The problem is, they have to go through this exchange 20 or 30 times before Delia will let them turn off the light. A few nights ago they decided not to follow the script and sent her to bed with just one "I love you" apiece. Delia got hysterical. "She was obviously in real pain," her father told me.

My last patient of the day was Tobias, age 16, who looked, from a distance, like a typical teenager—baggy clothes, huge athletic shoes, single earring, surly expression. Up close I could see that he was pale and tired, and I soon learned that the bagginess of his clothes wasn't just the latest fashion; Tobias had lost a lot of weight. He just didn't feel like eating. In fact, he didn't feel like doing much of anything. "Everything's just so boring" more or less summed it up for him. He didn't make eye contact when we spoke. His parents told me that Tobias stays up until all hours of the night and then takes four-hour naps after school. He's also missed a lot of school.

DISORDERS OF THE BRAIN

William, Margot, Kenny, Delia, and Tobias, like all the other children described in these pages, have many things in common. All of them have brain disorders; all of them have responded well to treatment, including medication; and all of them have parents who care. Their parents have something in common too. When they first brought their children to see me, virtually all of them thought, or at least suspected, that what was wrong with their children was their fault. Those worried, guilt-ridden parents couldn't be more wrong. What's troubling their children is *nobody's fault.*

According to a report issued recently by the Institute of Medicine, one quarter of the United States population is under the age of 18, and at least 12 percent of those under 18 have a diagnosable brain disorder. That's 7.5 million children and adolescents—boys, girls, rich, poor, black, white—with psychiatric disorders. That's roughly 15 million parents who feel guilty about it.

One of the reasons parents think that they're to blame for their children's emotional and behavioral problems is that people are always *telling* them that they are. Teachers, relatives, friends, even strangers aren't the least bit reluctant to share their opinions with the parents of troubled kids. The mother of Freddy, a six-year-old boy I was treating for attention deficit hyperactivity disorder, summed it up very well when she said, "My husband and I have gotten a lot unsolicited advice, and just about all of it has been bad. First people said all Freddy needed was discipline, and they blamed his illness on us. If I would just quit my job and stay home with him, he'd be fine. My sister thinks that Freddy has problems because I weaned him at three months. She breast-fed her two girls until they were nine months, and they're fine. My husband works long hours, so my family blames him too, saying that Freddy would be okay if my husband would take him to more baseball games. People made us feel like negligent, uncaring parents."

Old ideas die hard. Until 20 years ago there was a general belief that early childhood traumas and inadequate parenting were responsible for childhood psychiatric disorders. Although we know better today, that antiquated way of thinking is still supported by many mental health professionals, perpetuated by the media, accepted as gospel by too many teachers and other school officials, and espoused wholeheartedly by well-meaning relatives. People who wouldn't dream of blaming parents for a child's other diseases—asthma or diabetes or multiple sclerosis, for example—don't hesitate to embrace the notion that a child's behavioral difficulties are caused by working mothers, overly permissive parents, or absent dads.

The fact is, when a child has a brain disorder, it is *not* the parents' fault. It is also not the fault of teachers or camp counselors or the children themselves. A brain disorder is the result of what I call "DNA Roulette." In the same way a child comes into the world with large ears, a tendency to go gray in his twenties, or, like Kenny, beautiful hazel eyes and deep dimples, a child is born with a brain that functions in a particular way because of its chemical composition. (The chemistry of the brain is explained at length in Chapter 5.) *It is brain chemistry that is responsible for brain disorders, not bad parenting.*

At conception a child receives genes from his parents, half from his mother and half from his father. As parents with more than one child know very well, those genes aren't donated in exactly the same configuration every time. A child's precise genetic makeup is largely determined by chance. Genetic messages from both parents come together to create many different combinations. If that DNA Roulette wheel stops spinning on a "lucky" number, the brain works properly and the child is normal. If not, the brain is dysfunctional. There is no reason for parents to feel guilty about their child's psychiatric disorder. There's nothing that any of us can do about our genes. The good news is that there is a lot we can do to treat the problems that genes can cause in our children.

Over the past two decades genetic influences in psychiatric disorders among adults have been fairly carefully studied, but science has only recently begun to focus attention on brain disorders in children and adolescents. Still, the studies that we do have are quite persuasive. Studies comparing the frequency of brain disorders in identical twins (who share the exact same genetic makeup) to the frequency of brain disorders in fraternal twins (who are only as genetically similar as any siblings) show that if one twin had a psychiatric disorder, the other twin was more likely to have it too if he or she was an identical rather than fraternal twin. The conclusion: many childhood psychiatric disorders have a genetic component. Adoption studies that investigated the genetic influences of psychiatric disorders in children who were raised from a very early age by adoptive parents, and compared their incidence of psychiatric disorders with both their biological and their adoptive parents, came to the same conclusion.

Animal models, especially those conducted with Rhesus monkeys, who have a 94 percent genetic similarity to humans, also support the theory that brain chemistry is genetically transmitted. In studying the neurochemistry of these animals and their reactions to stress and other environmental factors, experts have established in yet another way that nature is a stronger force than nurture. Of course, nurture does play a part in determining how a child will feel and behave. An unfavorable environment, in which a child is abused or unloved, certainly will have a detrimental effect. If that child begins life with a brain that is vulnerable to a disorder, a demoralizing environment is strike two.

THE FINE ART OF STORYTELLING

"Right after my daughter Serena was born, I was very sick. I spent most of the first year of her life in bed. I gave the baby as much attention as I could, but I was way too sick to be the kind of mother I wanted to be. Serena was difficult as a baby, and over the years she got much worse. There were a lot of problems with her behavior. When she was four, we took her to a child psychiatrist, who told us that Serena had separation anxiety disorder. He said it was probably caused by my not being available to her when she was an infant. If I hadn't gotten sick, she probably would have been completely normal. One part of me didn't believe what the doctor said. It isn't as if I abandoned her or anything. But I felt tremendous guilt anyway. I cried for a week."

Serena's psychiatrist wasn't the first person to make up a story to explain away a child's problem, and he won't be the last. People do it all the time; they see a set of symptoms and create a story around them. What's the rationale of this disorder? they ask. What has happened in this child's life to explain this abnormal behavior? Traumatic birth, adoption, illness, parents' divorce, strong mother, weak mother, an overachieving older sister—all of these and many more have been used to rationalize children's psychiatric disorders. One mother told me that her 10-year-old son wet his bed every night because he had skipped second grade. The impossible behavior of a nine-year-old with obsessive compulsive disorder was attributed to the fact that the little boy, who was always bossing people around, was simply imitating his father, the CEO of a Fortune 500 company.

Even when these ingeniously fabricated stories make a small amount of sense, science is all but ignored. The psychiatrist who told Serena's mother that it was her sickness that brought on Serena's separation anxiety disorder was forgetting the fact that many children with sick mothers—or no mothers, for that matter—do *not* end up with SAD. What's more, there are many children with SAD whose mothers have never spent a single day in a sickbed. People who become convinced that A causes B often lose sight of the facts. For example, it is widely believed that bulimia is the result of sexual abuse, but there is little evidence to support this theory. Sexual abuse is a common phenomenon, and bulimia is a common disorder; it stands to reason, therefore, that there will be a substantial number of women with bulimia who have been sexually abused. That still doesn't prove a cause-and-effect relationship. Many women who have been sexually abused don't have bulimia or any other disorder, and many women with bulimia have not been abused.

There are millions of people who endure traumatic experiences—abuse, divorce, the death of a loved one, skipping second grade, and so on—without having to be treated for a psychiatric disorder. Naturally, all children are affected by the events of their lives. If a child is abandoned or beaten, it will most certainly change the way he looks at the world and reacts to it. If his parents get a divorce, it will unquestionably have an effect on him, probably a significant effect. But unless he has the brain chemistry that makes him vulnerable to a psychiatric disorder, the child will not end up with a disorder. By the same token, a brain disorder doesn't miraculously disappear if the unpleasant environmental factors are altered.

NORMAL DEVELOPMENT

Not all children develop at precisely the same rate, of course. Still, the developmental milestones that follow will give parents a rough idea of what to expect.

At *one month* a child will react to voices and be attentive to faces. By *four months* he'll smile at people and respond socially to both familiar and unfamiliar people. At *six months* a child will sleep through the night. At about *age one* he'll walk and say his first word, usually "Mama" or "Dada," and he'll have developed a clear attachment to a caretaker, usually but not necessarily the mother. Also at one year kids start "pretend play," having tea parties with imaginary food and pretending, for example, that a toy cup is real.

At *two years old* a child can draw a circle, and he starts to use symbolism: a pencil represents a person, or a block becomes a chair. At the same time kids have "idealized representations"; they don't like broken dolls or toys or anything that has something wrong with it. Kids develop empathy at about this time; if a child hears a baby crying, for example, he'll say that the baby's hungry or hurt. By the time a child is two, he'll be comfortable around strangers with his parents nearby and capable of parallel play: two or more children playing in the same room at the same time but not together. The kids may not speak or otherwise interact as they go about their tasks. Most two-year-olds have a hundred words in their vocabulary and speak in sentences of two words, such as "Big boy," "More food," or "Come here." Girls usually have a more advanced verbal ability than boys, so a two-year-old girl probably will have a much more extensive vocabulary than a hundred words.

At around age *three* most children are toilet-trained, and they have a thousand-word vocabulary. They move on to reciprocal play, building sand castles together or engaging in some other mutually enjoyable activity. With reciprocal play there's a connection between children, even if it *is* a fight. At three kids can sit for 20 minutes of story time or some other activity. By the age of *four* they stop wetting their beds at night and use complex grammatically correct sentences. At four a child can separate comfortably from his parents; he'll be able to stay at a birthday party for an hour without his mother in the room. He will also be able to share toys, follow the rules of a game, and function in a group with minimal aggression. A four-year-old might be afraid of the dark or of animals, but that fear is usually transient.

At *five years old* children like to hear stories read repeatedly and enjoy rituals throughout the day, such as having a snack as soon as they get home from school, playing with certain toys in the bath, and sleeping with the same teddy bear every night. At *six* kids have a vocabulary of about 10,000 words, and they learn to read. They frequently start to collect things—rocks, dolls, basketball cards, and so on—and may become fond of superheroes. At *seven* they may develop superstitions and rituals: step on a crack, break your mother's back.

From age eight through adolescence, children focus on school performance. Competition and ambition become more important in their lives. Boys and girls begin to develop a value system based largely on the beliefs learned from their family. Their social sphere widens, and friendships begin to take on greater meaning.

The developmental milestones associated with adolescence are less specific in terms of age; there are basically five *developmental tasks* that must be accomplished by a youngster between puberty—approximately age 11 for girls and 12 or 13 for boys—and the end of adolescence, about age 22. There are enormous physical changes that take place during adolescence, especially hormonal fluctuations, and brain chemistry goes through changes as well.

The first task youngsters must accomplish is to *separate* from their parents. Naturally, this separation process doesn't happen all at once; it comes about gradually, in steps, such as flirting with ideas that are different from those of their parents or favoring music and wearing clothes that adults hate. By age 22 a young person should be completely comfortable about being separate from his folks, regardless of geography. The second task that faces an adolescent is the *development of a network of friends.* At age 13 or 14 a child begins to find his peer group important. The greatest influences in his life remain Mom and Dad, but he's influenced by his friends and shares intimacy with them. The third task is *sexual orientation.* Sexual fantasies usually start at puberty; by the age of 22 a young person, even one who is not sexually active yet, should know which gender arouses him sexually. Task number four is the *setting of educational and vocational goals.* At age 12 that means finishing a math project or learning the history of Syria. When a youngster is 17 or 18, his goal may be to get into college or find a job. By the time he's 22, he should have a good idea of what he wants to be when he "grows up." The fifth and final developmental task of adolescence is *adjustment to the physical changes* that take place during this period. It's important for a child to adjust not just to the specific changes themselves but also to the fact that his changes are different from those of his friends and are taking place at a different rate.

Being mindful of the milestones of childhood and adolescence will help parents to identify problems their child might have. Parents should be on the lookout as well for specific abnormal behaviors that may indicate that a child has a psychological disorder. Some of them are: repetitive actions, such as tapping, hair-pulling, and hand-washing; unreasonable fears, such as not being able to sleep unless the parents are in the same room; agitation and excessive rigidity; nervousness about meeting people; motor or verbal tics; and extremely aggressive, disruptive behavior. The degree and the intensity of these symptoms are what really matter. Occasional lapses into peculiar behavior are not cause for concern.

Parents who have children with brain disorders tend to end up in hospital emergency rooms more often than the average parent—because of accidents, suicide attempts, and other crises—and they're always saying things like, "Whenever there's trouble in the classroom, my kid is bound to be in the middle of it." Being with these kids is challenging and terribly demanding. "I'm not having much fun with my child. I love him, but I'm exhausted after being with him. And no one else can stand him" is a statement I hear quite often from my patients' mothers and fathers. Many parents are embarrassed by the child's behavior.

Even though they are nobody's fault, there is a lot of parental guilt and blame attached to these disorders, and much of it comes about when parents are slow to notice a problem. One extremely conscientious mother of a boy with pervasive developmental disorder knew by the time her child was two years old that he needed some help, but she feels bad anyhow. She insists that she could have picked up the symptoms of PDD earlier if she had known what to look for. "Because of my son I got involved in a PDD program, and I saw babies who were four or five months old who were already showing signs of developmental delay. If I had known before what I know now, I would have taken him to the doctor much earlier than two."

Another mother and father whose child I've treated reproach themselves for not being aware of their daughter's depression. "She was so good at masking everything. She fooled us," they told me. And they're right. Some children, unable or unwilling or ashamed to ask for help, are masters at disguising the symptoms of their disorders.

A child should be evaluated by a child and adolescent psychiatrist if any of the items on this checklist describes his behavior for at least two weeks:

- Stomachaches or headaches with no physical cause
- Loss of interest in activities previously enjoyed
- Change in sleep patterns
- Change in eating patterns
- Social withdrawal
- Excessive anxiety or fearfulness upon separation from parents; refusal to sleep away from home or alone in his own bed
- Refusal to go to school
- Decline in school grades in several subjects
- Persistent underachievement at school
- Unacceptable behavior in the classroom
- Aggressive behavior
- Stealing, lying, breaking rules
- Inability to speak to peers or adults other than family
- Repetitive behavior; a child becomes overly upset if these actions are prevented or interrupted
- Avoidance of objects or activities not previously avoided

- Mood swings or a dramatic change in mood
- A preoccupation with death or dying; suicidal wishes or threats
- Change in personality, especially from cooperative to irritable or sullen
- Odd or bizarre behavior or verbalizations
- A tendency to confuse fantasy and reality

This checklist and the brief overview of a child's developmental milestones are not meant to be alarming to parents, but I do hope that if you see that your child is not developing normally or that he's exhibiting unusual behavior, you will be encouraged to do something about it. (Chapters 7 through 19 thoroughly examine the most common brain disorders in children and adolescents.) For example, if a child of two seems exceptionally uncomfortable with people, you should say, "You know what? My kid is supposed to be over this by now. Maybe I should talk to the pediatrician about it. Perhaps I'll get him to recommend a child psychiatrist." There's nothing to be lost by getting some professional advice. The only thing better than prompt treatment of a disorder is the reassurance that nothing is wrong.

DISTRESS AND DYSFUNCTION

Schoolteachers have the three Rs: reading, writing, and 'rithmetic. Child and adolescent psychiatrists have the two Ds: distress and dysfunction. In deciding whether or not a child needs treatment for a disorder, we look for one or both of the Ds. If a child's symptoms are not causing him or his parents distress or dysfunction, we watch and wait. Perhaps it's not a disorder but the child's style or an element of his personality. If and when the symptoms of a disorder increase and *do* cause distress or dysfunction, we establish a course of treatment, usually a combination of behavioral therapy and medication.

Child and adolescent psychiatrists are in the business of treating children who are sick, not medicating children who aren't sick so that they can become more popular, perform better at a music recital, or turn a B + average into an A average. Since most children's brain disorders are treated with medication and since all medications have some side effects, no physician is eager to put a child on medicine unless he really needs it.

The first line of attack should be and is psychosocial intervention. Medication isn't called for unless there is a diagnosable disorder.

Any physician must weigh the seriousness of a disease against the effects of the cure. Before he is treated with medication, a child has to be sick *enough*. If a boy bites his fingernails and the medicine to get him to stop doing it causes liver failure, we live with the chewed-up nails. After all, there's no dysfunction involved, and the distress is only on the part of the parents. On the other hand, a girl who's banging her head so hard and so often that she detaches her retinas needs a trial of medication to get her behavior under control, even with the risk of side effects.

Distress is not always obvious to spot in children. Some admit it, but many others deny that they're in pain. Distress may manifest itself in any number of ways, many of them in conflict with the others: agitation, depression, social isolation, boisterousness, silence, sleeplessness, giddiness, sadness, and lots of others. Identifying dysfunction is a little more clear-cut. A child is dysfunctional if he doesn't achieve and maintain developmental milestones; if he can't or won't go to school and pay attention; if he doesn't have friends; or if he does not have a satisfying, loving relationship with his parents.

TAKING CHARGE

"It's been really hard," said a father of a little boy with attention deficit hyperactivity disorder. "I was looking forward so much to being a dad, and when my son finally came along, I was incredibly happy and excited. I wanted to do millions of things with him—all the great stuff my dad did with me. I couldn't wait to play catch and go camping and that kind of thing. Then I found out I was living with a holy terror who was an absolute pain in the neck to spend time with. I hate to admit it, but I was pretty disappointed."

The father's statement is extremely blunt, true, but he's only expressing what many parents with problem children feel. When a baby is on the way, parents are expectant in more ways than one. They *are* excited, consumed with hopes and fantasies about what the child will look like and how he will be. Parents want their children to surpass them, to live better, more fulfilling lives than their own. They want them to be accomplished, beautiful, and happy. When parents are busy picking out layettes and narrowing down the list of possible baby names, they aren't anticipating illness. Brain disorders—even no-fault brain disorders—are *not* what they have in mind.

Accepting the fact that a child has a brain disorder is never easy for parents, even those who do finally realize that they're not at fault. It's even harder to cope with the realization that a child's problem is in his brain. After all, parents think optimistically, if the behavioral problem is caused by something environmental, perhaps the child will outgrow it. I've met some parents who are a little downhearted that it's *not* their fault. "I was hoping that it was our divorce that was making our daughter so crazy," another blunt parent said to me. "At least that way she would get over it in time." After all, if bad parenting is what is causing a child's disease, it stands to reason that good parenting can make it better.

Unfortunately, that's not how it works. Parents don't cause the disorders, and they can't cure them either. However, mothers and fathers can and should take responsibility for seeing that their children get professional help, and the sooner the better. The sooner a child's brain disorder is diagnosed and treated, the sooner he can get on with living a full, happy, satisfying life. And that, in the end, is what every loving parent wants.

CHAPTER 2

Brain Disorders and Personality

Several years ago I was part of a group of psychiatrists and other clinicians who studied the effects of the psychostimulant Ritalin on preschoolers with attention deficit hyperactivity disorder. One part of the study involved observing the children and their mothers at play before and after the child was given medication. A mother and child were left alone in a playroom full of toys and games for 25 minutes, and their activities were monitored—one of the walls was a two-way mirror—and videotaped.

The time allotted to mother and child was divided into three segments: 10 minutes of free play, 5 minutes of cleanup, and 10 minutes of structured tasks. During free play a youngster was allowed to play with whichever toy he chose, with no limit as to the number of toys or the kind of play. The mother was encouraged to play with him. The cleanup was to be done by the child, with the mother supervising the process if necessary. During the 10 minutes of structured tasks the child would sit at a table with his mother, and she would ask him to complete 40 tasks, or as many as the child could manage in the time allowed. The simple tasks—picking out circles, identifying the red triangles, pointing out everything that's blue, and so forth—tested the child's ability to distinguish colors and shapes. What we were really taking note of, however, was the child's ability to focus, pay attention, and follow instructions. We were also interested in the interaction between mother and child.

I'll never forget the day that Christopher, three years old, came in with his mother to be tested. Little Christopher had one of the most severe cases of ADHD most of us had ever encountered. He nearly tore up my office the first day I met him, climbing on the furniture, scribbling on the tables, and tossing books and papers around the room. I ended up having to hold him in my lap (quite firmly, I might add) in order to interview him, and even then our talk lasted only a few minutes. Not surprisingly, Christopher had long since been blacklisted by every baby-sitter in his neighborhood. My diagnosis was ADHD. Christopher's parents agreed to let him take part in our study, and his mother brought him to the playroom a couple of days after our first appointment.

Christopher was by far the most impulsive, inattentive child who took part in our study. During the 10 minutes of free play the boy played with *61* different toys. (Children with a normal attention span may play with as many as five toys in ten minutes, but many three-year-olds will spend the whole time with only one toy.) In truth, he didn't *play* with any of them; he'd just pick a toy up, throw it down, and move on to another. Christopher's mother tried to get him to settle down, running after him and making a strenuous effort to engage him, but nothing worked. The video camera caught it all: Christopher running from toy to toy, not even pausing to look at a toy; mom following along, calling out, "Christopher! Come here! Look at the truck! Christopher! Here's a beach ball! Don't you want to play catch with Mommy?" The faster Christopher moved, the louder and more agitated the mother became. There was complete chaos in the room.

After the time for free play had elapsed, one of my colleagues went into the playroom and told the boy and his mother that it was time for cleanup. That's when Christopher really went ballistic. He screamed, threw himself down on the ground, and categorically refused to have anything to do with picking up the 61 toys. Again the mother tried to get her son to follow orders. "Chris, honey, come on. Let's clean up," she said, first in a normal voice and then, as the boy's behavior grew into a full-fledged tantrum, more loudly. The noise on the tape is deafening. After a minute of the tantrum we asked Christopher's mother to handle the cleanup on her own.

The structured tasks were a total washout. Christopher would not even sit at the little table, let alone pick out red triangles and blue circles. His mother put him in the chair, but he kept getting up and running around the room. Mom kept trying—"Christopher! Come on! Let's sit down and play some games!" she cried, over and over again—but noth-ing worked. The mother became increasingly frustrated; she knew that Christopher was capable of accomplishing the tasks, but nothing she did could persuade him to sit down and do it. When the 10 minutes were up, the little boy had not completed one task. The mother was exhausted.

Almost exactly a month later Christopher and his mom came back to do the test again, but by this time the boy was taking 40 milligrams of Ritalin a day. Again, the whole thing was captured on videotape. During free play Christopher chose a Fisher-Price toolbox, and he and his mother sat on the floor playing with it, and *only* it, for the full 10 minutes. It was so quiet in the playroom that we had to adjust the microphones. "You really like this toy, don't you, Chris?" the mother asked softly. "Yes, I love it," the boy answered. Their conversation was lively and pleasant. Cleanup took only a few seconds; there was just the one toy to put away, and Christopher did it as soon as he was asked. Finally, during the structured-tasks portion of the test the youngster sat at the table with his mother and completed 32 of the 40 assignments. The interaction between the two of them was a pleasure to watch; there was give-and-take and lots of laughter. Voices were never raised.

A few months later I had occasion to show the two videotapes of Christopher and his mother—before and after—to a small group of medical students who were doing a rotation in child psychiatry. We asked the students, who knew nothing at all about the study, what they thought had happened in the month between sessions. All of the students came to the same conclusion: the *mother* was taking medication. "In the first tape she's a mess. She's practically driving the kid crazy, constantly yelling at him and giving him a hard time," one med student said. "She's so much calmer and quieter on the medication."

It's true: on the second tape the mother *is* quieter and calmer, thanks to medication, but she's not the one taking it, of course. The medication that brought on the changes in the mother's attitude and behavior, not to mention the tone and the decibel level of her voice, is her son's Ritalin. The "new" Christopher, the one who pays attention and enjoys laughing and playing and talking to his mother, is so much more pleasant to be with that his mother can't help being pleasanter right back. And the cycle continues from there. The mother's yelling and nagging are converted to praise and approval, and the child flourishes. The more his mother likes him, the more likable he becomes, not just to his mother but to everyone else around him as well. After a time, even the baby-sitters may have a change of heart.

I've described this study at length not to emphasize the effectiveness of Ritalin in the treatment of ADHD—I do that in Chapter 7—but to open a discussion of how a child's brain disorder affects the way he and the rest of the world interact. Christopher's ADHD did a lot more than make him impulsive and inattentive. It made him unpleasant and unlikable, even to the people who love him most. It made people avoid him, yell at him, and refuse to baby-sit for him. Furthermore, being constantly criticized and yelled at and infrequently praised probably made Christopher's situation even worse. One of the things we learned in our study is that the mothers of children with ADHD don't praise their children as often as other mothers do, even when the children do something eminently praiseworthy. The mothers of kids with ADHD are more attuned to their children's negative behavior than to their positive behavior; this is not surprising, since there's usually so much more *of* the negative than the positive.

Although it may not seem so, Christopher is one of the lucky ones. He was only three years old when his brain disorder was discovered and treated. He'd had a couple of years of negativity out there in the world, but it had been largely contained within the family. He hadn't started school, so he had not had a chance yet to alienate his teachers and annoy his classmates. With the help of the Ritalin and his conscientious parents we hope he never will.

A PERSONALITY IS BORN

Children are born with certain personality traits, which determine how they will behave in the world, how they will learn, and how they'll interact with others. Even newborn infants have personalities; intelligence, humor, and all the other elements that make up a personality are largely determined in the womb. But that is by no means the whole story. A child's personality development is affected, sometimes very strongly affected, by the environment in which he grows up. A child who is naturally cheerful and optimistic will not remain upbeat for long if the world is constantly giving him or her downbeat messages. Neglected and abused children find it more than a little difficult to maintain the sunny dispositions they were born with. In the same way, having a brain disorder has crucial and sometimes long-lasting effects on a child's personality development.

When Mario, an eight-year-old boy, came to see me, I asked him what he thought his problem was. "I'm a bad boy," he answered. "What do you mean you're a bad boy?" I asked. "I get into trouble all of the time," he explained. "Do you want to get into trouble all the time?" I asked. "I don't know if I want to, but I do. I'm just bad," Mario replied. At the ripe old age of eight, Mario is already convinced that he is a failure. Traveling through life surrounded by people who are forever impatient or enraged is bound to have an impact on a child's personality.

Mario is by no means the only child I've encountered with low self-esteem. I see kids every day who think they're bad or stupid or incompetent, who are convinced that they're a thorn in the side of their teachers and a severe disappointment to their parents. "My dad thinks I'm a real screw-up," 10-year-old Ross told me. "He's right. I *am* always screwing up." It's easy to understand what has brought Ross to this sad conclusion. His short life has consisted of one negative experience after another. He's known little else.

THE LONG-TERM EFFECTS OF A BRAIN DISORDER

Mario and Ross both had attention deficit hyperactivity disorder, ADHD, the most common and most studied of all children's brain disorders. There's a great deal of evidence to suggest that ADHD affects every aspect of a child's life: school, friendships, and family. School is an unpleasant place for these kids, filled as it is with demands and tasks that seem impossible. Some 25 percent of all children with ADHD drop out of high school (as opposed to 2 percent of those kids without ADHD). Obviously, that makes their prospects for employment less than ideal.

The stigma associated with academic failure can last a long, long time. Riley, the 32-year-old manager of a parking garage, recently told me, with some embarrassment, that he had dropped out of school in the ninth grade. "School was like prison to me," he said. "I couldn't sit still. I couldn't do the work. I couldn't *wait* to get out of there." Riley went on to tell me that he still doesn't read books, and he can't even sit through most movies. "I'm just not very intelligent," he concluded. He's wrong about being unintelligent. Riley reads two newspapers every day, runs a busy garage, and has great people skills. He's clearly smart. However, his early failures in school—a result, I believe, of untreated ADHD —left a mark on his self-esteem that may well be indelible. (See Chapter 7 for more about ADHD.)

All of the other no-fault brain disorders have secondary effects on a child's life as well, especially performance and self-esteem. A youngster with *separation anxiety disorder* will be reluctant to leave the comfort and solace of home, where his parents are, so his ability to make friends will be impaired. He'll miss out on many positive experiences, such as parties and sleepover dates. Later on the disorder may limit his college and job choices. (Chapter 9 focuses on SAD.)

Kids with *social phobia,* fearful of being mocked, will avoid social situations and with time will become socially incompetent. Many opportunities, both romantic and professional, will be lost. We live in a verbal world, and people who don't make themselves heard are at a distinct disadvantage; they often are thought to be "stupid" or "hostile" or both. (Social phobia is discussed in Chapter 10.)

The "overachiever" symptoms of *generalized anxiety disorder* may seem beneficial at first blush, but children with GAD, unable to relax or enjoy life, are often tiresome and irritating—not the most popular kids in the class. Not being liked by peers is intensely demoralizing, and it may lead to depression, especially if the disorder continues into adulthood. (GAD is the subject of Chapter 11.)

Obsessive compulsive disorder has a tremendous effect on a child's personality because of the secrecy and shame that usually are components of the disease. A child who spends all of his time hiding his irrational obsessions and compulsions from other people—even those people closest to him—shuts himself off from the world. OCD is time-consuming; it limits a child's ability to experience and enjoy other activities. It may also keep him away from his studies. Ashamed and guilty about his behavior, he doesn't let himself be open and honest with other people. Naturally that kind of covert behavior makes it difficult for the youngster to establish satisfying relationships. One adolescent girl I treated for OCD told me that she feels as if she's faking it all the time. Kids with OCD carry a very heavy burden. (For more about OCD, see Chapter 8.)

In some ways youngsters with *Tourette syndrome* have an even weightier load to bear than children with OCD, because many of them are hiding something even worse: they think they're freaks. The motor and phonic tics associated with TS are hard to disguise, so people with this disorder often become homebodies. They don't want to go out in public for fear of being stared at or mocked for what they themselves regard as "crazy" behavior. Again, love, marriage, and fulfilling employment may elude them because they keep their distance from other people. (TS is described fully in Chapter 13.)

Enuresis/bedwetting causes kids to feel ashamed, inadequate, and insecure and usually makes them avoid situations in which their disorder will be discovered, such as camping, pajama parties, and sleepover dates—all social activities that most young people enjoy. The effects may be felt for a long time. A 20-year-old man who's had untreated enuresis his entire life (he kept thinking he would "work through it") says he has never had a satisfying relationship with a woman. He had a girlfriend he was crazy about, but it didn't work out. He would have sex with her, he told me, but, because he didn't want to fall asleep, for fear of wetting the bed, he always got up and went home right afterward. His girlfriend, convinced he was thoughtless and uncaring, broke it off. The young man was convinced he'd never get married. (Chapter 12 focuses on enuresis.)

Having *major depressive disorder* has a formidable effect on how a youngster experiences and relates to the rest of the world. Teenagers with MDD tend to avoid going to school and being with other people, so they may fall behind academically, miss out on dating, and may not have a chance to develop friendships. Their hopelessness—the "glass is half-empty" approach to life—and their social isolation put them at greater risk for suicide. (MDD is the subject of Chapter 14.)

Kids with *bipolar disorder* have difficulty in every sphere of their lives: school performance is impaired; friendships are difficult to maintain; and their relationship with their parents is disturbed and filled with conflict. All of these problems have a huge impact on self-esteem. As time goes by, they are at serious risk for substance abuse and suicide. (For more about bipolar disorder, see Chapter 15.)

Adolescents with *schizophrenia* experience a deterioration of their personality; they become increasingly unresponsive and unable to initiate and maintain activities and friendships. Delusions and hallucinations play a more important part in their lives than the rest of the real world, and they may lose touch. (Chapter 16 focuses on schizophrenia.)

Like OCD, *eating disorders*—anorexia nervosa and bulimia—involve secrecy and activities that are all-consuming of time and energy. An adolescent girl with an eating disorder is limited in her ability and her inclination to interact with her friends and participate in age-appropriate activities. (Eating disorders are covered in Chapter 17.)

Children with *conduct disorder* have problems developing meaningful relationships—being devious, dishonest, and aggressive doesn't usually make children popular—and a lot of difficulty keeping up with their studies at school. The dropout rate for kids with CD is high, as is the likelihood of substance abuse. Not surprisingly, their employment opportunities are limited, and their chances of ending up on the wrong side of the law are better than even. (Conduct disorder is discussed in Chapter 8.)

Children with *autism* find it difficult or impossible to communicate —many can't speak, and others use language in peculiar ways—to learn, or to relate in any meaningful way to their parents or anyone else. Often avoided or ostracized by their peers for being so unusual, children with this and other *pervasive developmental disorders* suffer tremendous blows to their self-esteem. (PDD and autism are covered in Chapter 19.)

TEACHER'S PEST

Aside from his mother and his father, the most important adult in a child's life is his teacher. Just as it is essential for a youngster's well-being and self-esteem that he be cherished and highly regarded by his parents, it is crucial that he be well thought of by his teacher. When a child has a brain disorder that adversely affects his behavior in the classroom, he may be out of luck; even the most patient and understanding of teachers cannot always give him the positive reinforcement he needs.

Another study I was involved in illustrates just how hard it can be for a teacher to deal with a problem child. This time we were interested in finding out how teachers react to the behavior of their students. Our first challenge was to track down the very best teacher we could find— someone conscientious, caring, patient, creative, and skillful at getting the best out of children. We ended up in a grammar school in the Bronx with Ms. Leonard, a veteran first-grade teacher everyone said was the best in the business. When we asked Ms. Leonard if she would help us out, she agreed to leave her own class for a day and teach another group of first-graders a few miles away in Manhattan. We asked her to conduct the class as she usually did, but with two provisions: she was to ignore any negative behavior on the part of the children and praise all positive behavior.

Unbeknownst to Ms. Leonard, one of the kids in her temporary classroom was six-year-old Vincent, who had been diagnosed with ADHD but had not yet started taking medication for the disorder. Also in the classroom that day was a *blind observer*—someone who monitors behavior without knowing why. We asked our blind observer to monitor Ms. Leonard's reactions to four of the children in class, one of whom was Vincent. Every time any of the four children did or said anything, either positive or negative, the observer was to make a note of the child's behavior and describe the teacher's reaction to it in one of three ways: *ignore, criticize,* or *praise.*

Vincent hit the ground running that morning. Before class had even begun, he pulled the hair of the girl in front of him so hard she started to cry. Then he tripped one of his classmates on his way up to the blackboard. When Ms. Leonard gave instructions, he ignored most of them. Ms. Leonard, who richly deserved her reputation as "super-teacher," was flawless in her almost impossible mission. All day long she ignored all the bad things that Vincent did—shouting out, getting up from his seat, and so on. The behavior of the rest of the class was fine for the most part, and she praised and thanked each child who did something positive.

At about two o'clock in the afternoon, when the school day was just about over, Ms. Leonard handed out some papers to the first person in each row and asked the children to take one and pass the rest back. For the first time that day, Vincent did as he was asked, but Ms. Leonard did *not* praise him for his positive behavior. The blind observer made a note of the action and the reaction of the teacher. *"Ignore,"* he wrote. Soon thereafter class was dismissed.

After class we reviewed the events of the day with Ms. Leonard and congratulated her for her overall handling of the class and for her patience and restraint in the face of Vincent's impossible behavior. Then we asked her about her slip at the end of the day.

"At about two o'clock, when you asked the kids to pass the papers back, did you notice that Vincent followed instructions?" the interviewer asked her.

"Yes, I noticed," said Ms. Leonard.

"Oh, we were thinking you might have missed it," said the interviewer.

"No, I definitely saw him do it."

"But you didn't praise the behavior," the interviewer said. "Remember? You were supposed to praise the kids whenever they did something positive."

"Yes, I remember," Ms. Leonard replied. "But after the terrible way that child had behaved all day long, there was no way I was going to say anything nice to him!"

My colleagues and I could do a hundred more studies and dozens of more tests, but one thing is already crystal clear: brain disorders affect a child's behavior in many ways, directly and indirectly, and a child's behavior affects the way he is regarded and treated by the outside world. The longer a child goes without treatment, the more damage will be done to his self-esteem and his prospects for success. If Ms. Leonard, superteacher, can't say anything nice to poor little Vincent, nobody can.

CHAPTER 3

The Doctor-Patient-Parent Relationship

As I've said before in these pages, a child's brain disorder is not his or her parents' fault, but making sure that the youngster is cared for, promptly and properly, is their responsibility. One of the most important decisions that parents of children with brain disorders make in fulfilling this responsibility is choosing a child and adolescent psychiatrist.

There are other health care professionals besides child and adolescent psychiatrists who help troubled children, of course; psychologists, social workers, speech therapists, tutors, and others also play vital roles in helping these kids. Still, the first person a child with a suspected brain disorder should be examined by is a psychiatrist. That assertion leaves me open to accusations of bias, I know, but I'll stand firm in my conviction that in dealing with no-fault brain disorders, child and adolescent psychiatrists make the best diagnosticians. If a child has an ear infection or a stomach virus, he belongs in his pediatrician's office. If his problem is behavioral, he should consult a child and adolescent psychiatrist.

Because they are physicians—M.D.s—child and adolescent psychiatrists are able to evaluate all aspects of a child's development and behavior (including neurology, psychology, language, speech, and hearing), to make a diagnosis, and to recommend a course of treatment. If the recommended treatment includes medication, psychiatrists are able to prescribe the medicine and monitor its effects. If behavioral therapy is called for, psychiatrists can either do the job themselves or send a child to someone else more suitable. If other help is necessary, such as tutoring, speech therapy, social skills training, cognitive behavioral therapy, or family therapy, a psychiatrist is in an excellent position to direct the parents and child to the appropriate expert.

CHOOSING A CHILD AND
ADOLESCENT PSYCHIATRIST

Of course, not all child and adolescent psychiatrists are the same, and finding one who is suitable for the child and acceptable to you may take some time and effort. *Consumer Reports* doesn't cover the field of psychiatry, so parents in need of a child and adolescent psychiatrist will have to do their research the old-fashioned way, by asking for recommendations and checking out credentials.

Most pediatricians will be glad to point interested parents toward a good child and adolescent psychiatrist. School psychologists, principals, and guidance counselors may be able to help you as well, and the same goes for other parents whose children have similar problems. Parents' support groups (listed near the end of this book, in Appendix 2) are also an excellent resource, as are medical schools and university-affiliated medical centers. The American Academy of Child and Adolescent Psychiatry, a professional organization, fills requests for referrals across the nation all the time; it offers not just names but a physician's credentials as well.

Credentials *are* important. Parents owe it to themselves and their children to learn something about the training of the psychiatrist who is going to treat their child. Parents should look for someone trained and *board-certified* in child and adolescent psychiatry; this means that a physician has completed at least five years of training in general psychiatry and child and adolescent psychiatry as well as rotations in neurology and pediatrics or internal medicine, after which he passed an extensive written and oral exam in child and adolescent psychiatry. It is also useful to find out *where* the physician's training took place. Like doctors, some hospitals have a better reputation than others. Parents who aren't comfortable asking the psychiatrist about training and the reputation of a hospital may get the information from their child's pediatrician.

THE INTERVIEW

Many parents like to interview child and adolescent psychiatrists before their children are evaluated. Spending time talking to the doctor can satisfy parents in two important ways: first, you get a sense of the psychiatrist's breadth of skills; and second, you get a feeling for how well the psychiatrist communicates. A child and adolescent psychiatrist, like all physicians, should speak to you in language you can understand. I have little patience with any caregiver whose attitude is, "This is far too technical for you to understand. Why don't you let me, the expert, handle this?" Parents should be comfortable not only with what the psychiatrist has to say but also with how he says it.

There's a good chance that parents faced with this kind of decision are venturing into new, uncharted territory, and they need to be informed and reassured every step of the way. One way to accomplish this is to ask the child and adolescent psychiatrist how he works right up front. Don't be shy about asking questions: What is the procedure for making a diagnosis? Who will be involved? How many sessions will it take? The doctor should be able to give you an idea of the time and expense involved in the diagnostic evaluation.

It pays for parents to be as specific as possible about what is troubling their child. A description of a child's symptoms—"My daughter follows me from room to room and won't let me out of her sight," a parent might say, or "My son refuses to go to school," or "My child seems really depressed," or "He has these terrible temper tantrums all the time" —followed by, "How do you think you might approach the problem?" should give you the lay of the land in short order. Sometimes it makes sense to be even more specific about a child's disorder, asking such questions as:

"My son has tics. Have you ever treated Tourette syndrome?"

"Do you specialize in children with attentional problems?"

"My kid has a real language difficulty. Are you the right person for that?"

"Do you have experience with depression?"

"How many kids have you treated for schizophrenia?"

It's not essential that a child and adolescent psychiatrist specialize in a certain disorder—in fact, many people feel that "generalists" are preferable—but it is advisable to find someone who has some track record with a specific disease. The more familiar a doctor is with a given disorder, the more likely he is to be proficient in treating it. There are many ways of treating a disorder once it has been diagnosed. Practice does make perfect.

Parents would do well also to find out in advance if a psychiatrist has a particular therapeutic approach; that is, which kind of psychiatric treatment the doctor is likely to favor. Some child and adolescent psychiatrists rely exclusively on psychoanalysis or a specific type of psychotherapy. Others work only with medication. Most work with a combination of medication and psychotherapy. You shouldn't expect a psychiatrist to be committed to a specific course of treatment in advance, of course, but it is not unreasonable to expect a straight answer to these kinds of questions, in terms that make sense. Treating a child with a brain disorder is very much a collaborative effort between doctor and parents; mothers and fathers need and deserve to know what's going to happen between the psychiatrist and their child.

In my practice I am very much in favor of psychopharmacology—the use of medication as appropriate in the treatment of children's brain disorders. While nearly all of my patients undergo some sort of behavioral therapy as well, medications are often a very important part of the treatment package I recommend. I strongly advise parents to choose a child and adolescent psychiatrist who keeps an open mind about medicating children and adolescents and who knows how to prescribe medicine when the diagnosis suggests that it is indicated. The best way to find this out is to come right out and ask: "Do you use medication in your work? Is there a role for psychotherapy as well? What is your general approach to treating a problem?" Parents who send their children to doctors who "don't believe in giving drugs to children" are not giving them the chance for recovery that they require and deserve.

Child and adolescent psychiatrists should *listen* to parents as well as speak to them. It's not always easy for a professional, any professional, to take the time to read clippings that parents tear out of magazines or listen to the latest miracle cure that Uncle Henry read about in last week's Sunday supplement, but that's part of a physician's job. If you have something, *anything,* on your mind about the treatment that your child is receiving, the doctor should hear you out and respond accordingly. For example, if you've read about a new treatment for a child's disorder and want to talk about it, the best response from a psychiatrist is: "If you'll send me the information, I'll read it and discuss it with you. I'll tell you the pros and cons as I see them. I'll explain why I agree or disagree." Psychiatrists should be willing to discuss all aspects of a child's case with his parents—provided that the discussions don't violate doctor-patient confidentiality—without becoming defensive or annoyed. It comes with the territory.

THE EVALUATION

Ever since I was a kid I've liked mysteries, especially detective stories. One of the things I've enjoyed most about being in medicine is being able to solve mysteries every day. As far as I'm concerned, when a child comes to me with a problem, I'm a detective. It's my job to ferret out information and unravel the mystery, only instead of "Whodunit?" I'm faced with "What is it?" I've always been a firm believer in getting as much information about a patient as possible. The more information I have access to, the easier time I will have making a diagnosis.

I begin to gather data even before I see a new patient. When parents call for an appointment, I ask them to pull together reports from teachers, guidance counselors, and any physicians or mental health professionals the child has seen and send them to my office in advance. I ask both parents and child to fill out a questionnaire. The parents answer questions about themselves, their families, and their child; the child, assisted by his parents if necessary, provides information about himself. The child's questionnaire includes a "self-rating scale," which identifies the presence of various symptoms by asking for responses to nearly a hundred questions. The questionnaire addresses, among many other subjects, such physical symptoms as headaches, dizziness, chest pains, muscle soreness, numbness, and difficulty breathing; behavior patterns, such as overeating, shouting, throwing things, or having to repeat the same action over and over again; anxieties, such as worries about talking to other people, eating in public, or being watched; and delusions, such as irrational thoughts and ideas not shared by others.

And finally, I ask for the results of a recent physical examination conducted by a child's pediatrician and any cognitive and psychological evaluations a child might have undergone. By the time I meet a child for the first time, a picture of the little boy or girl has already begun to form in my head.

When a family comes to my office for the first time, I spend the first part of the session with the whole group, parents and child, explaining, first of all, what a child and adolescent psychiatrist does. "I help kids who are having problems with their behavior, their feelings, or their thinking" is how I usually put it. During this period I start a discussion of why the youngster has come to see me, making sure to ask the child directly: "Why are you here? What kind of problem do you have? Is it a thinking, feeling, or behaving problem?" Even if the child isn't verbal or responsive, the question has been asked, and the child has been given an opportunity, in his parents' presence, to express himself. Then I ask the parents what *they* think the problem is, and the child hears the answer. As much as possible I try to make everyone acknowledge that there is a problem and to define, however loosely, what it is.

I go on to say to parents and child that the talks I have with children are *private.* I tell parents that there are things that children and adolescents talk to me about that parents are not entitled to know. I'm quite direct with the child too, even if he's very young: "You are the patient," I say. "I will blow the whistle on you if you are going to hurt yourself or someone else, but otherwise everything you tell me about yourself is private. I may tell you what your parents say about you, but I won't tell Mom and Dad what you say unless you give me your permission." This policy occasionally is a source of frustration and irritation to parents, and I sympathize with the adults' desire for full disclosure when it comes to their kids. Still, patient-doctor confidentiality is essential, even when the patient is in kindergarten. A child has to feel he can trust his psychiatrist; it's the only way he'll feel comfortable enough to talk openly to him.

This group meeting should be reassuring to parents as well as the child. As a father myself, I would not want to leave my child alone with a psychiatrist until I had observed their interaction, at least for a few minutes. I would want to be secure in the knowledge that the doctor I've chosen knows how to relate to my child.

The ground rules having been set, I then ask the child to leave for a little while so that I can talk to his mother and father. I assure the youngster that after I talk to his parents, he'll get his chance to spend some time alone with me too. How the child leaves my office is important. Does he leave easily? Does she protest or cry? Does he become physically aggressive? Once he's gone, does he sit patiently in the waiting area, or does he keep interrupting and banging on the door? Does she disrupt the secretary or the physicians and patients in the other offices? I'm watchful for any clues that will help me solve the mystery.

When I am alone with the parents, the second stage of the information-gathering process may begin: taking the *history.* When I take a history, I ask questions about the development of the child's disorder, covering every detail about the child and his extended family. There's an old cliché about the game of baseball that comes to mind: pitching is 90 percent of the game. In my line of work taking the history is 90 percent of the game. Exploring the details of a child's behavior—especially his developmental milestones (described in Chapter 1)—and investigating the psychiatric histories of his mother and father, his grandparents, his aunts and uncles, and his siblings help to give me a very clear picture of the child.

I also use this time to put parents at their ease about the diagnostic process. Parents need time to describe fully and clearly what is bothering them about their child's behavior, and I want them to feel confident that their message is getting across, without feeling rushed by the clock or restricted by the presence of their child. During this encounter, as I take a detailed history from the child's mother and father, there is sometimes a "language barrier" between psychiatrist and parent that needs to be overcome. Words don't always mean the same thing to everyone. The word *depression* is used a lot, but it doesn't often mean "clinical depression"—a psychiatric disorder. *Anxiety* is another frequently used word, but it can be used to refer to any of a hundred different emotions, none of which necessarily indicates an anxiety disorder. Encouraging parents to be very specific is a vital part of taking a history. Parents who come prepared with details make the process go more smoothly.

After I've taken a history from the parents, I excuse the parents and ask the child to come back into the room. "It's time for Harry and me to have a private talk," I might say. Then I ask the child specific questions about his symptoms, ruling out various disorders and narrowing down the possibilities. I ask about his life at home and at school, about his worries, his eating habits, his sleep patterns. All the while I'm observing how the child behaves. Mood, eye contact, motor activity, use of language, comfort level—all are important factors as I evaluate a child's mental status. By the time I have finished talking to the child, I have usually confirmed my diagnosis, and I am ready to call the parents back into the room to talk about treatment.

If medication will be part of the treatment I recommend, I'll check the child's height, weight, blood pressure, and pulse and order blood tests, which rule out anemia and infection and tell me something about his kidney, thyroid, and liver function. Depending on which medication is to be used, I may ask for an electrocardiogram.

THE DIAGNOSIS

Another cliché is appropriate here, but it has nothing to do with baseball. It's strictly medical: *diagnosis drives treatment.* Parents should keep those words in the forefront of their minds as they seek help for their troubled children. In real estate, the saying goes, the three most important criteria are location, location, and location. In child and adolescent psychiatry they are diagnosis, diagnosis, and diagnosis. Before a child and adolescent psychiatrist recommends a course of treatment, he should give parents a diagnosis. Parents are entitled to know what's wrong with their child and how the psychiatrist plans to proceed before agreeing to any course of treatment.

Parents have a right to a full explanation of the recommended treatment. If there is to be medication involved, you should be made aware of what the drug is supposed to do and what the side effects might be. If you ask the question, "What will happen to my child if I do nothing?" you should get a straight answer. If a child needs behavioral therapy in addition to the medicine, parents should be told what the therapy will entail and how they can help. It is in the best interests of everyone—psychiatrist, parents, and child—for parents to be directly involved in a child's treatment, and by that I don't just mean giving him a pill twice a day. If a child needs a special diet, his mom and dad make changes in the kitchen and supervise his meals. When he needs physical therapy, his folks make sure he follows the regimen strictly. It should be the same with behavioral therapy.

Here's how I might put it to parents of a child in therapy. "As far as I'm concerned, you two are both co-therapists here. I can prescribe the medicine, and my psychologist colleague can work with your daughter for an hour a week, but we can't watch her all the time. Even on school days you're with her eight waking hours every day. You're in charge of making sure that things are different at home. I want to give you some strategies to try and things you can do to make the therapy more effective. With your help the therapeutic process will go a lot faster." Most parents gladly rise to the challenge and welcome the opportunity to be involved. (The role of parents is discussed further in Chapter 4.)

Mothers and fathers should be given an idea of how long any treatment is expected to last and how its success or failure will be determined. What are the goals of the treatment? When and how will we know if they have been reached? If you're told, "Oh, the therapy is going to take at least three years. We won't really know anything until then," you should demand a more specific description of the treatment and ask the therapist to describe some short-term goals. It is not unreasonable to ask a therapist for a progress report every three months. Some treatments *do* take years—I'm not disputing that—but three years is far too long to go without seeing substantial improvement. For a child, even six months is too long to wait. A child with a brain disorder cannot afford to waste time.

Parents who are dissatisfied with the progress that their child is making may find it necessary to find another doctor, or at least get a second opinion. If you're uncomfortable questioning the judgment of your child's doctor, you should know that in medicine this sort of thing is done all the time when a treatment doesn't seem to be working. You should tell the treating psychiatrist about the second evaluation and ask him to participate by giving a summary of the child's treatment and progress to the second physician. Sometimes the second doctor agrees with the first, but sometimes what is called for is a fresh approach.

I believe that parents should look for a psychiatrist whose reaction will define short-term goals and set limits, as in: "Listen, I expect the treatment to be finished in six months. We're going to give your child medication, and I'll want to see him once a week every week for four weeks. I may want him to see a psychologist for some behavioral therapy. If everything goes well, we'll switch to an appointment once a month. At the end of six months I expect to see a marked improvement. [Here the psychiatrist will get specific about symptoms.] If at the end of six months we haven't accomplished what we set out to do, we'll reevaluate and possibly take another tack."

A CHILD'S FIRST VISIT

Generally speaking, children aren't thrilled at the prospect of going to the doctor, any doctor. Most parents prepare them well in advance of the visit. Others go the other way, relying instead on the element of surprise. Very young children faced with a visit to a child and adolescent psychiatrist's office may well think nothing of it. In fact, once they have been reassured that they won't have to get an injection, they're usually just fine about the whole thing. Older kids, who may have preconceived notions about psychiatry or who fear that they'll be labeled "weird" or "crazy" if the word gets out to their friends, may have more problems with the first visit.

I believe that a child *should* be prepared, however casually, for his first visit to a psychiatrist. Tricking a child to get him into a doctor's office only adds to the problem by getting the doctor and patient off to a bad start. Kids should have at least a general idea of what they're getting into. In presenting the notion of seeing a psychiatrist to a child, I often suggest that instead of focusing on the child's problem, parents would do well to make it a family matter.

Here's how the conversation might go: "You know what? When one of us in this family has a problem, we all have a problem. We're a family. That's the good part about being a kid. If something is bothering you, we all try to find a way to make it better. If you had a rash, we would put some calamine lotion on it, right? If it still didn't go away, we would go to see Dr. Smith, your pediatrician. If the rash *still* didn't go away, Dr. Smith would send us to see a skin specialist. I'm your mommy, and it's my job to do everything I can to make you feel happy.

"Your dad and I can see that you haven't been very happy lately. You've been crying and upset all the time and fighting with your friends. I don't think you've been having fun in school either. Miss Jones says you seem sad in class. Your dad and I want you to feel better, so we're going to take you to see a special kind of doctor. His name is Dr. Koplewicz."

"What *kind* of doctor?" the child will ask at this point.

"He's a child psychiatrist," the mother might say. "He's the kind of doctor who takes care of children who are sad or upset about something. If kids are having trouble in school or fighting with their friends, he can help them. We've met Dr. Koplewicz already, and he seems very nice and smart. He told us that he's talked to a lot of kids who feel the same way you do. We're all going to see him together. He's going to help you and help us so that we can get over this and you can start feeling happy again."

"A *psychiatrist!*" an older child might say. "Psychiatrists are for people who are crazy. I'm not *crazy!*"

"No, of course, you're not crazy," the parent might say in response. "Anyone who says that people who go to psychiatrists are crazy is wrong. People sometimes say silly things. They don't mean it. They just don't know any better. Child psychiatrists like Dr. Koplewicz help kids who have thinking problems or feeling problems."

I'm not saying that all conversations will go as smoothly as this one. Imaginary dialogues with imaginary children *always* go wonderfully well. Real-life kids are so unpredictable! However, it has been my experience that in this, as in all things, children take their cues from their parents. If Mom and Dad are straightforward and upbeat about a visit to a psychiatrist—and they certainly should be—children will follow their lead.

CHAPTER 4

The Art of Parenting
a Troubled Child

In the course of writing this book I had occasion to spend time with many of the parents of the children and adolescents I have treated over the last ten years. We had talked in the past, of course, but this time around our conversations were different from those that went before. I wasn't taking a history from the parents, offering an opinion about whether or not their child was ready for sleepaway camp, or discussing the possibility of discontinuing a child's medication. This time I asked the mothers and fathers of my patients to talk about themselves, and especially about how it feels to have a child with a no-fault brain disorder. Many of the stories that those parents told me have made their way into this book, particularly the "Parenting" sections of the many chapters in Part Three. Still, some of what I learned during those conversations calls, I believe, for a brief summing up here.

As it turned out, the most revealing question I put to all of the parents who agreed to speak to me was, "What is the worst thing about having a child with a brain disorder?" Everyone had a different answer.

"Taking her out in public and seeing people's looks of disapproval," one parent said.

"Having to rethink the whole idea of what having a kid is all about. Before our son came along, we were living in a dream world," said another.

"I worry about what's going to become of her, like will she fall in love and get married and have kids of her own? I want all of that for her," a mother told me.

And from a frustrated father: "It's so hard to accept that I can't make my son happy all the time. I always thought I'd be able to do that."

The parents I've just quoted are managing quite well with their kids, all things considered, but like all moms and dads, they have their good days and their bad days. Faced with the increased demands associated with having a child with a brain disorder, they occasionally are demoralized, impatient, and just plain cranky. "I just get so tired of having to do everything the hard way," one mother told me, somewhat sheepishly. "I see other mothers with their perfect little kids, and it's all so easy for them. They get to relax with their kids. I don't get to do that. Being just a good mother isn't enough. I've got to be super-mom. There's so much work involved in getting through our daily life."

What that mother says is true, and nearly all parents of children with brain disorders are overcome, now and then, by that "How come everything is so hard for us?" feeling. Parents with problem kids *do* work harder than mothers and fathers whose children are normal. Parenting skills that are perfectly adequate for normal kids just don't cut it with children who have brain disorders. For example, if a normal child misbehaves, parents can ignore the behavior once in a while ("picking your battles," some parents call it), but parents of kids with brain disorders have to be so much more vigilant about their reactions, always praising positive behavior and always correcting negative behavior. If they let their guard down even for a minute, they may lose ground in the behavior modification battle. As one father put it, "With my kid there's less of a margin for error."

Parents of children with brain disorders have to be consistent, much more so than the average parent. The "good cop/bad cop" parenting approach that many mothers and fathers rely on is disastrous with these kids. There's no place whatsoever for the time-honored "Wait until your father gets home" or "Let's ask your mother and see what she says."

It's not easy to be "on duty" all the time. In fact, nothing about this process is easy. However, as the parents who shared their personal experiences with me made quite clear, it *can* be done. Being a good, responsible parent of a child with a brain disorder brings special challenges, certainly, but they are challenges that can be met, with style, grace, and even a sense of humor. Parents looking for answers should bear in mind the following words of advice from people who have been there.

ACKNOWLEDGE AND ACCEPT THAT THERE'S A PROBLEM. Coming to grips with the fact that a child has a brain disorder and needs psychiatric help—which may include medication—is not easy for any parent, but it has to be done. Parents who pretend that there's nothing wrong with their child only impede the treatment and hold their child back from a happier life. "It took us a long time—too long—to take our daughter to see a psychiatrist," a father said. "I was the problem. My wife wanted to go, but I kept saying, 'No, let's wait.' I can't imagine what I was waiting for. I just couldn't bring myself to admit that she was sick. I just couldn't deal with the fact that the problem was so serious."

One mother told me about her frustration in accepting that her son's anxiety disorder was something she couldn't fix herself. "I tried reasoning with him—I was *so* patient—but it was like talking to a wall. I used to have fantasies of those movies with people who act crazy until someone slaps them across the face and says, 'Snap out of it!' And the person would, of course. Eventually I had to accept the fact that my son's disease wasn't something that I could snap him out of."

LEARN ABOUT THE DISEASE. "I was amazed at how little I knew about why kids behave the way they do," a mother said. "I grew up in a spare-the-rod-spoil-the-child kind of family. If my brothers and sisters and I didn't do what we were told, we got smacked, good and hard, by both of our parents. I'll never forget—one of my sisters, who was 13 years old at the time, used to wet her bed almost every night. Whenever she did it, my father would hit her the next morning.

"I feel terrible saying this, but that was my first reaction when our little boy started giving us so much trouble. I never hit him, but I sure was tempted. Once I knew what was wrong with him, once I understood that the trouble was in his brain, I felt a lot calmer about it, and I could be reasonable. I doubt that I can ever make my family understand, but that's okay. All that really matters is that *we* get it."

Another mother talked about how important it was for her and her husband to do their homework about their child's disorder. "If my husband could have found a way not to be a part of this whole thing, I think he would have. But I got him to go for family therapy, and then I brought home all kinds of literature about our son's disease. I got him hooked. Before he knew what hit him, he became a vital part of our child's treatment. Understanding the disease was the key."

BE REALISTIC. Parents with children who have brain disorders don't live in a "Leave It to Beaver" world, and the sooner they come to terms with that fact of life, the better off everyone will be. "I tried so hard to be like everybody else," said the mother of one of my patients. "I kept thinking that if I planned ahead enough, if I anticipated absolutely every contingency, then we could have a perfectly *normal* life. When I finally got over trying to control everything, we started having our own life. It wasn't exactly what anybody would consider normal, but it was good and we liked it. We were a lot happier after I lightened up."

DON'T TAKE IT PERSONALLY. Every parent carries around some emotional baggage, and it's not always simple to set it aside when dealing with problem kids. Some parents regard their kids' imperfections as a personal insult and react accordingly. One father who felt that way at first described his feelings to me quite candidly: "This is going to make me sound really shallow and like some kind an egomaniac, I know, but it was really hard for me to accept that there was something wrong with my kid. Image is very important to me, in my business and in the rest of my life. I really had to work hard at accepting that my kid is not me. I am not living my life through him. When I finally got that into my head, I did a much better job of helping him. I learned a lot from this."

Most brain disorders have a genetic component, so many parents' reactions are complicated by the fact that they themselves grew up with a disorder similar to that of their children or have a close relative with the same problem. "I had terrible social phobia when I was a kid," a mother said. "I still do, really. So it was sheer torture to watch my daughter go through it. I felt sorry for her, and I hated myself for giving it to her. Sometimes I think I even hated her a little. Making sure that I was thinking about *her* and not myself was one of the hardest things I've ever had to do."

BE PREPARED. As I say more than once in these pages, parents should be co-therapists for their child, and that means working, hard, with qualified professionals to learn parenting techniques designed to bring about the desired changes in a child's behavior. "I feel as if I have a doctorate in child psychology," a bemused father said to me. "My wife and I now have gotten so good at handling our son that I'm thinking of turning pro. I used to think that all you need when you deal with kids is common sense, but I was wrong. Common sense doesn't always work with these kids. We had to memorize all kinds of new methods. Now we know exactly what to say and how to react whenever our little boy does something he's not supposed to do. I guess we're not very spontaneous, but at least we're getting on with our lives. It used to be World War III around here every day."

KEEP THE HOME FIRES BURNING. Children's brain disorders are rough on marriages, and it's not difficult to see why. Anger, guilt, blame, feelings of inadequacy, recrimination—none of these is likely to strengthen and solidify a relationship between husband and wife. Strained relationships are all but inevitable as parents come to terms with a child's disorder. Disharmony comes in as many forms as there are marriages. One of the most common sources of tension is a situation in which one parent makes the other do all the work. Here's how one mother described her husband's reaction to her son's problem. "Years ago, when we first found out that Grant was quite sick—the diagnosis was depression—my husband basically checked out for a time. He's a wonderful man and a terrific father, but he just couldn't handle having a child with a mental illness. For three months he barely talked to Grant. He'd come home from work and stick his nose in the newspaper or a book until it was time for Grant to go to bed. I was the one out in the backyard playing catch with Grant or trying to get him to talk. My husband found Grant so difficult that he kind of withdrew. He wouldn't engage him, or maybe he couldn't. He said he felt as if he were walking on eggs with his own son. And it's true: Grant did fly off the handle really easily with his father. The least little thing would set him off. Eventually we went to parent counseling for a couple of sessions and really talked things out. My husband checked back in. We're fine now, but it was rough there for a while. I can definitely see how a marriage could just fall apart."

The feelings of another father were more mixed. "I'd go off to work every morning feeling like a monster. There I was, abandoning my wife and my poor crazy daughter. Part of me wanted to stay home and help, but another part was glad to be out of there, away from all the sadness and stress. But then things got better. The medication really helped, and I got more involved. I stopped feeling that I was letting my family down all the time."

Once in a while a crisis brings families together right away. "We were like a tag team," one mother told me. "Both of us would get discouraged now and then, but somehow it was never at the same time. We would kind of take turns. When I gave out, he was always there to take over. I quit my job for a year to look after Samantha when she was first diagnosed with pervasive developmental disorder, but my husband came home from the office whenever I needed a break. All I had to do was call. I can't say that the house looked all that great—we were too busy caring for Samantha to do much dusting or vacuuming—but we managed. There were plenty of times that we were unhappy, plenty of times when we cried ourselves to sleep. But we never had a fight about it. We always stuck together."

The story that Samantha's mother tells is unusual. Most parents *do* have arguments as a result of their child's brain disorder. That's why I often give a prescription for parents as well as the children. The child gets medicine. For the parents I often recommend dinner and a movie or, even better, a night in a hotel. (We call it *relationship hygiene*.) Even perfect parents need a break once in a while.

When parents find it necessary to spend a lot of time focusing on the problems of one child, the other children in the family may feel slighted. When a child has a brain disorder, it affects the entire family, and it is often difficult for parents to keep the nurturing scale in balance, tending to the needs of the children *without* problems. As complicated as it may seem, I recommend that parents set aside time to be with each of their children.

DON'T TRY TO DO IT ALONE. Some parents need help coping with guilt. Others need to talk about how hard it is to keep their tempers when their children try their patience. ("I know he can't help himself when he behaves like a lunatic, but sometimes I want to swat him so badly my hands itch," more than one rueful parent has said to me.) Speaking openly about a child's condition and involving others—teachers, friends, relatives—in the process of making him well can be a big help to parents in crisis. "I really didn't want to talk to anybody about this, but I finally broke down and told a close friend that my daughter was taking Prozac for her anxiety disorder," one mother told me. "It turns out that she has a son who has ADHD. It was such a relief to talk to somebody who knew what I was going through."

Parent counseling, individual therapy, and group therapy can all be helpful to parents in distress. Newsletters and support groups aimed at parents whose children have specific brain disorders are excellent sources of both practical information and emotional solace. (See Appendix 2 for a list of useful publications and support groups.) Not every parent I've spoken to feels the need to join a group—in fact, some would never dream of doing such a thing—but for those who feel they would benefit from the company of other parents who are going through similar experiences, support groups are quite wonderful.

"I always feel really great after I've been to one of the meetings," one mother told me enthusiastically. "Everyone is so open about sharing information about doctors and medication, and nobody's embarrassed. Being there always makes me feel as if I'm doing the right thing for my daughter. There are parents with kids who are worse off than mine and some with kids whose cases are more mild. All the people in that room have nearly the same life as mine and the same difficulties. We talk about our marriages. We talk about our horrible relatives and our nasty neighbors and exchange tips about getting teachers to cooperate. Knowing that I'm not alone, that someone else just like me is going through this, really means a lot to me."

DNA Roulette
and the
Role of Medication

The two chapters that make up Part Two of this book explain what causes a child's brain disorder and why medication may well be the solution to a very serious problem.

CHAPTER 5

The Chemistry of the Brain

Over the last 20 years there has been a major breakthrough in the understanding of emotional and behavioral disorders in children and adolescents. In the past, childhood psychiatric disorders were thought to be caused by early childhood traumas or bad parenting or sometimes both. Today we recognize the vital role of the brain itself. The effects of brain chemistry on mood, emotions, and behavior are part of the standard psychiatric curriculum in medical schools and university training hospitals all around the world. We know that children don't just develop psychiatric disorders as a result of outside stimuli. They're born with them, or at least with a vulnerability to them. It's a function of the brain.

Just as a baby is born with brown eyes or blood that's type B positive, he or she comes into this world with a certain genetically determined neuroanatomy and brain chemistry. Each of these elements contributes to the way that a child develops, learns, and behaves. With luck the child's brain will be "perfect"—sufficiently adaptable and not vulnerable to a disorder—so that he won't be anxious, depressed, inattentive, or compulsive. When luck fails and there's a severe imbalance in the brain, the child will experience emotional or behavioral difficulties. Contrary to what we used to think, these are not "emotional problems." These are brain disorders with emotional and behavioral symptoms. There's a big difference.

Children with brain disorders—attention deficit hyperactivity disorder, separation anxiety disorder, obsessive compulsive disorder, depression, and the many other disorders examined at length in the pages that follow—have these disorders largely because of the way their brains work. The fact that the symptoms of these disorders are behavioral doesn't change the fact that there is a neurobiological basis to them. Parents are no more to "blame" for a child's psychiatric disorder than they are to "blame" for his epilepsy or his red hair.

The parents of the children I treat aren't always eager to learn about brain chemistry, I know. Some, like the mother who showed up at my office with her own personal copy of *Diagnostic and Statistical Manual of Mental Disorders,* the diagnostic bible of the American Psychiatric Association, enjoy speaking the language and embrace the technicalities of their child's disorder. Others take the tack of the impatient father whose reaction was just the opposite: "Look, Doctor, when my watch is broken, I don't want to know why. I just want the jeweler to fix it!" Most parents are somewhere in the middle. "I really care about what's wrong with my kid, but this brain chemistry stuff is so *complicated*" is the comment I hear most frequently, and for good reason.

The workings of the brain *are* complicated. Even so, I encourage parents of children with a brain disorder to know a little something about the chemistry of the brain—not enough to diagnose disease or prescribe medicine, naturally, but enough to understand their child's disorder and sympathize with it. Even the most data-resistant parents will find it comforting to know that their child's bad mood or his alarming behavior is not willful or based on whim; the child is behaving that way because of his brain. What follows is a brief look at the basics.

THE NEUROTRANSMITTERS

It is useful to think of the brain as a system of message networks that are connected to one another, like a telephone network. Behavior is determined when one part of the brain dials the "phone number" of another part of the brain. The "phone call" is transmitted through the nerves. A message from one nerve cell to another nerve cell in the brain is transmitted by means of chemicals. These chemicals, called *neurotransmitters,* trigger the electrical signals that produce our thoughts, our emotions, our memories, our sleep patterns, and our will. When everything goes as it should, the phone calls made in our brains are completed as dialed; when something goes wrong—when there's too much or too little of one of the necessary neurotransmitters—we get a wrong number or a busy signal.

The brain has literally millions of nerve cells, each of which sends messages within itself by means of electricity. That electricity, which is generated chemically, moves from one end of the nerve to the other end. When it gets to the end, the nerve does not connect directly to another nerve. Nerves end in a space called a *synapse*. That's where the neurotransmitters come in. They float across that space, touch other nerves, and cause a chemical reaction that creates more electricity and sends the message on. The body is very careful about protecting and saving everything it produces, so once a nerve has sent its signal, it will attempt to take the chemicals back and store them until they're needed again—a kind of "recycling" project in the brain. The process is called *reuptake*.

The messages that the neurotransmitters send from nerve to nerve are governed by three factors: first, which specific nerves are connected by these chemicals; second, the intensity of the connection, which in turn governs the strength of the signal; and third, the pattern of connections: where a set of nerves goes and to what part of the brain it sends messages. In describing the significance of the signal's strength, a colleague of mine uses a model he calls "I'm a Little Teapot." As he describes it, the rate at which someone pouring tea from a teapot sends the liquid into the cup depends on how much he tips the teapot; similarly, a strong signal in the brain results in a lot of messages. If the pourer of the tea puts his finger in the spout, no tea will come out no matter how much he tips the teapot, not unlike what happens when a brain signal is blocked by chemicals. If he tips the teapot over too fast, the tea will probably slosh out over the lid. Again, too strong a signal will send too many messages in the brain, and to the wrong destination.

The critical factor here is to regulate the strength of the signal that is "poured" into the synapse. While there are literally dozens of chemicals capable of transmitting their own messages, three seem to be the most critical, because we can measure them easily, because their actions are consistent with our hypotheses about the physiology of brain disorders, and because we have medications that can alter their functions. The three basic chemicals—neurotransmitters—that affect the process are:

- *Serotonin.* This neurotransmitter is related to anxiety, depression, and aggression.
- *Dopamine.* This neurotransmitter affects the perception of reality.
- *Norepinephrine.* This neurotransmitter affects attention and concentration.

There are other important neurotransmitters in the brain, such as hormones, which send messages that bring on a woman's premenstrual syndrome, among other things; catecholamines (including adrenaline), which affect arousal patterns (the "fight or flight" reactions) and raise blood pressure; and histamine, which stops up the ears and makes the nose run. All of these neurotransmitters can be affected and often are (with hormone replacement therapy or antihistamines, for instance), but in the treatment of child and adolescent psychiatric disorders we are dealing mostly with the Big Three: serotonin, dopamine, and norepinephrine. Those words will come up many times in these pages as we examine the psychiatric disorders that affect children and adolescents.

THE DELICATE BALANCE

Every muscle in the body has an opposing muscle. For example, the biceps muscle makes the arm go up, and the triceps muscle makes it go down. The same is true for the central nervous system. Every nerve or nerve action has an opposing nerve action. When the sides are evenly balanced, everything runs smoothly; but when one side is stronger than the other, there are problems. In *psychopharmacology*—the treatment of psychiatric disorders with medication—we try to restore the brain's chemical balance, so that the body and the brain may maintain some equilibrium. Someone driving a car on which the wheels on the right are spinning faster than the wheels on the left will go around in circles, never getting anywhere. The only way to get the car moving forward is to balance the motion of the wheels. That's roughly what we try to do—adjust the brain so that all of its wheels are spinning forward at the same rate of speed.

Good psychopharmacology effects changes that are subtle. It doesn't mean sedating a patient or making him super-alert; it involves getting the patient back on an even keel. When we treat a child with attention deficit hyperactivity disorder (see Chapter 7), our goal is to increase the child's ability to pay attention. If he pays too much attention, he may become suspicious or obsessive and not be able to get anything done. If he pays too little attention, he can't be productive either. In treating the child with ADHD, usually with daily doses of Ritalin or some other stimulant, we try to find the middle ground, where balance is restored and a child is paying exactly the right amount of attention. This is true of all the brain disorders that we treat with medication. Our aim is always the same: to restore a chemical balance in the brain.

Pulling off this balancing act is often easier said than done. The body has many ways to regulate itself. In correcting a balance problem we choose one place to regulate the neurotransmission, but that one place is not necessarily the only spot that will work. There's more than one way to increase or decrease a specific neurotransmitter. Different drugs may work at different sites on the brain and achieve the same effect.

Furthermore, there is virtually no such thing as a "norepinephrine disease" or a "serotonin disorder" or a "dopamine disease." Most disorders are the result of more than one neurotransmitter malfunction. It's as if we have a man and a woman in an office building in different elevators, and we want them to get to the same floor at the same time so that they can meet and work together. The man is on an elevator—the serotonin elevator—that is stopped on the fourth floor; the woman is on the eighth floor in the dopamine elevator. In order to get them to the same level, we can do one of three things: raise the serotonin elevator up to the eighth floor; bring the dopamine elevator down to the fourth floor; or adjust both elevators so that the man and woman have their meeting on the sixth floor. Any of these is a satisfactory solution; any is possible. Our job is to find the best strategy to restore balance.

It's important to realize that we are talking about very small amounts of chemicals here. We measure the neurotransmitter serotonin in nanograms, which is about one 10-billionth of a pound. Dopamine is measured in picograms, roughly 10 trillionths of a pound. Brain chemicals are powerful stuff, and a minute discrepancy can have a substantial impact on a child's behavior.

Every brain is different, of course. A drug may work beautifully for one child and do nothing for another even if both children have exactly the same disorder. Sometimes drugs have only a temporary effect. The medicines increase the level of a neurotransmitter, but over time the brain compensates for the change and says, "Wait. There's too much of that chemical coming through," and instinctively makes the adjustment by cutting it back. The short-term result of treatment is an increase of that neurotransmitter, but over the long term there may be an actual decrease. For all of these reasons and more it takes time and sometimes several careful trials to determine which medication, at which dosage, a child needs. The challenge is to find the right balance for each child.

OUTSIDE AGITATORS

Medicine isn't the only thing that can bring about a chemical change in the brain. Environmental experiences may also have an effect on the neurotransmitters. There is strong evidence that stress alters brain chemistry, especially in a brain that is vulnerable. Not everyone reacts the same way to a stressful or painful situation. The death of a loved one makes everyone sad, sometimes very sad for an extended period of time, but only in a few people does such an event lead to the persistent, debilitating symptoms of clinical depression (see Chapter 14). Severe illness, divorce, a change of location, physical or mental abuse—all of these will take their toll on a child's brain. If the chemical makeup of his brain makes him vulnerable to a psychiatric disorder, outside stimuli may well bring it on.

The brain is not a constant. It adapts and changes according to the environment. One of my colleagues compares the process to a home thermostat that is always set at 68 degrees. In the winter the temperature starts to drop, so the heat goes on, brings the house back to 68 degrees, and shuts off. In the heat of summer, when the temperature rises, the air conditioner kicks on and cools the house to 68 degrees again. The brain has a kind of thermostat too. In times of stress we may get anxious or sad, but our thermostats keep us from straying too far away from our ideal set point. We're anxious when we have to give a speech or a little depressed when we go to a funeral, but we bounce back.

Those unpleasant feelings don't last forever, any more than the elation associated with good news lasts forever. A man who gets a promotion and a raise is ecstatic. He and his wife go out to dinner to celebrate, and they drink champagne. For a few days he's on top of the world, but a week later things are pretty much back to normal. He doesn't stay on top of the world for the rest of his life. His thermostat does its job.

However, some children have thermostats that aren't set quite right, so their ability to keep their emotions and their behavior within normal boundaries is seriously impaired. Perhaps they can't sit still or pay attention in class. Maybe they're overanxious or depressed. They could be compulsive or have involuntary tics. In psychopharmacology we're in the business of resetting children's thermostats so that their heating and air conditioning systems keep the temperature just right.

PSYCHOPHARMACOLOGY 101

Our lives are basically divided into three spheres: love, fun, and work. In the case of children those spheres are translated into the relationship with their parents, social interactions with their friends, and learning in school. A mild imbalance in a child's brain—a little too much norepinephrine, for instance—usually will not cause any real distress or dysfunction. He'll still love his parents, he'll have friends, and he'll function perfectly well in school. No treatment will be necessary. However, if the chemical imbalance is severe and a child's activities in any of these areas are significantly altered for an extended period of time, we take a closer look. We may decide to alter the chemical makeup of the child's brain with medication.

Each of the three essential chemicals in the brain is affected by different categories of drugs:

- Serotonin is affected by groups of drugs called *SSRIs* (selective serotonin reuptake inhibitors). The best known of the SSRIs are Prozac, Zoloft, and Paxil.
- Dopamine is affected by drugs called *neuroleptics,* among them Haldol, Thorazine, and Mellaril.
- Norepinephrine and dopamine are affected by a group of drugs called *psychostimulants* or, more often, just *stimulants.* Ritalin and Dexedrine are the two most frequently prescribed stimulants.
- Norepinephrine and serotonin are affected by the *TCAs* (tricyclic antidepressants). The best known of the TCAs are Tofranil, Elavil, and Norpramin.
- Norepinephrine is affected by the *antihypertensive agents.* Developed originally for patients with high blood pressure, the antihypertensives, especially Catapres and Tenex, are now used in the treatment of children's brain disorders.
- Serotonin and dopamine are affected by the *atypical antipsychotics.* The most commonly prescribed drugs in this category are Risperdal and Clozaril.

- All three of the neurotransmitters—serotonin, dopamine, and norepinephrine—are affected by a category of drugs called the *MAOIs* (monamine oxidase inhibitors), which slow the metabolism of the brain's neurotransmitters. Nardil and Parnate are the most commonly prescribed MAOIs.

(When I talk about various medicines in these pages, I usually refer to them by brand name, because in my experience that is the name with which people are most familiar. Appendix 3, Psychopharmacology at a Glance, lists the generic as well as the brand names of all the major psychiatric drugs.)

All the medicines prescribed for the treatment of brain disorders do one of four things: (1) they block the metabolism of the neurotransmitter, so that more of the neurotransmitter is available; (2) they block the place where the neurotransmitter connects, making it more difficult for the message to be sent; (3) they block the reuptake of the neurotransmitter, making the neurotransmitter more available; and (4) they block the release of the neurotransmitter. We can put this even more simply and reduce the functions to two. Either the drugs increase the availability of these chemicals and send more of a message, or they decrease the availability of the chemicals and send less of a message. We prescribe a medicine depending on whether we want to facilitate or to block the neurotransmitter message. Ritalin is a facilitator. Thorazine and Haldol are blockers. Prozac and Paxil block the reuptake, or recycling, of the neurotransmitter.

In a perfect world we would be able to zero in on a specific chemical in a particular synapse and make the change that's needed, but the drugs available to us aren't advanced enough at this point to treat a specific disorder. The brain is complex, and very few medications are "clean"; that is, when a patient takes a drug, it is rare that the level of only one brain chemical is affected in only one part of the brain. If a drug we prescribe affects serotonin, it will affect the serotonin everywhere in the brain, not just in the areas of the brain that are responsible for a child's compulsions or his depression. A drug that affects dopamine levels won't work its magic just on the area of the brain that is responsible for schizophrenia; it affects all the parts of the brain that use dopamine.

Brain disorders aren't "clean" either. We often encounter *co-*

morbidity, a situation in which children have two or even more brain disorders at the same time. For example, attention deficit hyperactivity disorder may be *co-morbid* with conduct disorder; separation anxiety disorder is often *co-morbid* with major depressive disorder; and obsessive compulsive disorder is sometimes linked with Tourette syndrome. To complicate matters even further, brain disorders often involve more than one neurotransmitter, and there is interaction among the neurotransmitters; when we change the level of one, it may have an impact on the others. These neurotransmitters don't react in a vacuum. Increasing the brain's level of serotonin may, as a side effect, decrease the level of dopamine.

Unfortunately, much of what we know about brain chemistry can't be diagnosed with blood tests, X rays, or other tools. If there's something wrong with a child's liver, we can give him a local anesthetic, use a long needle, do a biopsy, and find out exactly what the problem is. There's no such thing as a routine brain biopsy; that procedure would be far too drastic for these purposes. Still, there has been some progress in the field, largely in the *neuroimaging techniques,* which give us new insights by allowing us to examine certain physiological and chemical processes that take place in the brain basically by producing three-dimensional images of the brain.

Neuroimaging techniques have helped us reach an important conclusion: there are brain abnormalities in adults who have brain disorders. Although studies of children and adolescents are in the very early stages, there is already reason to think that they have brain differences too. These techniques can also be very useful in helping us understand how the brain works and especially how various medicines affect the brain's function. For all of their value, however, neuroimaging techniques are not used for diagnosis. For diagnosis the best tool always has been and probably always will be behavioral observation. No matter how many tests a child undergoes, we base our diagnosis on a child's history and his behavioral symptoms. These tools allow us to diagnose a brain disorder as precisely and as reliably as physicians diagnose diabetes and hypertension.

The fact is, there is a lot of information about the brain that we don't yet have. We know that children with psychiatric disorders have a chemical imbalance in the brain that is caused by a genetic abnormality, but we don't know what the specific abnormality is. And we don't know precisely *why* these medicines work. We just know that they *do* work. That's nothing new to medicine, of course. Digitalis has been around for hundreds of years. We've been using it for heart attacks for decades, but until relatively recently we had no idea why it works. We just knew that it did.

CHAPTER 6

The Great Medication Debate

According to his mother, 10-year-old Adam had always been a "difficult child." When Adam and his parents came to my office for the first time, I learned that the little boy had been seeing a psychologist three times a week for five years. That's roughly *750 sessions*. Adam was still having serious trouble with his behavior. He wasn't doing well in school, and he didn't have any friends to speak of. I asked the parents what had taken them so long to bring their child to a psychiatrist.

"Well, Adam's psychologist has been telling us for several years that he probably needs medication for his attention deficit hyperactivity disorder, but we were afraid to do it," the mother replied. "We thought that it would change his personality," added the father. "And besides, we don't like the idea of medicating a child."

I've met a lot of parents who don't like the idea of medicating a child for a brain disorder—or anything else, for that matter—but that was the first time I had ever encountered parents who preferred 750 sessions of psychotherapy that didn't work to a daily dose of medication that does work. After two weeks of a moderate dose of Ritalin Adam was a lot better. His parents, his teacher, and his friends noticed the change right away.

FOOLING MOTHER NATURE

Adam's parents are not alone, of course. Many fathers and mothers are adamantly opposed to the idea of psychopharmacology for their children. "My kid on drugs? *Never!*" is something I've heard more than a few times. Parents who wouldn't think twice about giving their children insulin to treat diabetes or an inhaler to ease the symptoms of asthma balk at the prospect of giving their child medication for a mental disorder, for any number of reasons. They worry that the child will become addicted to the medication or will be encouraged to abuse other drugs. They fear that the child will be stigmatized by taking medication. They're concerned about the negative side effects. Some parents regard giving a child medication as taking the easy way out. They think that a more "natural" approach—for example, withholding sugar and caffeine, or using discipline, or trying to get to the root cause of every problem— is the more desirable, even the morally superior, course of treatment.

"Isn't it a crutch?" some concerned parents ask, and I have to say yes, I suppose medication is a kind of crutch. But if a child's leg is broken, what's wrong with a crutch? If a youngster has a broken limb, he can't be expected to get around without some help. If a child has an infection, doesn't he take antibiotics? If a child's brain isn't functioning the way it's supposed to, shouldn't he be given whatever assistance is available to make it easier for him to lead a normal life, free of distress and dysfunction? Parents have to understand that brain disorders must be taken as seriously as asthma, diabetes, or any other organic problem. A child with a brain disorder is suffering, and there is nothing wrong with using medication to relieve a child's suffering.

Many parents who come to see me don't need to be persuaded about the virtues of medication. This is especially true of parents who have been helped by some of these medications themselves. When I recently prescribed a low dosage of Zoloft, an antidepressant, for a little girl with selective mutism, her parents didn't hesitate for a moment to follow my advice. "You know, a year ago I started taking Zoloft for depression, and it completely changed my life," the little girl's mother said. "There was a time I would never have dreamed of giving my child psychiatric medicine, but I don't feel that way anymore."

The father of a little boy with severe obsessive compulsive disorder put his feelings about medication even more succinctly: "Our son's life began the day he started taking his medicine."

THE STIGMA OF MEDICINE

It's all very well for my colleagues and me to equate brain disorders with diabetes and to say that giving a child Ritalin shouldn't be any different from making sure he takes his insulin. We know that there *is* a difference. A pediatrician looks in a child's ears, detects an infection, and prescribes ampicillin. Parents give the child his medicine without missing a beat. Do they ask the pediatrician about its long-term side effects or question him closely about what caused the infection? Probably not, or at least not at any length. They might even tell their friends about it. There's no stigma attached to having an ear infection. Most parents won't keep a child's diabetes a secret. There is, unfortunately, a stigma attached to having a brain disorder, and as a result many parents are secretive about their children's problems and the fact that they're taking medication.

When I hear stories of how some people react, I can't really blame parents for keeping the news to themselves. One worried mother called me because the principal at her child's school said her son shouldn't be taking the Ritalin I had prescribed (and to which he was responding wonderfully well). The Ritalin is a crutch, the principal said; what the child really needed was a lighter school schedule and a different teacher. I was shocked by the principal's ignorance, not to mention his colossal nerve. If I had prescribed two puffs of an inhaler to keep a child with asthma from wheezing during gym class, I doubt that the principal would have suggested that the child forget the medicine and be excused from gym instead.

Another mother showed up at my office in tears. Her daughter's teacher had told her that medicine—in this case an antidepressant for separation anxiety disorder—is the worst possible thing for a growing child. "I can't believe you're giving her drugs," the teacher said to the mother. (This was the same teacher who, only a few months earlier, had told the mother that her six-year-old daughter Ellen had some real problems, that all she did all day in class was stare down at her desk, cry, and ask to go home to her mommy.) Ellen's mother sputtered a response to the teacher: "But you told me there was a problem. I'm trying to fix it." The teacher's response: "I told you to do something, but I didn't mean this." The fact that with the medication Ellen was able to attend class all day without chronic worries and fears didn't affect the teacher's attitude.

Teachers aren't the only people who routinely second-guess child and adolescent psychiatrists who prescribe medication. Most relatives aren't shy about giving their medical opinions either. We're always being told that Aunt Judy heard that Zoloft is better than Prozac or Grandpa read somewhere that lithium doesn't really work. And then there are the well-meaning family members who just blame the parents.

"When we told my family that Josh is taking medication, they completely flipped out," said the mother of a four-year-old. "They think that we should be able to handle Josh ourselves. My sister gave me a long lecture about how I spoil my son and how he would be perfectly fine if I would just stop paying so much attention to him." The attention that she'd been lavishing on her son involved preventing Josh from overturning tables and pulling down drapes at family gatherings. Before the medication she couldn't turn her back on Josh for a minute. He would literally climb the walls.

When children are on medication, it's not just the parents who are judged. Teachers and others sometimes look askance at the children themselves. That's why one mother waited until halfway through the school year to tell the school that her eight-year-old daughter was taking Prozac. "I wanted them to get to know Maria first, without hearing about the Prozac. If they knew about the medicine from the beginning, they'd have all these preconceived notions about her. That's all they would think about. Once they know she's a great kid, they won't think about her as the little girl who takes the medicine. When I finally got around to telling them she was taking Prozac, their reaction was, 'Why? She seems fine to us.'"

Other parents flatly refuse to tell the school about a child's medication. The father of a 13-year-old girl who has been taking Cylert for many years says that he has been burned so often by unsupportive, uncooperative school officials that he has decided not to tell them about it anymore. "We lied on the health form, and we've encouraged our daughter not to say anything about her treatment," the man, himself a doctor, said to me. "This isn't how we want it to be, but we're tired of hearing lectures from people who don't know what they're talking about. I don't want my daughter to suffer because people are ignorant and prejudiced."

Naturally no one can force parents to confide in teachers or other school officials, but schools do usually require full disclosure, and I recommend it too, in theory at least. A collaborative approach should be the goal. I advise the parents of my patients to let me work with the school psychologist and the school nurse to coordinate the child's treatment. I believe that teachers should be involved in the treatment whenever possible, especially if a child's symptoms affect his behavior in the classroom. It is a teacher's job to help *all* the kids in class, but before teachers can help, they have to know what the problem is.

I've known many teachers who are immensely helpful to these troubled kids; it's not unusual, in fact, for a teacher to be instrumental in identifying problems or persuading parents to seek help. One school principal I know, a seasoned professional, arranged to meet two parents near the end of their eight-year-old son's academic year. The principal suggested gently to the parents that their child's behavior was out of the normal range and that he should be evaluated by a child and adolescent psychiatrist. The principal went on to say that the child might need medication.

"Oh, we've had him looked at," the mother said.

"Yes, the psychiatrist said he needed drugs, but we don't believe in them for kids," the father added.

"I believe you should reconsider," countered the principal. "If your son had a vision problem, you'd get glasses, wouldn't you? You wouldn't just expect him to *squint.*" The parents showed up in my office the following week.

Most very young children in treatment for a brain disorder hardly give a thought to the fact that they have to take medication on a regular basis, except perhaps to regard it as a minor inconvenience. However, as kids get a little older, they may become embarrassed or even ashamed about needing medicine. Many children don't want their friends to find out. They're fearful that what happened to a 14-year-old boy I treated will happen to them: when he told his friends he was taking medicine, they laughed at him and called him "Psycho." No one ever said that children are overly sensitive to the vulnerabilities and shortcomings of their peers. Kids can be brutal sometimes. They can also be remarkably supportive, especially if a good example is set for them. Children follow the lead of the significant adults in their lives—Mom, Dad, teacher. If the adults treat taking medication as perfectly normal, children will usually follow suit.

Each child is different, of course, but in general I find nothing wrong with a child's desire to keep his illness and medication private, provided that the child truly understands and appreciates that there's nothing wrong with taking a medicine that fixes the brain. The way I explain it is that people, grown-ups as well as children, aren't always educated about these kinds of disorders. They don't understand what makes people sick and why they need medicine to get well. That's why they call people names and say silly things that hurt other people's feelings. Perhaps it *is* better not even to tell them about it. Besides, it's none of their business. A visit to any doctor is a private matter. Many of the kids I treat with medication never even mention it to their friends and classmates. Others are very open about it. The decision about how to handle this should be made by the parents, the child, and the psychiatrist.

Children, even very young ones, usually find it easier to accept the fact that they take medication if they understand their disorder and accept some responsibility for taking the medicine. One of my colleagues says that when he prescribes medication, he makes a speech to his young patients that goes something like this: "This is *your* medicine. It is not your mom's medicine. It's not your dad's medicine. It is not your teacher's medicine. It is your medicine, and it's going to make you feel better. It will help you stop worrying all the time. Even if you don't always want to, you have to take it every day, so I want you to know the name of the medicine. It's called *Zoloft*. I don't want you coming in here next time and telling me that you take little blue pills. I want you to tell me you take Zoloft. And I want you to know how much you are taking, when you take it, and what it's doing for you." Involving a child in his own treatment in this way helps to remove the stigma.

THE MEDICATION Q AND A

Not all mental disorders should be treated with medication, of course. Sometimes the recommended treatment is psychotherapy, and most often a combination of medication and psychotherapy is the solution. The psychotherapy I recommend most strongly for children and adolescents is behavioral therapy, which is characterized by its direct, supportive quality. In this kind of therapy we target specific symptoms and goals, and every aspect of the treatment is geared toward minimizing symptoms and achieving those goals. This is not psychoanalysis. We don't try to unearth trauma and repair it. We don't "regrow" the child. We focus on getting rid of a child's symptoms and improving his ability to function. This kind of therapy may involve relaxation techniques (which include deep breathing and visual imagery), behavior modification, parent counseling, and family therapy. A child's problems aren't just a child's problems. They affect the entire family.

Medication should be prescribed only after careful diagnostic evaluation. Just as antibiotics are prescribed for bacterial infections but not for viruses, the medicines I prescribe are effective only for specific disorders. *Diagnosis drives treatment* is one of the most important maxims of any physician. Before any treatment begins, a physician must make a diagnosis.

Parents have to make it their business to understand their child's disorder and the recommended treatment by asking questions. Here are a handful of drug-related questions that any child and adolescent psychiatrist should be prepared to answer when prescribing medication:

- What is the diagnosis?
- What is the medicine, and how does it work?
- Have studies been done on the medication?
- Which tests need to be done before my child starts the medication?
- How soon will I see an improvement?
- How often will his progress be monitored, and by whom?
- How long will he have to take the medicine?
- How will the decision be made to stop it?
- What are the negative side effects of the medicine?
- What will happen if my child doesn't take it?

Doctors won't be able to answer all of the questions with precision, of course. "How long will he have to take the medicine?" is an especially hard one. Adults who take medication for high blood pressure can never be sure how long they'll have to keep taking it. With diet and exercise and a lot of luck perhaps they can discontinue the medication after six months or a year, but it's also possible they'll have to take it for the rest of their lives. Regular checkups with the doctor tell the tale. The same goes for children's brain disorders. Many kids need medication for an extended period of time; others thrive without it after a short "trial." Regular evaluation and monitoring of a child's progress will tell the physician and the parents what they need to know.

Careful, individual *titration* is also vital to the treatment; the prescribed dose of any psychiatric medication given to a child may have to be adjusted, perhaps many times, before we get the results we're looking for. Too often a child is given a dose of a medicine that is not sufficient. When the behavior doesn't change and the child doesn't get better, it shouldn't be assumed that the drug isn't working. The child may simply need a little more of it.

The answer to another question, "Have studies been done on the medication?" may not be what parents want to hear. We have several ways of gauging the effectiveness of a medicine. The simplest is the *case study* method, in which we follow the progress of one case. We give a child medicine, see what effect it has on certain symptoms, stop the medicine, see what happens, and then start it again. *Open clinical trials* are more sophisticated. We take a group of kids with the same disorder, give them all the same medicine, and measure their progress after six weeks. The gold standard of tests is the *placebo-controlled double-blind trial.* We choose a fairly large group of children with the same disorder —96 children from ages 8 to 18 who have major depressive disorder, for instance—and give half of them medication and half of them a placebo. Neither doctor nor patient knows who is getting what. That's why the study is called *double-blind.* After eight weeks we measure and compare the progress of both groups.

Unfortunately we do not have placebo-controlled double-blind trials for many of the drugs we routinely prescribe for children's brain disorders, but this doesn't mean that a child or adolescent shouldn't take them. It does mean that both parents and physicians should be careful to examine all options before starting a child on any medication.

DRUGS AND PERSONALITY

Here's how one mother reacted to the changes in her son that were brought about by medication: "When Allen takes his medicine, he's so much quieter than he was before. He seems to listen to me a lot more carefully, and our conversations are much deeper and more enjoyable. He's practically a different person. I hate to admit it, but I like him better when he's on the medicine. He's more in tune, more attentive, more interesting. What worries me is, *Is this really my child?*"

The answer is yes, the new Allen is really her child. The medications that we prescribe don't change children's personalities; they simply free kids up so that they can be themselves. A brain disorder disguises a child's true nature and hampers his abilities. Medicine lets him use his assets.

Children with brains that don't work quite right are like kids whose thermostats are out of whack. They're always a little colder than everyone else. The other kids are running around in the sunshine in shorts and T-shirts, but the child with the disorder always has on a bulky sweater, mittens, a scarf, perhaps even a coat. Because he's weighed down by all the extra clothing, the child with the disorder finds it difficult to run and play with the other kids. He looks different. He tends to stand on the outskirts of the activity, away from the others. He knows how to run and play, of course, but it's a lot harder for him to manage than it is for his peers. When this child takes the medication that repairs his thermostat, he's finally able to take off the coat, the mittens, and the extra layers. Unencumbered, he can run faster and play more vigorously, more happily, than he did before. He seems different, and in some ways he is different.

The real question is: Who's the *real* child—the unhappy, sluggish one swathed in sweaters or the carefree, gleeful one running around in his shirtsleeves? As far as I'm concerned, there's no contest; the one without the sweater is the child as he is meant to be. He's the one who's functioning properly. He pays attention in school, interacts well with his friends, and, like the new Allen, has a fruitful, fulfilling, loving relationship with his parents. He's the one with a real chance for a happy, healthy life.

Once in a while parents give undue credit to their child's medicine. That was certainly the case with the mother and father of 12-year-old Libby. "I remember the first year we sent Libby to camp after she started taking her medication," her father told me. "When we went to see her for Parents Day, she seemed very subdued. All the other kids were running around, but she was quiet. I said to my wife, 'It's the medicine that's making her like this. What are we doing to our child?' My wife looked at me with a funny expression on her face and said, 'She didn't take the medicine today. She knew we were coming, so she didn't take it.'"

THE SIDE EFFECTS

"What will this medicine do to my kid?" is almost always the first question that passes any parent's lips, and it's a good one. If a child with a fever takes too much Tylenol, it may cause inflammation of the kidneys. The ampicillin that cures a child's ear infection often causes diarrhea. All medicines, including those prescribed for children's brain disorders, have side effects, and parents should know in advance what to expect. (Specific medications and specific side effects are described in Part Three, which covers individual disorders, and summarized in Appendix 3, Psychopharmacology at a Glance.)

However, parents should also be mindful that the adverse effects of *not* taking a drug are often far more unpleasant than the possible side effects of taking it. The long-term effects of an *untreated* brain disorder —distress, low self-esteem, dropping out of school, unsatisfying interpersonal relationships, and many others—can be truly devastating.

Little Billy, a seven-year-old child with a brain disorder—attention deficit hyperactivity disorder—comes to me in severe distress and obvious dysfunction. He's inattentive, hyperactive, agitated. He can't focus on anything in school, and he drives everyone crazy with his obnoxious behavior. His teacher doesn't like him; the other kids don't want to play with him; even his parents find his behavior intolerable. He's the only one in the class who doesn't get invited to the birthday parties. He's not learning anything, and he's not having any fun. With the correct dose of a stimulant he can focus in school and follow the lessons. He can play with his friends and go places with his parents.

To be sure, the stimulant may cause a decrease in little Billy's appetite, alter his sleep patterns slightly, or cause an occasional headache. But without the stimulant this child is heading for trouble that's a lot more serious than a headache. To me the choice seems clear: the child needs the medication.

THE BOTTOM LINE

A colleague of mine says that the most important task that children have is to choose the right parents. Carefully chosen parents not only accept their children's assets and deficits; they also do whatever is necessary to make sure that their kids have plenty of opportunities to use their assets and are given whatever help they need to compensate for those deficits. That's what parenting is all about.

A child's brain disorder is not a parent's fault, but finding the right treatment for the disorder is a parent's responsibility. If a son is diagnosed with diabetes, it is a parent's job to give the child his medication, work out a proper diet, and give him the moral support he needs to keep himself well. If a daughter has an allergy, a parent should make sure she takes her shots, keep the house allergen-free, and offer moral support. The same rules apply to a brain disorder. A parent's job is to find the right treatment, work with the doctor and the child to implement it, build the child's self-confidence, and make the child's life easier along the way. Often the right treatment will include medication.

There are hundreds of thousands of success stories associated with pediatric psychopharmacology. "We got our life back" and "We finally could think about having another child" and "It was a miracle" are the kinds of comments heard every day from parents whose children's lives have been turned around by medication. Like Adam's parents, who took their child to a therapist 750 times before deciding to give medicine a try, they probably don't *like* the idea of giving a child medicine, but they like it a lot more than the alternative. The story that Margaret's parents tell, which describes a journey from despair to optimism, sums it all up.

"Our daughter Margaret was always different, not like the other kids. When she was six—that's seven years ago now—we had her independently tested, and we got this 28-page report telling us that she had terrible problems and needed full-day special education. At this point Margaret was completely miserable. She didn't have any friends, and everything she did was wrong. Her self-esteem was incredibly low. I remember asking the psychologist who tested her what class or activity we could sign Margaret up for that she would be most likely to succeed at. We wanted to make her feel good about herself. I'll never forget his answer: 'Don't sign her up for anything. She will never succeed at anything.' Those were his exact words. We were completely devastated.

"That was in January. By April we had seen a psychiatrist who put Margaret on Ritalin, and after two days on the medicine she was able to focus for the first time. The change in her was so dramatic that we called her the new Margaret. It was as if she rose from the dead. By the end of the school year she was getting perfect scores on all her tests and having sleepover dates with her classmates. Today, seven years later, she makes straight As in school, plays French horn in the band, and has plenty of friends. She still takes Ritalin three times a day for her ADHD. I can't say we like giving her the medicine, but we know she needs it. We can't imagine her life without it."

No-Fault
Brain Disorders

Each of the chapters in Part Three addresses a different brain disorder, focusing on the symptoms, the diagnosis, the recommended course of treatment, the prognosis, and the effects of a disorder on a child's personality and on his relationships with others. I also talk about the special parenting concerns associated with each disorder.

CHAPTER 7

Attention Deficit Hyperactivity Disorder

Nicholas, nearly three, still slept in the crib he used when he was a baby. His parents hoped that the high sides of the crib would discourage him from getting up in the middle of the night and wandering around the house. When that didn't work, and when he took to going downstairs to the kitchen and playing with the stove, his mother and father tied a cowbell to his door. When he opened the door, the bell would ring and wake his parents. During the day Nicholas was fidgety, unable to sit for even the shortest time. He had no interest in the TV shows most children like; he watched only the commercials. A lovely, lovable little boy with a keen sense of humor and a real zest for living, Nicholas was like an engine that wouldn't stop running. Everywhere he went, accidents happened, and little things got broken. His grandparents, who doted on Nicholas, nicknamed him "Sweet Destructo."

• • •

"He's been difficult since the day he was born." That's what Theo's mother said about her 11-year-old son the day we first met. He'd been a very demanding infant, with lots of sleep problems. He walked at eight months and was a whirlwind of activity from the start. When Theo was two, he and his mother were politely asked to leave a "Mommy and Me" program at the local YMCA; Theo just took up too much room. Theo never did get along with the other children. He was always grabbing their toys, pulling their hair, and cutting ahead of them in line. Even now, at 11, Theo pokes at his younger brothers during meals. In a restaurant he plays with the sugar and knocks over the water glass. He's been going to the same sleepaway camp for three years, and he hasn't made a single friend. This year complaints from his school have been coming almost daily. The teachers say that Theo fidgets constantly, rips papers, shouts out comments in class, and gets up every ten minutes to walk around the room. The parents are frankly embarrassed to take Theo anywhere. In a private moment Theo's father confesses to me: "I just don't like him."

• • •

When Peter's parents brought their 10-year-old son to my office, he fought them every inch of the way. Two appointments had already been canceled. Peter didn't think he had a problem, although everyone who came into contact with him strongly disagreed. He was getting bad grades in school, and his teachers said he was constantly missing assignments and losing papers. He was always looking for trouble with the other kids in school. He had a fight with a boy in his neighborhood that was so bad, he had been socially ostracized by his classmates ever since. None of the other kids wanted to play with him. His father, who was the coach of Peter's soccer team, told me that his son was always ending up in the wrong place on the soccer field. Peter was a terrific athlete otherwise, but he kept getting lost out there.

THE TERRIBLE TWOS, THREES, FOURS, FIVES, SIXES, ETC.

If the statistics are to be believed, there's one in every crowd—a child who's different from all the others. He's more accident-prone and more difficult to manage. In all likelihood he ran as soon as he started to walk. In a playground he refuses to leave the jungle gym when it's time to go home. While all the other toddlers are sitting still on Mom's lap during "Mommy and Me," he's squirming or running around. He needs more supervision than all the other kids put together as he shouts out answers and fights with his classmates. When the rest of the moms leave their kids to enjoy their hour or two of fun and games at a birthday party, his mother is asked to stay on to make sure he doesn't tear the place apart.

The disorder I'm describing is attention deficit hyperactivity disorder —ADHD—the most common of all the childhood psychiatric illnesses. More than a million children in this country have ADHD. According to the most conservative estimate, 3 to 5 percent of all children have the disorder, and some estimates put it as high as 9 percent. The overwhelming majority of kids with ADHD are boys. The male-female ratio is anywhere from 4–1 to 9–1, depending on the study. As we become more aware of the symptoms in girls, that balance will shift.

ADHD is a behavioral disorder with three major symptoms: inattention, impulsitivity, and hyperactivity. Like all disorders, ADHD can be mild, moderate, or severe. Some children are somewhat fidgety (in fact, we expect all toddlers and preschoolers to be a *little* fidgety), while others can't sit still for even a minute. There are kids who are terrors in large groups but do fine when the interactions are one-on-one. The children with the most severe ADHD have problems constantly and in all settings: at home, at school, and at play.

Although signs of this disorder are often evident during toddlerhood or even earlier, most children who have ADHD make their way to the office of a mental health professional a little later, most often when they start school. Parents and other loved ones may be willing and able to cope with or even ignore the behavior associated with ADHD, like the grandparents who indulge their "Sweet Destructo," but teachers cannot and will not put up with it.

ADHD is a chronic, not an episodic, illness; the inattention, impulsivity, and hyperactivity don't come and go as a result of circumstances. Normal children may have any or all of the ADHD symptoms temporarily as a result of something that happens in their lives—if their parents divorce, for instance—but that behavior will disappear after a short time. The symptoms of true ADHD won't make a sudden appearance after a child is in school. The disorder usually starts early and gets worse over time.

Over the last few years ADHD has developed a high profile, and many misconceptions connected with ADHD have surfaced. The most widely held, and the most alarming, is the belief that children will outgrow the disorder. For example, if a child is physically aggressive at the age of two, a well-meaning pediatrician might tell his parents, "He's just being negative and oppositional because he's going through the terrible twos." A year later, when that same child is even more badly behaved—more aggressive, more unpleasant, more active and inattentive—the pediatrician may well stick to his original interpretation: "He's immature," he might say. "It's the terrible twos at three. He'll outgrow it." Three years later the child is six and in first grade, unable to stay in his seat and driving everyone crazy with his antics. Not only has he not outgrown his symptoms; things have gotten a lot worse.

Some children do leave the symptoms of ADHD behind once they reach puberty, but that fact doesn't mean that this serious disorder should go untreated for ten years. If ADHD is ignored, a child may well end up going through puberty with rotten grades, no friends, and a terrible attitude. Studies have shown that more than half of all kids with ADHD will continue to have difficulties associated with the disorder as they get older. The most common problems are continued inattention, impulsivity, restlessness, learning difficulties, poor social relationships, and low self-esteem. The high school dropout rate for kids with ADHD is more than 12 times that found among high school students without ADHD. Further findings suggest that youngsters with ADHD who are aggressive in childhood are more likely to show antisocial behavior during adolescence and adulthood.

As far as I'm concerned, whether a child outgrows ADHD is beside the point. The point is that every child should be given the chance to enjoy school, to be liked by his parents, and to go to his friends' birthday parties—without his mother or father. Children who can't pay attention to their studies, who spend their childhood being yelled at and considered stupid, lazy, or just plain bad by family, friends, and teachers are not getting the start in life that they need and deserve.

THE SYMPTOMS

There are three different types of ADHD. The first type, and the least common, features behavior that is predominantly hyperactive and impulsive, characterized by fidgetiness and restlessness. (Theo, back at the beginning of this chapter, has this type of ADHD.) The kids in this category are the ones who can't wait in line, have trouble remaining seated, and are likely to blurt out answers in class.

The children with the second type are predominantly inattentive, distractable, and disorganized—ADHD without the *H*, hyperactivity. Children with ADD make a lot of mistakes, often forget or lose their possessions, daydream, procrastinate, and fail to complete their work. (Peter, the boy who's always getting lost on the soccer field, falls into this category.) They may be impulsive, but they're not as active as the first type, so ADD is somewhat more difficult to diagnose than ADHD. Children and especially adolescents with ADD (no hyperactivity) may be perceived as lazy, willful, frustrated, and academically limited. Parents often describe children with ADD as charming in two-way conversations with friends and family but "a little off" in large groups. These kids aren't disruptive, but they miss social cues and often seem out of step with the rest of the world. These kids may get by in elementary school, but the increased demands of junior high usually bring about their downfall.

The third type of this disorder—and the most common form—combines the symptoms of the first two, hyperactivity and inattention. Nicholas, alias "Sweet Destructo," falls into this category.

One mother of two children has two types of ADHD in her own family: a son, Carl, who's 11; and Amy, a daughter who recently turned eight. Both kids are in treatment now, but their mother, a schoolteacher accustomed to observing and reporting on the behavior of children, remembers very well what it was like in the bad old days. Here's how she describes the differences in their behavior before they started their treatment:

"You'd never know they have the same disorder. It manifested itself so differently. Carl was impulsive but not hyperactive. If he saw something he wanted, he would just get up and help himself to it, without any thought for the consequences. With other children, if you say 'don't,' they don't. If I said 'don't' to Carl, he did anyway. It was almost as if he didn't even hear me. He was always getting himself into awful situations. He was easily distractable, but periodically he could get it together and seem fine. Amy was much more hyperactive. Even when she was really small, she went nonstop. If I didn't bolt the front door, she'd fly outside and into the street. When she was two years old, she climbed up the drawers of the dresser to reach something. Of course, the dresser came over on top of her, and she ended up in the hospital. Carl was afraid of a lot of things, so he was usually safe, but for a while my husband and I lived in terror because we just couldn't seem to keep Amy safe. If we didn't watch her every second, she'd run out into traffic. I'll never forget the day a photographer asked me if Amy, who's a pale blonde and very pretty, would be available to do some modeling. I had to laugh. I said, 'Go ahead if you want, but I doubt you can get her to stand still long enough to take a picture.' "

Carl and Amy's mom is right: ADHD doesn't look the same on

everyone. It's the class bully who punches the other kids, grabs their books, and steals their cookies at lunchtime. It's also the "nerdy" kid who always seems out of it, the one who forgets to do his homework or loses it on the way to school and never even realizes that his shirt isn't tucked in. It's the little girl who can't swim but keeps jumping into the pool anyhow and the pre-kindergartner who shouts profanities at his teacher. It's the child at the carnival who gets so stimulated that he moves from one ride to another without ever settling on anything.

Generally speaking, no matter how ADHD is manifested, all of these children are difficult and demanding, to say the least. One mother summed it up this way: "He wants what he wants when he wants it, and that means *now*. And everything has the same intensity. When he wants something, there's no difference between a candy bar and a bicycle."

THE DIAGNOSIS

We make a diagnosis of ADHD the old-fashioned way, by talking to the parents, the teachers, and the child himself. We learn as much as we can about the child's functioning since birth, paying special attention to his development, his activity level, and especially his interactions with others. (We know that children with ADHD have more trouble in groups than they do in one-to-one situations.) We compare the level, frequency, and intensity of their symptoms with those of normal children of the same age. Along the way we look for the crucial telltale signs of any disorder: distress and dysfunction.

ADHD is tricky in this regard because children with this disorder don't always recognize that they're in distress. Kids with behavioral disorders, as opposed to anxiety disorders, tend to be unreliable historians. As far as many of these kids are concerned, they're fine; it's their parents or their teachers who have the real problem. "There's nothing wrong with me. I'm great," they tell me, and often they really mean it. One of the best ways we have of persuading a child to acknowledge that something might be wrong is to ask one of the standard child and adolescent psychiatrist's questions: if you could have three wishes, what would they be? Most kids with ADHD will offer a variation on these three themes:

"I wish I didn't have to go to school."

"I wish I had more friends."

"I wish my parents would stop yelling at me."

On the other hand, parents make excellent historians when it comes to children's behavioral disorders. When we ask mothers and fathers about the actions of a child with ADHD, the facts come pouring out: the child has terrible grades; he's always losing things; he gets into fights with the other kids; teachers complain about him nearly every day. Things usually aren't too rosy at home either. A child with ADHD rarely has a good, well-rounded relationship with his parents. The relationship often consists in large part of constant criticism of a child's behavior. Furthermore, the tension created by the disorder in the household may lead to disharmony between Mom and Dad. It's not easy keeping romance alive when everyone is shouting and upset all the time.

Parents are not always infallible in their observations, of course. Many first-time parents don't recognize that their youngster is more inattentive or hyperactive than the average child; after all, this is their only child. Other parents think that their child's inattention is more willful than chemical. "He pays attention just fine when he's watching television or playing video games, but somehow he just can't focus on his homework" is something I hear often from cranky, frustrated parents, and what they say is true as far as it goes. What those parents don't realize is that the type of attention needed for watching TV and playing Nintendo is actually different from the type required for doing homework. Everyone has an easier time paying attention when he is directly engaged. That explains why many children with ADHD are much more responsive when they interact one-on-one than when they are in groups. If an activity doesn't engage a child or if the setting is distracting, he'll find it nearly impossible to focus. Willfulness has nothing to do with it.

We look to a child's teachers for an assessment of his behavior as well. Teachers can be excellent sources of significant facts about how a child is functioning and how his behavior compares with that of others; teachers have a *lot* of experience with normal children. When we suspect that a youngster has ADHD, we ask teachers to provide information about the child's academic performance, his behavior in class, and his social interactions. We also ask teachers to fill out standardized rating scales designed to elicit information that's relevant to this disorder. The form most often used is the *Conners Teacher Questionnaire,* which helps a teacher to evaluate a child's hyperactivity, passivity/inattention, and conduct problems. The 28 questions in the form I use ask teachers to assess a child's behavior, learning ability, and social skills in the classroom. Is he restless? Does he make inappropriate noises? Does he insist that his demands be met immediately? Does he daydream, pout, or disturb the other children? Does he deny his mistakes or blame others for them? Does he make excessive demands on the teacher? Does he fail to finish what he starts? And so on. Because the Conners questionnaire has been used for thousands of normal children as well as those suspected of ADHD, the Conners score provides yet another piece of useful evidence in the diagnostic process. Once a child diagnosed with ADHD is on medication, Conners forms are sent regularly to teachers and used to help monitor the effects of the medicine.

It's also important to review and interpret correctly any tests given by schools, psychologists, or independent testing services, such as IQ tests, standardized achievement tests, and tests for learning disabilities. Far too often my colleagues and I hear the sad tales of parents who have been misled by faulty test results. One couple in particular got the runaround for several years before their child finally got the help she needed. Here's the story they tell: "We had an inkling that something was wrong with Carrie well before she was two years old. She was slow to walk and slow to talk compared with her peers and her older brother. And she was difficult. When she started nursery school, we began what we now understand is a typical adventure. First we were told she was okay. Then we were told she had some serious problems. Then we were told she was okay but *we* had some problems—namely, we were overprotective and neurotic. We had her tested by two different, very reputable places, and they gave us totally different results. One said she was normal, and the other said she had speech delays and learning disabilities. When she started kindergarten, the teacher said she was a perfectly normal kid, but by the end of the year she was saying that Carrie was immature. It took us another two years before we got the right diagnosis and the right treatment. Carrie definitely has ADD."

Early identification of ADHD and early intervention are extremely important. There's a huge difference between diagnosing a child early, when all he has is a little impulsivity and inattention, and seeing him later, when his parents are angry at him, his teachers are fed up with him, and his every encounter since early childhood has been negative. It's not unusual to see kids of 12 or 13 with ADHD who don't want to be in school anymore. It's also not difficult to understand why they feel that way. If I were being picked on and berated at the office every day, I'd want to quit my job too. Studies have shown that teachers are not only more short-tempered with kids who have ADHD; they're less patient with everyone in the class.

THE BRAIN CHEMISTRY

Too much sugar and too little discipline: those are just two of the things that do *not* cause ADHD, no matter what Uncle Frank says he thinks he read in last week's *Parade* magazine or what the well-meaning but ill-informed math teacher announced at the last parent-teacher conference. I've never met parents of a child with ADHD who haven't been told, somewhere along the line, that their child wouldn't be acting this way if he just got a little discipline at home.

ADHD has nothing to do with diet or with parenting. It's also not caused by chronic exposure to lead, another theory that has been proposed but not substantiated. ADHD is a disorder of the brain. Children are born with a vulnerability to the disorder.

There is a great deal of evidence to suggest that ADHD is genetic. For one thing, parents of children with ADHD tended to show symptoms associated with the disorder when they themselves were kids. For another, ADHD is more prevalent among the siblings of kids with ADHD than in the general population. And finally, there is a higher rate of hyperactivity and restlessness between identical twins than between fraternal twins.

There's a strong suspicion that brain chemistry, and specifically the level of the neurotransmitters dopamine and norepinephrine, is an important determining factor for ADHD. All of the medications that have been effective in the treatment of ADHD affect the regulation of one or both of these chemicals. Neuroimaging techniques—especially magnetic resonance imaging (MRI), positron emission topography (PET) scans, and single photon emission computer topography (SPECT)—have demonstrated that children with ADHD have brains that are different from the brains of kids who don't have it—specifically, dysfunction in the areas of the brain that have high concentrations of dopamine. PET scans performed on adults with ADHD have shown some evidence that a particular area of the brain is undermetabolizing or underutilizing energy. When those adults were treated with Ritalin, a dopamine-increasing stimulant discussed in detail later in this chapter, the PET scan returned to normal. This result indicates—indirectly, to be sure—that dopamine plays a part in ADHD.

THE TREATMENT

The good news is that ADHD is relatively easy to treat. There are more than 200 studies showing that a stimulant called Ritalin (generic name: methylphenidate) works wonders for children with ADHD. Stimulants have been used in the treatment of ADHD for more than 90 years. Adults feel more focused and alert after a cup of coffee in the morning. That's roughly how Ritalin works on children. Ritalin and other stimulants increase the alertness of the brain and nervous system, stimulating it to produce more dopamine and norepinephrine. The medication increases the child's attention and reduces excess fidgetiness and hyperactivity, allowing him to focus on his work. Children with ADHD who take Ritalin make fewer errors on a variety of tasks than untreated children do. They are less impulsive and more attentive, both in the classroom and in social situations. They're better able to control themselves. Kids with ADHD taking Ritalin receive more praise and less criticism from parents and teachers, and they get along a lot better with the other kids. Their grades go up, they become more popular, and they feel better about themselves.

A myth surrounding the treatment of ADHD is the "paradoxical calming effect" of stimulants such as Ritalin. It is a commonly held misconception that if a stimulant calms a child, then he must have ADHD; if he didn't have the disorder, the thinking goes, the medication wouldn't have any effect. That is categorically not true. Stimulants increase attention span in normal children as well as those with ADHD.

The recommended dosage of Ritalin varies widely. I've seen kids who respond to as little as 10 milligrams of the medicine and others who require 80 milligrams. Most children I see take from 30 to 70 milligrams of Ritalin; we start with the low doses and build up if necessary, taking into account the decrease in symptoms and the occurrence of side effects. Children nearly always take their Ritalin twice or three times a day: first thing in the morning, at lunchtime, and right after school. (This third dose helps kids to focus as they do their homework.) A dose of Ritalin lasts about four hours.

A child should have had a complete physical examination within the last year before a stimulant is prescribed. (We want a baseline of a child's physical condition before the medication begins, so that we won't mistakenly conclude that the stimulant is causing adverse effects.) Ritalin usually decreases appetite and may affect a child's growth, so we pay special attention to a child's height and weight, checking both every four to six months to monitor his growth rate. Most kids take ADHD medication for a minimum of nine to twelve months.

A decrease in a child's rate of growth is a possible side effect of Ritalin, but that doesn't happen very often. Most youngsters experience minimal negative side effects or none at all. The most common side effects are reduction in appetite, delay in falling asleep, headaches, and tearfulness. These side effects almost always disappear over time or with an adjustment in either the timing or the dosage of medication. Stimulants have been known, rarely, to cause tics, usually in children whose families have a history of tics. When a child is genetically vulnerable to tic disorders, particularly Tourette syndrome (described in Chapter 13), we look to other medications for treatment.

Ritalin is unquestionably the medication of choice—the first line of attack—with ADHD; but when Ritalin doesn't get results or when the negative side effects are such that it must be discontinued, several other medications are routinely prescribed. The other stimulants that have proven to be effective are Dexedrine and Cylert. Dexedrine lasts longer than Ritalin and has similar, more frequent side effects: decrease in rate of growth, decrease in appetite, and delay in onset of sleep. Both Ritalin and Dexedrine are available in sustained release (SR) pills, which have the advantage of not requiring a school nurse to give the lunchtime dose. Frequently children taking Ritalin SR will also need to take regular Ritalin with their morning dose and an additional dose of regular Ritalin after school. Cylert lasts about ten hours, so it can be given once a day. Unlike the other stimulants, which work very quickly, Cylert may require two weeks before the full effects are felt. Cylert's side effects are a little different from the others; appetite, sleep patterns, blood pressure, and heart are less often affected, but inflammation of the liver may occur in a small number of children. (Liver changes are rare and reversible once the medicine is stopped.)

There are three tricyclic antidepressants (TCAs) that psychiatrists turn to in treating ADHD, especially when the child being treated is vulnerable to tics: Norpramin, Pamelor, and Tofranil. These antidepressants have their own side effects, of course. They may cause tiredness, dry mouth, and constipation. More important, they may have an effect on heart rate; a child taking any of these medications must have an electrocardiogram before starting the medicine and before the dose is increased. Until recently Norpramin was the TCA used most frequently because it has fewer of the bothersome side effects, but over the last year or so several sudden deaths have been reported in children taking this medicine. Although there is not sufficient evidence to link those deaths with the Norpramin, it is rarely prescribed; Pamelor and Tofranil are now the medications of choice. The doses of Pamelor and Tofranil that are prescribed for children with ADHD are lower than those prescribed in the treatment of depression, and they need from one to four weeks to take effect. Because the medicine lasts a long time, it is taken in the morning and at bedtime. Wellbutrin, a new antidepressant, has proven to be effective in children with ADHD who have had a poor response to stimulants. The side effects are similar but less frequent than those associated with the stimulants.

Two antihypertensives, Catapres and Tenex, have been used when children have tics as well as ADHD. (An antihypertensive is frequently given in combination with a stimulant.) The medicine lasts a short time, so children must take it three or even four times a day. Catapres is available in a skin patch, which eliminates the necessity for the multiple doses. Side effects of Catapres and Tenex are minimal—sedation, headaches, nausea, dry mouth, and constipation—and they usually disappear with time. Antihypertensives don't have the same cardiac effects on children as they do on adults, who take the medicine for high blood pressure, but an electrocardiogram is necessary before the medication is started. The child's blood pressure and heart rate should be checked on each visit.

Some antipsychotic medications, especially Haldol, Thorazine, and Mellaril, reduce the symptoms of ADHD, but their side effects are such that they're not ordinarily prescribed for this disorder.

We prescribe "drug holidays" for children who take stimulants, suggesting that parents discontinue the medication for at least four weeks each year. There are two reasons for a drug holiday: first, it allows kids whose rate of growth or weight has been affected to catch up; and second, it lets us know if the medicine is no longer necessary. (Some children with ADHD do get better.) Most parents are inclined to declare the drug holiday in the summer, when a child's school work won't suffer, but it's harder to assess a child's progress in the summertime, because there is relatively little pressure on him to perform when school is not in session.

No matter when the drug holiday comes, most parents *dread* it. "I have a very hard time with drug holidays," said one mother of a 10-year-old boy being treated for ADHD. "My whole life turns upside down, and the rest of the family goes a little crazy too. He is so different off the medicine, and by *different* I don't mean *better.* July is the longest month of the year."

Another mother wanted to give her son the summer off between fifth and sixth grade, but the child's baseball coach pleaded with her to put him back on. The medication made a critical difference in his performance. Since playing the game well also made a critical difference in the child's happiness and self-esteem, the mother gave him back his Ritalin after two weeks.

I've known parents who flat-out refuse to give their children a drug holiday. "We just couldn't take drug holidays," said one such mother, whose 11-year-old daughter has been taking Dexedrine for five years. "It's not just that she's incredibly unpleasant. We could deal with that. It's that she's so reckless. She gets into terrible trouble. She can't make rational decisions and get on with her life without the medication. We worry about her too much to take her off it for any length of time."

Then there are the parents of children with ADHD who say that their kids seem to take a drug holiday every day, when the lunchtime dose of Ritalin wears off. (Some children taking stimulants experience *behavioral rebound:* several hours after the last dose of the stimulant taken, there's a dramatic increase in hyperactivity, hypertalkativeness, and irritability.) I've often talked to parents who disagree about their child's diagnosis depending on the time of day they're most likely to interact with him. For example, a mother says her son needs an extra dose of Ritalin. At the moment he takes it twice a day: in the morning and at lunch. Mom tells me that her son has trouble following directions after school; he has temper tantrums at home; he doesn't always behave on the bus in the afternoon; he loses his focus when he's doing his homework. Dad says that the twice-a-day regimen is just fine. "He's great at Little League, and he's fun to be with. We wrestle together and have a terrific time. My wife is making too big a deal out of this," says the father. The explanation for their difference of opinion is quite simple: the father nearly always spends time with his son on weekend mornings, when he's on Ritalin. By the time Dad gets home from work every day, and the medication has worn off, the child is in bed asleep. Mom is there when the little boy gets off the school bus, already a little out of control. She was right about the extra after-school dose of Ritalin.

Stimulants and the other medications used for ADHD have many miraculous powers, but they cannot and do not solve all the problems associated with ADHD. Stimulants help a child to pay attention, but they don't automatically make him more organized. However, they do make him more able to benefit from other interventions. A child with ADHD may need to work on improving his organizational skills and study habits, ideally with a tutor who specializes in psychoeducational tutoring. Parents can help with this too, of course, by working with the child and the tutor to come up with new strategies for behavior and then reinforcing the new behavior with a system of rewards. For instance, parents may tell a child: "If you come home, have a snack, and then settle down to do your homework right away, you get a star. If you don't have a fight with your brothers and sisters today, you get a star. For every day your teacher says you worked quietly without interrupting in class, you get a star. For every three stars you earn, you get to play a half-hour of video games at the arcade." The reward will be different for every child, of course, but the principle stays the same.

Most children with ADHD will need some social skills training as well. Unlike children with social phobia (see Chapter 10), who must be encouraged to take part in the events around them and learn how to do *more* in the way of socializing, kids with ADHD have to learn to do *less*. In all probability they've been accustomed to leaping before they look; they have to learn that their social actions have consequences. ("Stop. Listen. Look. Think. Act." That's the cognitive behavioral mantra taught to children with ADHD.) Being in control takes practice; most of these kids don't even know what it feels like. A child psychologist who specializes in behavioral therapy or a social worker with a specialty in social skills training can be of great help to a child just learning how to behave in social situations. As strange as it may seem, some children don't know the first thing about how to act at a birthday party. Professionals can show them the way.

A psychologist can help with parent training and counseling too. A child with ADHD on medication is more attentive, less hyperactive, and less impulsive, but he still has to be managed, and the job of child management falls primarily to the parents. Parents have to learn to exercise control over their children without losing control themselves. The message a parent must convey to children who misbehave is: "This is unacceptable behavior. It will not be tolerated. It keeps you from functioning in the world."

When that doesn't work—and everyone knows that it sometimes doesn't—parents have to know when and how to go to the next level: "Look, I just gave you a warning. You didn't listen to me. Now you've lost 15 minutes of television for tonight. Please get up and go to your room now. You've already lost 15 minutes. The next time I tell you to leave, it'll be 30 minutes. Are you leaving? No? Okay, you just lost 30 minutes." The parents' request and the consequences for noncompliance are both clear. The parent is calm and in control, and the punishment is meted out without rancor or malice.

If and when the battle escalates, a parent moves to level three: "Now you need a time-out. Your behavior is intolerable. I won't put up with that kind of talk. You know you're not allowed to bang on the furniture." By now the parent is taking the child by the arm and walking him to his room. "You have to stay in your room for five minutes." The older the child, the longer the time period should be. At the end of the time period the child is asked, "Are you ready to come out and join us?" If the child is still not in control, he goes back for another five minutes.

When the child comes out of the room, the punishment still stands, of course. He still loses 30 minutes of television. The final message from Mom and Dad should reinforce all the others. "We still love you. We still want to hug you and give you a kiss. Life will go on. But tonight it will go on without television."

These kinds of parenting skills don't come naturally; they have to be learned and practiced. Children with ADHD need an immediate response from their parents. "If you do that one more time, you'll be punished" doesn't work with them. Parents have to be ready to respond to any and all situations. With normal children parents can get away with, "I'm not sure yet what your punishment is going to be, but it's going to be a whopper." With these children parents have to be ready with specifics. Parents of children with ADHD also have to be absolutely consistent. Kids who have ADHD need structure, because it helps them to learn rules and establish limits.

Another aspect of ADHD that therapy can address is the youngster's self-esteem. There's no empirical evidence at the moment that being liked by parents and teachers is good for a child, but we don't need statistics to know that being yelled at and put down on a regular basis doesn't make a child feel good about himself. Unfortunately there is no medicine that works on a child's self-esteem. Some of these kids become so accustomed to failure that it's hard for them to acknowledge anything else.

I was reminded of this fact when Teddy, a seven-year-old boy I was treating for ADHD, came to my office for a checkup after three months of Dexedrine. He was responding beautifully; his parents and teachers were delighted with his behavior. I asked Teddy how he was feeling. He told me that he felt the same as always. Then came the kicker: "Since I started taking medicine, my teacher and my parents are much nicer," he told me.

PARENTING AND ADHD

"I wasn't prepared for this," said the mother of Cheryl, a five-year-old girl with severe ADHD. This was before her daughter started taking medication. "My idea of having kids used to be dressing them up in cute little outfits. Then I thought we'd all do things together as a big happy family. I never knew so many things could go wrong. We went to Disney World for vacation, and it was a nightmare. Cheryl was impossible. She didn't want to wait in line. She didn't want to sit still when we got on one of the rides. When we went to the gift shop, she couldn't make a decision; she wanted everything, and she didn't want anything. Sometimes my husband and I play a game called 'Normal Family.' We take the kids out to dinner, sit down at the table, and pretend that we're totally relaxed, not at all worried that Cheryl is going to pick up the butter dish and throw it across the room. We always wonder if people can tell how much work it takes just to keep her in her seat."

Being the parent of a child with ADHD *is* a lot of work, perhaps more demanding and more challenging in terms of time and attention than any of the other disorders. When the kids are little, finding children for them to play with can be a full-time job; they tend not to be on anyone's "A" list. As they get older, helping them with their schoolwork is usually extraordinarily time- and energy-consuming. The hard work usually pays off, though. The mother of one 13-year-old girl I've treated works closely with her daughter on her homework every night and helps her to prepare for tests, and the results have been spectacular. Last report card the girl came home with straight As. Her mother says that if any of the kids in the class have a question about the homework assignment, they always call Kelly. "Everybody knows that Kelly is the most organized child in her class," she says. That's because they work long and hard at it. Some nights after Kelly's medication wears off, her mother sits in a chair next to Kelly and rubs her back while she studies. It's the only thing that helps the girl concentrate.

Kelly's parents think that they have the school situation pretty much under control, but as their daughter reaches puberty, they're starting to have serious worries of a different kind. So far Kelly is not allowed to date, but they know that the day will come. "We're a little nervous about her with boys," her father told me. "She really needs her medicine. She's the kind of kid who has terrible judgment and no impulse control without it. If somebody offered her a drink or a some marijuana, I could see her accepting if she hadn't taken her medicine. She would think it was 'neat.' If some guy says, 'Let's go for a ride' or 'Let me put my hand there,' I'm afraid she'll do it. She knows the rules, but rules don't really work for her if she's not on her medicine."

Parents of children with ADHD often drastically rearrange their lives, sometimes without even acknowledging that they're doing it. "We don't mind not eating together as a family," one mother of a nine-year-old told me. "If we try to have dinner together, he just knocks everything over. It's better for everyone if I just stand and watch while he has his dinner."

Before the parents of five-year-old Gary started their son on Ritalin, they had stopped taking him anywhere—no movies, no restaurants, nothing. Two weeks into the Ritalin treatment they took him to a puppet show at the local college, and he sat through the whole thing. "I had forgotten that these family outings could be fun," Gary's father told me.

Parents should understand that when they change their lives to suit the symptoms of their child's disorder, they are not doing the child any favors. A kid who lives in a world in which everyone accommodates him is in for an extremely rude awakening. Parents can't and shouldn't shelter their kids forever. The sooner they teach their children to follow the rules of polite society, the better off everyone, especially the child, will be.

This disorder is tough on everyone in the family, including the other siblings. First of all, mothers and fathers of children with ADHD tend to be more short-tempered with *all* their kids, not just the one with the irritating symptoms. Second, kids with ADHD require and demand so much attention that there's not always enough to go around for the others.

"Seth is so well behaved that I take him for granted," a mother says about her son who *doesn't* have ADHD. "When he does misbehave, I know I'm too hard on him. I count on him not to give me any trouble."

Another mother feels similarly guilty about her ADHD-free son, who is a couple of years older than the child with ADHD. "The other day they both came home with grades. Casey got 100 percent on his test— which he always does—and Ben got 80. I'm sure I made much more of a fuss about Ben's 80. Casey never complains. In fact, he's a wonderful, caring older brother, and he really helps Ben. But I'm sure he feels slighted sometimes." Family therapy can help a family deal with the child's disorder and its impact on the whole family.

One of the biggest problems that parents of children with ADHD face is that the kids get labeled by the rest of the world. "Troublemaker" is the usual epithet they're given, and it doesn't take long for the word to spread. Fortunately a bad reputation is relatively easy to shake, at least as far as teachers are concerned. Kids who get treated for ADHD are almost always regarded as "new and improved" by their teachers, with no hard feelings. Classmates tend to be less forgiving, however, and there are instances in which a kid with ADHD alienates his peers beyond redemption. When that is the case, it may be necessary to ask the school to place the child in a different class for the next academic year. A fresh start may be just the ticket for a child being treated for ADHD.

Teachers and other school officials, who should be part of a strong support system for these troubled children, sometimes make this problem worse. Kids with ADHD are disorganized and easily distracted, so re-membering to take their medicine every day at school can be tricky. One of the children I treated set his watch so that it would beep, reminding him to take his medication at noon. The teacher complained that the beeper disrupted the class and wouldn't let him use it. Another teacher routinely made fun of the fact that one of his students needed Ritalin. If the boy did anything out of the ordinary in class, the teacher would say, "I bet you forgot your medicine today, Tommy. Look how you're acting." I've encountered nurses who give a child his medicine if he remembers to come to their office but refuse to track him down to make sure he gets there.

Most schools will listen to reason, especially if parents enlist the help of the child's psychiatrist, psychologist, or social worker to get their attention. High school guidance counselors are looking more favorably on the idea of untimed SAT tests—allowing kids with ADHD to complete the tests at their own speed—and many colleges feature special resource centers for their students with ADHD. The U.S. Office of Education has started a major campaign to inform school personnel about ADHD, including its identification, its treatment, and the special needs of children who have it. As more school systems become enlightened about this no-fault brain disorder, the same kinds of accommodations will be made for these kids as are made for children with any medical disorder.

The Age of Enlightenment may already be underway in the schools. I came to that conclusion when, quite recently, I evaluated a child with ADHD and faxed a letter to the school with instructions on how the medication was to be given. I was floored when, the very same day, the school nurse called to ask me how often I wanted the Conners questionnaire to be filled out by the child's teacher. I told her that I'd like the form filled out every two weeks and that I would send her some forms. "No, don't bother," she told me. "We have our own supply right here."

For sound practical advice about coping with ADHD many parents turn to ADHD support groups. The best known of them is CH.A.D.D. —Children and Adults with Attention Deficit Disorder—the largest organization of its kind in the country. The members of CH.A.D.D. have helped to identify ADHD as a real disability, forcing school districts and insurance companies, among others, to acknowledge its existence. They have enormous resources and can be helpful to parents who come up against teachers, camp counselors, or other authorities who are reluctant to cooperate with the treatment of a child with ADHD.

I said earlier in this chapter that ADHD is relatively easy to treat. I wish I could say that it's easy to live with. Still, with active treatment and a lot of hard work, a child with ADHD can have a well-rounded, happy, productive life even if his symptoms never disappear entirely. He'll probably have to make some allowances; he'll do best to choose a profession that lets him move quickly from task to task rather than one requiring long periods of concentrating and sitting still. Theater critic is probably out, but he'd probably make a terrific stockbroker or salesman. I know one young man with ADHD who's a physician. His specialty? Ears, nose, and throat. He told me he needed a practice with lots of action and quick results.

One mother whose child I've been treating for seven years is cautiously optimistic about the prospects of her 12-year-old son, more so than she ever thought possible. "When Max was first diagnosed with ADHD, I spent a month crying," she told me. "I would drive to school with the tears rolling down my face, wondering what in the world we were all going to do. I just kept thinking that I wanted him to be like all the other kids. I wanted him to be treated like everyone else. It hasn't been easy, but I think he really *is* treated like the others. He does all the things that the other kids do. It just takes a lot more effort."

CHAPTER 8

Obsessive Compulsive Disorder

James was 12 years old when he came to see me. Earlier that week he and his family had been on vacation, skiing in Colorado. One evening just before dinner James bolted out of the bathroom wrapped in a towel. Still wet from his shower, he stood in the middle of his parents' bedroom and moved his head methodically from side to side, touching his chin to each shoulder over and over again. He said he couldn't stop. The family, who'd never witnessed anything like this before, watched helplessly as he kept moving his head back and forth, sobbing. Soon the parents were crying too. Finally James's older brother grabbed the bedspread off the hotel bed, wrapped his brother in it, and rocked him until he calmed down. A half-hour later they all went down to dinner, and James refused to talk about what had happened. During my first meeting with James I discovered that the chin-to-shoulder motion was only one of his inexplicable repetitive actions, things he did on a regular basis. He also tied his shoelaces repeatedly, checked his eyeglasses for cleanliness dozens of times a day, and kept on bending his fingers back, one by one, until he felt exactly the right amount of tension in each.

• • •

Five-year-old Mary likes to tear things. If the pictures she draws aren't absolutely perfect—and they never are—she rips them into dozens of pieces. She also tears her clothing, particularly her underwear. If her parents don't monitor her carefully, she'll go to nursery school literally in rags. In the bathroom she constantly touches the walls and tightens the faucets. The barrettes in her hair have to be equally tight on each side. When her parents take her out to a restaurant, she checks for gum under the table 20 or more times during a meal. Her parents say she's been doing some of these things since she was two years old.

STEP ON A CRACK, BREAK YOUR MOTHER'S BACK

When I was in junior high school, a boy from my homeroom used to fascinate me in the school cafeteria every day. Like the rest of us, Norman would stand in line, fill his tray with food, and carry it back to the table. That's when it got interesting. I would stare, mesmerized, as Norman proceeded to eat his lunch one quadrant at a time. He was incredibly precise about it; first he'd eat what was directly in front of him. Then he'd carefully rotate the plate 90 degrees and eat the contents of the second quarter. He went on like this until his plate was clean. Kids teased him about it, of course, but during the time I knew him he didn't change his eating habits. Back then I thought Norman was weird. Today I'm reasonably sure that he had obsessive compulsive disorder, or OCD.

Childhood rituals and superstitions are perfectly normal. At about two and a half years of age children begin to follow and indeed expect a regular routine, especially at mealtimes or in preparation for bed. "Before I go to bed, I brush my teeth. Then Daddy reads me a story, and Mommy rubs my back," a child might recite. Another kid says: "When I take a bath, I have six toys in the tub with me. Daddy sings 'Rubber Ducky' while he washes my hair." Any change in routine can create discomfort in a small child. Between five and six children develop group rituals, during which they play games. These games nearly always have rules, and most kids are as strict as Marine drill sergeants about them. Anyone who tries to circumvent or break the rules will face an extremely irate kindergartner. As children get older—from seven to 11 or so—they begin to take up hobbies and start collections: stamps, coins, baseball cards, dolls, and so on. They often appear overly preoccupied with their hobbies, but that too is normal. Obsessiveness is part of any hobby or collection.

Ritualized behavior helps to relieve anxiety and eases socialization in children as well as in adults. Anyone who has ever worn a "lucky shirt" to watch the World Series on television or knocked on wood to ward off bad luck knows about the stability that pointless rituals can bring. At any age we derive comfort from following a routine, waking up, going to school or work, eating meals, going to bed for the night. Some people are more obsessive-compulsive about their actions than others, like the man who checks his keys half a dozen times or the woman who has to lock the front door exactly three times before she can leave the house. "Checking" is a common behavior: locks, lights, ovens, faucets. It often verges on obsessive-compulsive, but if it doesn't interfere with functioning, it isn't considered a symptom of the disorder. When obsessive thoughts and compulsive acts become so frequent or so intense that they cause distress or dysfunction, a diagnosis of obsessive compulsive disorder is made.

Two eight-year-old girls are skipping down the street, and bystanders can hear their familiar refrain: "Step on a crack, break your mother's back." Both are avoiding the cracks in the sidewalk, but one little girl loses interest after covering less than a block. The other keeps going, refuses to stop. When the second little girl is asked why, she seems distressed. "I can't stop because I haven't done it enough times," she says, and keeps on skipping. There's nothing carefree or cheerful about her actions. She's an eight-year-old with a mission. The first little girl is playing a simple fantasy game. The second child has OCD.

THE SYMPTOMS

Obsessive compulsive disorder is an anxiety disorder characterized by pathological obsessions (involuntary thoughts, ideas, urges, impulses, or worries that run through a person's mind repeatedly) and compulsions (purposeless repetitive behaviors). OCD affects as many as 3 percent of the general population, roughly 1 million of whom are children and adolescents. That translates into three or five youngsters with OCD per average-sized elementary school and as many as twenty in a large urban high school. The onset of OCD may be as early as preschool—age three or four—with a peak onset at age 10. Adults with OCD almost certainly had the disorder as children or adolescents; research has revealed that more than 50 percent of the adults with this disorder had symptoms before age 15. More boys have OCD than girls. Other anxiety disorders are more common in females, but with OCD the ratio of boys to girls is 2 to 1.

OCD has a wide range of symptoms, from seemingly benign to obviously bizarre. (Every time I think I've seen everything, a child will show up with a new wrinkle.) Many children become obsessed about precision, demanding that things be done a certain way or, quite often, that questions be answered over and over again. Other common obsessions are germs, lucky or unlucky numbers, religion, and bodily functions. Some of the most common compulsions are hand-washing, touching, counting, and hoarding.

Some kids have violent temper outbursts if their rituals are blocked or their questions don't receive the proper responses. Nine-year-old Manuel had a long history of temper tantrums. When I asked his parents what was likely to set Manuel off, they gave me a succinct answer: "Anything." When I asked them to be more specific, I learned that what made Manuel lose his temper was not typical. "What time is dinner?" he would ask. "In a couple of hours," Mom would answer. "No. *When* is dinner?" he repeated. Only when his parents were specific to the minute was Manuel satisfied, and even then he needed to hear the answer many times before he could feel reassured.

In the first few moments of my meeting with Manuel I got firsthand confirmation of his parents' reports. I asked Manuel to get on the scale so that I could weigh him. "How much do I weigh?" he inquired. I told him. "Is that the right weight for me?" he asked. I said, "Well, we have a range of weights, and yes, you're in the right category." "But is that *really* the right weight? Is it exactly the right weight?" he asked. I could sense his anxiety. It all but overwhelmed him. "This is *exactly* the right weight for you," I told him. He calmed down almost immediately.

Taking his first ride on an airplane, Stuart, age 10, kept peppering the flight attendant with questions.

"What kind of plane is this?"

"This is a 727," she answered.

"Is this the safest type of plane?"

"Yes, it's very safe."

"But is it the *safest* plane?"

"All of our planes are safe."

"But is this the *safest* plane?"

When the stewardess didn't answer Stuart's question for the third time, he became extremely agitated. "Is this the *safest* plane?" he repeated. "If you don't answer me, I'm going to kill you."

At this point Stuart was shouting and waving his arms around, and his nervous parents began to reassure him, telling him that yes, their plane was indeed the safest. The flight attendant had the presence of mind to agree that the plane they were flying in was absolutely the safest in the skies. Stuart's tantrum subsided.

Outbursts of temper don't always end in a truce. OCD has been known to lead to violence. An adolescent girl with an obsession about tearing and breaking things nearly flattened the OCD unit in a midwestern hospital last year. Before being restrained she had shredded the curtains, shattered the windows, and completely destroyed three sinks.

Anyone familiar with Judith Rapoport's important 1989 book about OCD, *The Boy Who Couldn't Stop Washing,* knows that one of the most common symptoms associated with OCD is an obsession with cleanliness and fear of contamination, often manifested by the constant washing of hands or compulsive wiping after using the toilet. Lately my colleagues and I have been seeing a new, related obsession connected to OCD: fear of AIDS. As many as half the people diagnosed with OCD who come through our hospital are overly (and illogically) concerned about the virus. I especially remember a 14-year-old girl who had persuaded herself that she was dying of AIDS. Six months earlier she had been walking on the beach and had stepped on something sharp. Convinced that the pointed object was a contaminated needle, she had been washing her foot 50 times a day ever since, until it was raw and bleeding. I've seen other youngsters with OCD who call AIDS hotlines 50 times a day.

There is no relationship between OCD and IQ. Jake was an extremely bright kid with a high IQ, who eventually became class valedictorian. In fact, Jake's anxieties had to do with his intelligence; he was obsessed with the idea that he was becoming stupid, that he was literally losing his intelligence. "My brain cells are dying," he told me, sobbing. To keep this from happening Jake had developed a series of rituals that only he knew about: opening his locker while standing on one foot, putting his socks on before his underwear, touching the four corners of a room before leaving, and at least a half-dozen others. Jake was 16 when his parents brought him to see me, because he had had a problem taking his SATs. He wrote his answer, erased it, wrote it again, and erased it again, so that he finished only a quarter of the test. His parents knew that there was something very wrong. What they didn't realize was that Jake had been having similar problems since the age of 10. It's not unusual for parents to be kept in the dark about OCD. Many children, realizing that their symptoms make no sense and feeling a sense of shame about them, keep their symptoms secret.

THE DIAGNOSIS

There is no biological test for OCD. The diagnosis of OCD in children and adolescents requires a systematic, comprehensive evaluation. That means questions, questions, and more questions. If the child is eight years or older and the therapist suspects OCD, he'll probably begin by filling out the Yale Brown Obsessive-Compulsive Scale and the Leyton Obsessional Inventory, tests that measure not just the presence or absence of obsessive thoughts and compulsive behaviors but also dysfunction and the degree to which a youngster tries to resist his symptoms. There are 20 items in the Leyton form, including: Do you have to check things several times? Do thoughts or words keep going over and over in your mind? Do you hate dirt and dirty things? Do you get angry if other students mess up your desk? Do you ever have trouble finishing your schoolwork or chores because you have to do something over and over again? Do you move or talk in a special way to avoid bad luck?

The interviewing process with a child with OCD is often an uphill battle, with a slow pace and a great deal of reassurance on the part of the therapist. A child has to be made to feel safe and secure; he has to be persuaded that the secret thoughts he has and the secret things he does are nothing to be ashamed of. "I am not going to be surprised by anything you say," I might tell a child. "Tell me about the silly things you do. I'll understand. I've talked to lots of kids who have the same problem as yours. I'm going to try to make it better."

Some children are unwilling to acknowledge that anything is wrong. I've met kids who try to explain away their peculiar habits as a matter of "lifestyle." "Sure, I wash my hands 50 times a day and I use a whole tube of toothpaste to brush my teeth, but that's just me. That's the way I like it." Others are terrified that they're going crazy. Still others know that there's something wrong with them, but they're too embarrassed to talk about it. The word "silly" comes up a lot, as in "I do a lot of silly things." There's a lot of shame associated with OCD. One boy I treated was caught "cheating" in class. His teacher noticed that he was turning his head from side to side during a spelling test, and, little knowing that the boy had a compulsion to touch his chin to his shoulder (five times on each side or else something terrible would happen), she called him on it. The boy denied cheating—he wasn't cheating, of course—but he was too ashamed to tell her what he *was* doing. His unexplained denials got him sent to the principal's office.

An interviewer has to be persistent in his questioning. It can take a while to persuade a child to talk about his problems, even when he's obviously in pain. Here's how a conversation might go.

"Everyone has silly habits. Do you have any silly habits?"

"What do you mean?"

"Well, some people feel as if they have to check themselves. Sometimes they have to check themselves more than once even though they know they've got it right."

"You mean like when I have to check my homework to make sure I didn't make any mistakes?"

"Well, that's a good habit. What about the times when you check and you don't need to, like when you leave your room and you go back to check that the light is off."

"My mother always tells me to make sure the light is turned off."

"Yes, that's good. But what about when you check to make sure the light's off even though you already know it's off?"

Very young children present a special challenge during these interviews. A three-year-old who makes his parents tie and untie his shoelaces five times on each foot every morning, until they feel equally tight, is unlikely to be able to explain why he needs it. He doesn't know either why the closet door has to be closed a certain way. A four-year-old child whose compulsion was turning in a circle, always four times in one direction and four times the opposite way, couldn't come close to formulating an explanation. When I asked him what would happen if he stopped, the best he could come up with was: "If I don't go in a circle, I feel like crying."

Children often appreciate and benefit from an explanation of their disorder. I find it useful to talk to a child about habits, discussing various bad habits that people might have. I go on to say that once you start a bad habit, it's very difficult to break it, and it will probably get worse and worse. I talk about OCD as a *disease,* like chicken pox, only this time it's caused by a problem in the brain. I may tell a child that his brain is just forgetting to give him the right messages—for example, that he has already checked to see if the door is locked and that he has washed his hands enough. He is not crazy, and his symptoms are not a reflection of the child any more than the blemishes associated with chicken pox define him. Thus demystified, the symptoms a child has been experiencing can be dealt with with considerably less anxiety.

In the end, when a child is finally persuaded to tell the truth about what he's been thinking and doing, he's nearly always incredibly relieved to be rid of his secret. Once the floodgates are opened, most kids can't stop talking about their problems. After all, they've probably never said some of these things out loud before. That little boy whose mother told him to make sure the light was off finally blurted out the truth in a great rush—"Every day I have to touch the light switch a hundred times!"—and then burst into tears. Nearly every child I talk to about OCD ends up crying with relief at some point during the interview.

OCD is a disorder in which symptoms can wax and wane, so it's important to get information about a child's behavior from several different sources. We look to parents to provide information about the child's early development and to describe his current behavior. Perhaps Mom and Dad have noticed that it's taking longer than usual for the kid to get out in the morning, for instance, or that a child is asking more than the average number of anxious questions: "Did you lock the doors?" "Do you really love me?" Mothers and fathers often interpret this kind of behavior in a child as garden-variety insecurity. Only when they realize that their kid is taking two hours to get ready for school in the morning do they acknowledge that something might be amiss.

Over the course of a day, children may be able to control their obsessions and compulsions for a time. Teachers are often not aware of OCD symptoms because many kids keep their strange behavior under wraps during school; fear of ridicule by your peers is very strong. A teacher may notice oddities—a kid who repeats himself all the time or uses the bathroom more than usual or pays an excessive amount of attention to the arrangement of the items on and in his desk—but in general the school is not a particularly good source for information regarding OCD.

Before a final diagnosis of OCD is made, other disorders with similar symptoms must be ruled out. For instance, children with separation anxiety disorder (see Chapter 9) may appear to have OCD. One example was a schoolboy who would get down on his knees in the classroom several times every day and rock back and forth. At first he was thought to have OCD, but he eventually explained that he was just praying that his parents were all right.

Schizophrenia (see Chapter 16), which is very rare in children, may include symptoms similar to those of OCD. Kids with schizophrenia usually look withdrawn. They're living in an internal world, unlike children with OCD, who are very much with us. A child with OCD recognizes that his fear of germs is illogical, but the child with schizophrenia believes that those germs are a real threat to him or others. OCD may also look like Tourette syndrome (TS; see Chapter 13), an illness in which children have a variety of motor and vocal tics. Unlike the actions associated with OCD, Tourette's tics are involuntary. OCD often occurs with TS; that is, a child may have both brain disorders at once.

Patients with OCD who are obsessed with fears of contamination may refuse to eat and begin to lose weight, behavior that must be distinguished from that associated with anorexia nervosa. (Some 20 to 40 percent of all adolescents with eating disorders will also have OCD.) A 13-year-old boy named Brian was brought to our emergency room because he was dehydrated. According to his parents, he had basically stopped eating. Anorexia was the first diagnosis that came to mind, naturally, but after taking a history the doctor learned the real story about Brian's food avoidance. It all started when he refused to eat Reese's Pieces candies (prominently featured in the movie *E.T.*, Brian's favorite). Brian was preoccupied with the idea that if he ate Reese's Pieces, something terrible would happen to him. The fear of Reese's Pieces led to a fear of peanut butter and then, gradually, to a fear of just about all food. The diagnosis became clear: OCD.

THE BRAIN CHEMISTRY

Animal studies have indicated a neurological basis for many OCD symptoms. These ideas were reinforced by an association between certain neurological illnesses and OCD. For example, there are numerous case reports of people who developed OCD after recovering from encephalitis, an inflammation of the brain caused by a virus or bacteria. We also know that patients who have Sydenham's chorea tend to have a higher than usual incidence of OCD. (Sydenham's chorea is a disease of the basal ganglia. Basal ganglia contain a lot of serotonin.) Neuroimaging devices, such as CAT and PET scans, reveal specific differences in the brains of patients with OCD and those without the disorder. All of the differences are in the basal ganglia and the frontal lobes. Neurosurgery treatment in which the basal ganglia are disconnected from the frontal lobes has been successful in severely ill patients with OCD who did not respond to other treatment. Put together, this evidence strongly suggests that OCD is caused by a deficiency of serotonin in the brain. That theory is strengthened even further when we see that medicine that increases serotonin is extremely effective in treating OCD.

The brain disorder that causes OCD runs in families; recent studies show that 20 percent of all youngsters with OCD have a family member with the disorder. Sometimes it takes a little digging to discover who the "donor" in the family is. I've talked to parents who at first claim that there's no family history of OCD, but nine times out of ten they change their minds. "Wait a minute," someone will eventually say. "What about your brother? Didn't he used to shrug his shoulders all the time?" or "Don't you remember? Cousin Betty used to go up to the attic 20 times a day to see if the fan was on."

More often the family connection is more obvious and immediate. One mother whose little girl I diagnosed with OCD wakes up at five o'clock every morning and cleans the entire house, scrubbing the bathrooms at least twice. Her husband says that the family spends more money on cleaning products than on groceries.

THE TREATMENT

The recommended treatment for OCD is a combination of behavioral therapy—most notably *exposure* and *response prevention*—and medication. If children are not in great distress, a doctor may find it worthwhile to try behavioral therapy first without the medicine, but most kids who end up in a doctor's office because of OCD symptoms need the relief that medicine affords.

One child with OCD I treated, an 11-year-old boy named Daniel, used to spend hours getting ready for school in the morning. He said he "got stuck" in the shower; he'd start washing and almost couldn't stop. Despite his symptoms Daniel wanted to go to sleepaway camp for a couple of weeks, and his parents decided to let him give it a try. It's not difficult to imagine what his fellow campers and his counselors thought the first time they saw Daniel "stuck" in the shower. After about ten minutes under the spray Daniel was dragged bodily out of the shower and berated. "You're nuts!" the campers shouted. "Get dressed right now!" said the counselors. "If you don't dress yourself, we're gonna dress you."

Those young campers had no way of knowing that they had invented their own variation of one of the most effective forms of behavioral therapy for OCD: response prevention. In response prevention the patient is forced to confront his worst fears and, ideally, work his way through the anxiety created by a given situation. Some experts call it "letting the anxiety burn itself out." Response prevention is based on the fact that the body can't maintain a state of anxiety for more than 90 minutes; most people can manage only about 45 minutes.

In treating a child with OCD a therapist will conduct an extended session in which a child has to live through the anxiety. For example, a little girl who can't bear to have dirty hands is forced to make mud pies and then sit quietly for an hour without washing. Another child terrified of germs is led to a chair and then told that someone very sick has just been sitting there. The goal: to teach a child to break the connection between anxiety and that condition. Obviously it's necessary to involve the parents in a child's treatment for OCD—as always, mothers and fathers are indispensable co-therapists—but a qualified behavioral therapist is necessary to guide and monitor this sensitive process. A manual and a 16-week behavioral treatment program—both called "How I Ran OCD Off My Land"—have been developed for the treatment of children and adolescents with OCD.

Most experts agree that behavioral therapy is especially effective in combination with medicine. The drugs prescribed for OCD most often are the SSRIs (selective serotonin reuptake inhibitors): Prozac, Zoloft, Paxil, and Luvox. Anafranil, a tricyclic antidepressant (TCA) that inhibits serotonin, is also effective in treating OCD. Normally we see the results of medication within two to six weeks. The most common side effects of the SSRIs are nausea, diarrhea, insomnia, and sleepiness. Anafranil's side effects include sleepiness, dry mouth, constipation, and the more serious cardiac effects of all TCAs. To be on the safe side, we always measure a child's heart rate and blood pressure and do an electrocardiogram before starting a child on Anafranil and before increasing the dosage.

Just about all children will need to stay on the medication for six to nine months, during which time they should undergo behavioral therapy as well. After they're taken off the medicine, children should get follow-up evaluations on a regular basis, and they will also benefit from "booster shots" of behavioral therapy.

Some children being treated for OCD with medication will demonstrate only a partial response or will respond fully but then "break through" the medication with a recurrence of symptoms. When either of those things happens, we first try to improve the response by increasing the dose of the original medicine. If that fails to achieve the result we're looking for, we'll try *augmentation:* that is, we'll prescribe an additional medicine that will makes the original drug more effective. (Some people think of it as a "chaser.") The second medicine we prescribe will also take aim at any secondary symptoms that are associated with a child's OCD. If he's moody, we'll add lithium; if he also has ADHD symptoms, we'll try Dexedrine; Haldol will be added if the child has tics; and we prescribe BuSpar or Klonipin if the child's secondary symptom is anxiety. It may take a few tries to find the right combination, but some combination nearly always works.

As I've said earlier, parents who are reluctant to give medicine to their children, especially very young children, should be mindful that while there may be negative side effects of the medicine, there are also negative effects connected to *not* taking the medication. The youngest child I've ever treated with this disease was four years old, and I prescribed Prozac for him. What are the long-term effects of giving a kid Prozac (and thus changing his serotonin metabolism) at the age of four? No one knows for sure. What we do know is that a child in pain has to have some relief. That four-year-old I treated was completely unable to function; his many habits—turning in circles, shrugging, hopping, and scratching—had completely taken over. After four weeks on low doses of Prozac he was behaving like a normal, happy four-year-old.

Recent studies show that cognitive behavioral therapy is not particularly useful in the treatment of young children with OCD, age five and under. Cognitive therapy requires the active participation of the patient, and small children simply aren't up to the task. For the little ones—as young as three—we recommend medication alone.

The prognosis for OCD is quite good; the overwhelming majority of kids receiving medicine get better. However, their relapse rate is high. A combination of medication and cognitive behavioral therapy makes a relapse less likely once the medicine is stopped. For obvious reasons, the more promptly the disorder is treated, the better the results are likely to be. The longer a child holds onto a symptom, the more the undesirable behavior will be reinforced. A habit can quickly grow into a way of life.

Left untreated, OCD can be virtually crippling to a child. Symptoms will probably increase and grow, until he can't function properly at school or enjoy time with friends. Scholastically and socially OCD takes its toll on a child, seriously limiting his ability to develop and thrive. Also, not surprisingly, OCD creates serious problems with self-esteem. After all, it's hard for a kid to feel really good about himself if he thinks he's going crazy.

PARENTING AND OCD

I walked out into the waiting room of my office one day and saw a teenage girl with her mother. The girl was sitting in a chair with her mouth wide open, and her mother was standing over her, peering into her open mouth. "No, your tooth is smooth," I could hear the mother saying. "Your tooth is smooth," she repeated. Then the mother said it a third time. As I learned moments later, the daughter was obsessed with the notion that her teeth were jagged, and she needed to check them often. When the girl was by herself, she used a mirror that she carried with her all the time. When her mother was around, the mother conducted regular checkups.

A 10-year-old boy with a cleanliness obsession takes several showers a day. His mother stands outside the door and hands in fresh towels to the boy, sometimes as many as half a dozen per shower.

Whenever she walks outside, a six-year-old girl has to keep checking the bottom of her shoes to see if she has stepped in something. Several times a block she stops dead in her tracks to take a look. Her increasingly impatient parents have taken to carrying her to and from the school bus and the car.

Many children with OCD involve their parents in their rituals, and parents, eager to keep the peace, may become unwitting accomplices, important players in a child's disorder. (Alcoholics Anonymous calls such people "enablers"—people who make it possible and even easy for an alcoholic to live with his disease.) Parents should resist the temptation to make it easier for a child to indulge in rituals. If the treatment of OCD is going to be effective, parents have to help their children *give up the symptoms.* Doling out clean towels to a germ-obsessed kid or carrying a child down the street so that her shoes don't touch the sidewalk isn't a solution; chances are it contributes to the problem.

Of course, it's not always easy for parents—or anyone else, for that matter—to take a hard line with a child obviously in distress, but most families have their limits. Nathan, nine years old, was obsessed with the idea that his family was using too much water and electricity. "That's too expensive. Turn that off," he would say to his father, who was using an electric razor to shave, or to his mother, trying to toast frozen waffles for the family's breakfast. "Don't take a bath. It wastes water," he screamed to his older sister. Just before they came in to see me, Nathan had begun walking around the house in the evening and turning off all the lights. When anyone complained, he would usually have a tantrum. His parents knew that Nathan's behavior was unacceptable, and we worked together to come up with a plan to deal with Nathan's demands as well as a trial of medication to alleviate his symptoms.

Kids with OCD can be remarkably dislikable, even to their loving parents. "I know this is going to sound cold and awful, but it's gotten so I really don't like my son," a sorrowful mom said to me not long ago. The boy she came to see me about, Lonnie, age ten, was indeed not likely to win any popularity contests. Exceptionally good-looking, with olive skin, green eyes, and dark curly hair, Lonnie was also exceptionally obnoxious. He had a persistent shoulder shrug, but when I asked him about it, he denied it, quite rudely. Throughout our conversation he was fidgety and provocative. When I asked him what he enjoys, he said, "I love sharks. I love violent movies. I love seeing heads being ripped off." Then he started imitating the voice of Chuckie, the evil doll from the movie *Child's Play.* His parents told me he fights with them and his siblings all the time, and he's recently been having trouble at school with both his classmates and his teachers.

To all outward appearances Lonnie was a difficult, oppositional, spoiled brat. It was only when he made some very unusual demands on me—the strangest was asking me to curse at him loudly from across the room—and explained that he wanted me to do it to keep something bad from happening that I looked past the bad behavior and detected the symptoms of OCD.

Once in a while a parent faced with a child's OCD just snaps. One distraught father, his eyes filled with tears, told me about the night he lost his temper with his 11-year-old daughter, Renée. Night after night Renée would bang on her parents' bedroom door, screaming, "Do you love me? Am I attractive?" "Yes, you're very attractive. Go back to bed," Mom and Dad would tell her. "Do you mean attractive or do you mean pretty?" she'd ask. "Do you mean pretty or do you mean beautiful?" was next. They kept responding and kept telling her to go to sleep, but it was never enough. The banging and crying went on for hours. Completely frustrated, the father finally dragged Renée back to her room and locked her in. When he described wedging a chair against his daughter's door, he broke down.

As amazing as it may seem, some parents are unaware of OCD in their children. Even parents who realize that their kids have some pretty strange habits are very often stunned to find out just how bad the situation is. A 16-year-old girl with crippling fears about germs and dirt came to see me. She washes her hands dozens of times a day. She's disgusted by and scared of bodily functions; she's never had sexual intercourse but is terrified of getting pregnant. Her mother does the laundry for the family, but the girl says her clothes are never clean enough to suit her. For a year now, without her mother's knowledge, she has been washing her own clothes, sometimes as often as five times a day. The week before she came to see me she finally let down her guard and told her parents.

According to the mother of 12-year-old Howard, he's always been "fussy about his clothes." His undershirts have to be skintight, and he'll wear only one brand and color of pants. He has five pairs of identical pants and wears a pair every day to school. No one in the family thought too much about Howard's strange notions about wardrobe. After all, everything else about him was normal, or so his family assumed. One day Howard was typing out a report for school. Somewhere in the middle of the paper he realized that every time he typed the letter s, he felt compelled to hit the space bar. Soon he couldn't stop doing it, and he got scared. Fortunately he confided his fears to his mother and father, and soon thereafter he was in my office. It turns out that Howard had a host of other painful habits that he had never told anybody about.

There is some debate among professionals about whether or not to involve teachers and other school officials in the treatment of OCD. As a general rule I'm in favor of full disclosure, of letting the school know about a diagnosis of OCD and working out a strategy for managing the problem, but only if the symptoms are affecting a child's performance or behavior while he's in school. There's no question that OCD can manifest itself in behavioral problems—for instance, a child who keeps jumping up out of his seat and running to the bathroom to wash his hands is more than a little disruptive to the rest of the class—and a teacher is entitled to know why the kid is doing it. Once the lines of communication with the school are open, decisions can be made about how a teacher will respond. On the one hand, a child should not be punished for behavior over which he has no control. On the other hand, teachers must maintain order in the classroom, and there's no way they can do that without holding children responsible for their actions. OCD or no OCD, actions must have consequences. With the help of a professional, parent and teacher should be able to work out some realistic guidelines.

I always suggest that teachers choose their battles carefully when confronted with a child who has OCD. Some children will write only with a pen, drink from only one special water fountain, or use only one bathroom. Those behaviors, while certainly not ideal, do not significantly disrupt the classroom, nor do they interfere with the child's learning, and I recommend that a teacher ignore them if possible. However, the more disruptive behaviors—talking out of turn, making broad gestures, and especially leaving the classroom—must be dealt with more directly.

CHAPTER 9

Separation Anxiety Disorder

The first time I saw Jenny, age seven, it was a late Thursday afternoon at her school in a suburb of Boston. She was sitting on her teacher's lap, crying. When I asked her what was wrong, Jenny said she had a stomachache. I volunteered to help her, but she told me not to bother. "This is my Monday through Friday stomachache," she told me. "Today is Thursday, so I just have one more day to feel bad." I asked if there was anything that would make the pain go away, and she answered immediately: "Bring my mother here." A few weeks later Jenny's parents told me more about their daughter—how she'd sneak into their room at night and sleep on the floor, how she had to be forced onto the school bus every morning, how she would often ask them when they're going to die. When Jenny's goldfish died, she mourned for weeks.

• • •

Nine-year-old Ernie came to see me after he'd missed four months of school. He had had trouble with school ever since kindergarten, but by the fourth grade he was in terrible distress. When his parents tried to get Ernie to go to school, he complained of headaches, stomachaches, and fatigue. In the previous four months he had been in and out of the hospital with various infections. Ernie was inordinately anxious, especially about leaving his parents. He had trouble sleeping in his own bed and crept into his parents' room nearly every night. He didn't want to be with his friends after school because he worried about what would happen to Mom and Dad; even when he was away from home for a short time, he'd become homesick. Recently he wasn't sleeping even on weekends, and his appetite had decreased dramatically.

THE SUNDAY NIGHT BLUES

Nearly everyone knows what separation anxiety feels like. Changing jobs, taking a vacation, even spending the night away from home can cause discomfort. When I was a kid, I used to get a lump in my throat every time I heard the theme song from *Bonanza,* not because I was moved by the adventures of the Cartwrights but because that music, coming as it did on Sunday night, meant that it was almost Monday morning. My weekend was nearly over, and I wasn't prepared for school. I didn't know then that I was suffering from the "Sunday Night Blues," a common response.

The anxiety that Jenny and Ernie feel is, of course, more serious than my Sunday Night Blues. On Sunday nights Jenny is anxious not because she hasn't done her homework for the next day but because she knows she is about to lose access to her mother. Ernie is not fretting over a forthcoming spelling test. He's worried that something terrible is going to happen to his parents. My diagnosis was the same for both kids: separation anxiety disorder, or SAD.

THE SYMPTOMS

There is an important difference between separation anxiety and separation anxiety disorder. Children between seven months and 11 months experience *stranger anxiety:* when they see somebody unfamiliar—not Mom, Dad, a relative, or a regular caregiver—they become alarmed. Most children have *separation anxiety* between 18 months and three years. For instance, a normal two-year-old whose father goes outside for a few minutes, leaving the child with a family friend, will probably have some separation anxiety. As he leaves, the father might say, "I'll be right back, Sam. I'm going to the car to get something. Talk to Carol." Almost immediately, Sam will start to get anxious, thinking, "Wait. I don't know this person. Where's my father?" That reaction is normal, provided that Carol is able to console or distract Sam so that the anxiety doesn't last more than a few minutes. Another two-year-old playing comfortably outside might well take a break, touch base with Mom, and then resume playing after a few minutes. That's normal too. So is some weepiness in the early days of nursery school.

However, by the age of four, a child should be able to leave his parents or his home without distress or anxiety, and about 96 percent of all children can do so without a problem. (The fact that many children start nursery school at age four is no accident.) It is estimated that 4 percent of all children have SAD.

Every once in a while SAD makes its first appearance not in the early days of nursery school or in first or second grade but later, during adolescence. The disorder seems almost to "spring up," with no earlier evidence that there was a problem. Often what brings on the symptoms of SAD is a change or a loss. That was the case with two young people I treated for late-onset SAD. Amelia, 15 years old, showed the first signs of SAD when she and her family moved to a new state in the middle of her sophomore year of high school. Amelia had always loved school, but she just couldn't adjust to the new setting. Every day there were tearful phone calls home, in which Amelia would beg her mother to come and get her. By the time I met Amelia, she had stopped going to school. In fact, she was refusing to leave her front yard. Her parents were completely baffled by the change in their daughter.

Another "late bloomer" with SAD was 13-year-old Rafael, whose SAD came on after he missed a few weeks of school because of a case of mononucleosis. When he was finally well enough to go back to class, Rafael didn't feel comfortable being there any more. He told his parents he was tired and light-headed, and he insisted on staying home, where he would spend the day watching TV and sleeping. When I saw Rafael for the first time, it had been nine weeks since he'd been to school and almost that long since he'd left the house. Before the mono he had seemed perfectly normal, with no symptoms of SAD.

Children suffering from SAD are preoccupied with thoughts that harm is going to come to them or their parents. They feel distress when they have to leave their parents, to go to bed at night or to school in the morning. At school during the day or if they have to go away overnight, they're terribly homesick. Sometimes they experience physical symptoms. Younger children often get stomachaches and diarrhea; older kids may experience dizziness and rapid heartbeat. Their nightmares have a recurring theme: something bad is happening to their family. The house burns down; Mom gets sick and has to go to the hospital; someone evil is chasing the child. Children with SAD don't like to be alone in the house and may shadow their parents, following them from attic to basement. One mother I spoke to said she literally could not go anywhere in the house without having her six-year-old daughter tag along. Children with SAD can have worries that aren't obviously associated with the disorder; an eight-year-old boy named Eddie told me he was worried that someone was going to break into his apartment and steal the silver. Why the silver? The family always used the good silver for their special Sunday night suppers.

Kids with SAD can have extremely high IQs. John was one of the smartest children I've ever met. At the age of 10 he had verbal skills way above the norm. He was also one of the best-natured, sweetest kids I have come across. Dressed in his school uniform with his blond Dutch boy haircut, he looked like a youngster right out of a Norman Rockwell illustration. A few minutes into our meeting it became obvious that something wasn't quite right. Increasingly fidgety, John kept looking toward the door, behind which his mother was waiting. Suddenly he ran to the door and opened it to make sure Mom was still there, an act he repeated many times during the visit. I soon learned that John was preoccupied with the thought that his mom and dad were going to die. When he was in school, the idea sometimes upset him so much that he would get down on his knees and pray that nothing bad would happen to his parents.

THE DIAGNOSIS

The morning nine-year-old Elizabeth stepped into my office, the first thing I noticed were large patches missing from her curly red hair. My first thought was that she was being treated for cancer. I soon learned that her hair loss had nothing to do with chemotherapy. Every night, after she went to bed and was left alone in her room, she would pull out clumps of her own hair. There was nothing compulsive or ritualistic about the hair-pulling; she didn't pull three strands on one side and then three on the other, for instance. She pulled her hair out because she was worried. Elizabeth was convinced that as she slept, someone was going to break into her apartment and do something terrible to her mother and father. Lately her fears had been getting worse, and she'd been refusing to go to school. She was afraid of what would happen if she left her parents at home alone.

SAD can be and often is mistaken for other disorders. SAD is often called school phobia, but that's a misnomer. A child with SAD may not want to go to school, but he isn't afraid of it. Being in school—without Mom and Dad—is what he's afraid of. SAD is sometimes confused with depression. The child may look and act depressed—SAD may result in loss of concentration, sleep and appetite disturbance, and a demoralized state, all symptoms of major depressive disorder (see Chapter 14)—but, it's crucial to note, those symptoms nearly always disappear when Mom and Dad are around. A child who has no appetite for his lunch at school may eat perfectly well at dinner, when he's at home with his parents. By contrast, the loss of appetite associated with clinical depression doesn't come and go. A youngster with SAD may be perceived as defiant, especially when he has to be dragged kicking and screaming onto a school bus. Attention deficit hyperactivity disorder (see Chapter 7) may also be suspected, since children with SAD are so worried that they often appear inattentive and distracted in school. One mother whose daughter I treated received a succinct but less than helpful diagnosis from her neighbor: "spoiled brat."

Jenny, Ernie, John, and Elizabeth demonstrate a wide variety of anxiety symptoms, but at the core of each is the most important factor in SAD: a threat to the integrity of the family. That's what we look for when we examine a troubled child. And we look for it the old-fashioned way: by taking a detailed developmental history from the parents and interviewing the child. Here's how an interview with a child might go.

DOCTOR: "Everyone worries about something. What do you worry about?"

CHILD: "I don't know."

DOCTOR: "Some kids worry about tests in school. Do you worry about them?"

CHILD: "No."

DOCTOR: "Some kids worry about their parents not having enough money. Do you worry about that?"

CHILD: "No."

DOCTOR: "Some kids worry about their parents' health."

CHILD: "Yeah, I kind of worry about that."

The child doesn't always directly acknowledge worrying about his parents. He might talk about kidnappers or burglars or voice concerns about the security of his house. But it doesn't take too long to get to the real fear.

Here's another line of questioning I might try.

DR. K: "When you're at school, tell me what it feels like."

CHILD: "I don't know."

DR. K: "What does it feel like when you see your mother when you come home from school?"

CHILD: "Sometimes I feel like I could cry."

DR. K: "You feel sad?"

CHILD: "No, I feel happy."

DR. K: "Do you ever feel as if there's something pushing on your chest?"

CHILD: "Yes, but it goes away after school."

A child need not have all of the symptoms of SAD to qualify for a diagnosis; if a child is suffering, even one or two symptoms are sufficient. As is the case with all brain disorders, SAD is a spectrum disorder, ranging from mild to severe, so along with any diagnosis should come an evaluation of *distress* and *dysfunction*. There is a critical difference between a child who is a little uncomfortable sleeping with the lights off and one who is so pained to leave his home and family that he avoids going outside, refuses to accept sleepover dates with friends, or, worst of all, won't go to school. It's not enough for a child to have a rewarding, secure home life. Like a healthy adult, a healthy child should have an active social and "work" life as well.

THE BRAIN CHEMISTRY

Stephen, 10 years old, had one of the most severe cases of SAD I've seen. I'll never forget the day he first came to my office; rather, I should say *they* came to my office. When I opened the door, three generations were sitting in my waiting room, staring up at me: Grandma, Mom, and little Stephen. Stephen was refusing to go to school by himself. He agreed to attend school if his mother would drive him and then sit in the car right outside his classroom so that he could see the car through the window. The mother had been doing just that, and the school was remarkably cooperative; the staff agreed to the unusual parking setup and even let Stephen make calls (on the cellular phone he carried) to his mother on the car phone. This strategy had been going on for six months when I met Stephen, but now there was a crisis: Stephen's mother was finding the arrangement more difficult all the time. When she told Stephen that she couldn't take him to school any longer, he threatened to kill himself. When it was time to go to school, he cried hysterically, saying: "I'm going to die. You're going to die."

Stephen had SAD, and it doesn't take a world-class diagnostician to see where it came from. As I soon discovered, both Grandma and Mom had it as well. They lived a block away from each other and were inseparable. They had never spent a day apart and went everywhere together, including my waiting room. Obviously, the DNA Roulette wheel had spun, and Stephen had an unlucky number. Stephen had inherited his brain chemistry from his mother.

What is it about the chemical composition of that family's brains that results in SAD? What causes SAD? As always, it's difficult to answer precisely, but the most likely answer is an imbalance of serotonin and norepinephrine.

Eve, a 30-year old computer programmer, was waiting for the bus that would take her to work. It was a cool autumn day, but Eve felt hot and clammy. Her heart was racing, and the street seemed to be spinning. She felt dizzy and lightheaded. She was sure she was having a heart attack, so she sat down on the sidewalk. When her fellow commuters asked her what was wrong, she couldn't speak. In fact, she was having trouble breathing. Someone took out a cellular phone and called 911. Moments later Eve was evaluated in the emergency room of a nearby hospital. Her cardiogram was normal, and so, it seemed, was everything else. Eve's symptoms had subsided by then, and more than anything else she was embarrassed. This was the second time that Eve had gone through this, and it looked as if "nothing" was wrong. But the emergency room doctor told her that something was indeed wrong. Eve had had a panic attack. The psychiatrist on call confirmed the diagnosis and took it a step further; she told Eve that she had panic disorder: an adult psychiatric disorder (seen occasionally in adolescents) consisting of panic attacks and worry about future attacks.

SAD seems to be the childhood version of panic disorder. There are all sorts of data to support this theory: landmark studies (conducted by Donald Klein) show that 50 percent of patients with panic disorder had separation anxiety disorder as children; moreover, other studies indicate that the children of adults with panic disorder have separation anxiety disorder more than three times as often as the children of depressed or normal adults; and finally, the same medicines are effective in the treatment of both disorders.

Studying the causes of panic disorder has added immeasurably to our knowledge of what causes SAD. We know that both disorders are caused by a defect in the way the brain recognizes and responds to danger. It all happens in the *locus ceruleus,* the part of the brain that alerts the body when there is danger by producing norepinephrine. In people who have panic disorder and, more to the point, children with SAD, the locus ceruleus basically gives the "Danger!" signal when there is no danger, thereby upsetting the balance of norepinephrine and serotonin.

THE TREATMENT

If a child diagnosed with SAD is in extraordinary distress, it may be advisable to medicate him right away, but behavioral therapy without medicine is usually the first line of attack against SAD. Sometimes behavioral therapy is all that's necessary; in a recent study 40 percent of the kids diagnosed with SAD were determined to be functioning quite well (although only about half were symptom-free) after four weeks of behavioral psychotherapy.

In behavioral therapy we concentrate on modifying the way a child acts under various circumstances, addressing both the child's separation anxiety and his *anticipatory anxiety*—the worries he has about something that is going to happen. The goals are quite specific: for example, a child must sleep in his own bed, play with his friends, and, most important, go to school. He must not follow his mother from room to room or cry when he can't see her. He must allow a baby-sitter to care for him once in a while.

Therapists have tried many different ways of working with children to achieve these goals, but the one with which I have had the most success is the contract. This is a formal written agreement signed by the parents and the child and witnessed by me. To make it even more official, everyone gets a typed copy. (I've never gone so far as to get the documents notarized, but I'd gladly do so if I thought I'd get better results.) To my way of thinking the contract offers a perfect way to let a child know what is expected of him, to reassure a child that there are things he can count on from his parents, and to reward him for positive behavior. What's more, if the child doesn't live up to his part of the bargain, we don't have to blame him. We can blame the contract.

Here are a few contracts I've drawn up.

"Jennifer agrees to go to bed by eight o'clock. She will stay in bed with the light on for 15 minutes. During this 15 minutes Mom will come three times to check on her. Jennifer will not leave the bed. At the end of 15 minutes Mom will turn off the light and Mom will continue to check on her every five minutes until Jennifer is asleep and twice after she's asleep. For every night that Jennifer does this, she gets a star. If she gets three stars, she gets a prize. If she gets five stars, she gets a prize and a half. With seven stars she gets two prizes." Jennifer traded in her stars for TV shows.

"Sara agrees to go to school every day. Sara will not cry during school or when Mom leaves. Sara will go to sleep without Mom or Dad in the room. Mom promises to take Sara to school and pick her up each day. Dad promises to tell Sara one five-minute story and will check on her every five minutes before she falls asleep and twice after she's asleep." Sara asked for tickets instead of stars. When she earned five tickets, she got a package of stickers.

"Roger agrees to go to bed quickly without complaining. Roger will stay in his own bed and not go to Mom and Dad's bed or his brother's bed during the night. Mom and Dad promise to let Roger keep his bedside light on. Roger can play or read quietly in bed." Roger used his stars to play video games.

"Cynthia agrees to stay in school from the beginning to the end of lunch. Two stars. She will not cry when she gets on the bus. One star. She agrees to stay with the baby-sitter on a weekend night, without Mom and Dad, for three hours. One star. Without crying, two stars. Going to bed before the parents come home, three stars." With 11 stars Cynthia may rent the video of her choice.

Obviously no one wants a child to fail—the last thing he needs is to feel worse about himself than he already does—so some contracts have to be especially easy and very specific, like the one I drew up for little eight-year-old Karen: "Karen agrees to brush her teeth, wash her face, and prepare for bed by eight o'clock. Karen will get into bed by 8:30 and turn off the lights by 8:45. Mom and Dad promise to let Karen watch TV until 8:30, tuck Karen in at 8:45, check on her for ten minutes till she's asleep. If Karen wakes up, she can call Mom. Mom promises to go to her room and sit in a chair for a few minutes." Once Karen has mastered these simple tasks, we'll draw up a more ambitious contract for her.

A few of my colleagues oppose the idea of attaching rewards to behavior with these contracts, but I'm in favor of them, provided they're not too lavish. Books, videos, baseball cards, doll clothes, or any other relatively small items that a child values make these kinds of contracts that much more effective. Rewards do a lot to increase a child's motivation, and children enjoy looking at their "trophies," tangible evidence of their accomplishments.

Behavioral therapy works relatively fast. If it doesn't work right away, it's probably not going to work, at least not without adding medication. To persist with this type of treatment without adding medicine becomes painful for the parents, the therapist, and, most of all, the child. If a child hasn't responded to behavioral therapy after about four weeks, it's probably time to add medication to the treatment. The drugs that have been used to best effect are Tofranil (a tricyclic antidepressant, or TCA), Prozac, Zoloft, and Paxil (all selective serotonin reuptake inhibitors, or SSRIs), Xanax (an antianxiety agent), and Nardil and Parnate (monamine oxidase inhibitors, or MAOIs). All of these have been used to excellent effect, sometimes in a matter of days. One mother I know thinks that Prozac worked miracles, and she is not alone.

There can be negative side effects with some of these medications. Tofranil may cause dryness of mouth, constipation, and urinary retention, and there may be some behavioral disinhibition; children can become giddy or oppositional. Tofranil may also affect heart rhythm, so it's important for a child to have an electrocardiogram at the beginning and with each dose increase. Xanax, which treats anticipatory anxiety as well as separation anxiety, has no effect on the heart rhythm, but it may cause drowsiness and disinhibition in children. MAOIs carry dietary restrictions because the medicine may cause a reaction when taken with foods rich in a chemical called *tyramine* (aged cheese, red wine, beer, smoked fish, and aged meats). The SSRIs have the fewest side effects. When the dose of an SSRI is started low and increased slowly, there are few side effects. The most common ones are nausea, diarrhea, insomnia, and drowsiness.

Under normal circumstances the medication will take effect within six weeks. A child should continue to take the medicine for at least six months, at which time he should be taken off the medication—gradually, over a period of several weeks—and reevaluated. (I suggest that parents continue the contract policy during this time.) Some children taken off the medicine will redevelop their symptoms, in which case we gradually put them back on medication, enough to make the symptoms disappear; others will continue to be symptom-free without it. It is unlikely that a child will need medicine steadily for a very long period of time—more than a year—but many people diagnosed with SAD require medicine intermittently for many years.

SAD is a serious disorder, but the prognosis for someone with SAD who gets treated is excellent. Left untreated, however, SAD may damage a child permanently over time. If a child can't separate from his parents, he can't play with his friends or concentrate at school. If he avoids school, he will fall behind in his studies and lose ground academically, and that in turn will create another group of problems. He may become socially isolated, demoralized, even depressed. (Close to 50 percent of all adolescents who are clinically depressed also have an anxiety disorder. In 85 percent of the cases the anxiety disorder came first.) Twenty-year follow-up studies of children with SAD show that these children are at a higher risk for panic disorder as adults (like Eve, described a few pages back). Parents who don't take their child's distress about separation seriously and seek professional help are making a mistake.

PARENTING AND SAD

"Either *she's* going into an institution, or *I'm* going into an institution."

Those are strong words, especially coming from a mother talking about her intelligent, sweet-faced six-year-old daughter, Melissa. But this, as I soon discovered, was no ordinary six-year-old; this little girl was afraid of just about everything, including loud noises, Hulk Hogan, Big Bird, and the cashier at the local supermarket. She couldn't look at a newspaper or magazine because she might see a disturbing picture. She became anxious if anything, even a scrap of garbage, was thrown into the trash. At the gas station she was terrified if someone tried to put gas into the car. When she started kindergarten, her mother spent the first two months in the classroom with her. By the time I met Melissa, she refused to leave her mother's side, even for a moment. She almost never smiled. It's no wonder her mother was at the end of her rope.

Eight-year-old Matthew was terrorizing his family too. He had been fine in the first and second grades, but starting with third grade he was having difficulty getting up and out in the morning. At the same time he began trailing his mother as she took out the trash, prepared meals, and made the family's beds. He stood outside the bathroom door until his mother came out, and he crept into his parents' bed nearly every night. When things were at their worst, Matthew was getting up in the middle of the night with a mirror to make sure his mother was breathing. He couldn't fall asleep unless his mother was sitting in the room. He always went to school—that's a firm rule in the family—but he was constantly in the nurse's office, complaining of headaches and stomach-aches. When he got home, he called his dad and stayed on the phone with him for an hour, until Mom got home. Dad has taken to putting Matthew on the speaker phone while he goes about his work.

Another boy with SAD has a mother who is never without her beeper, not because of her work as a real estate broker but because her 13-year-old son must be able to call her a dozen times a day to make sure she hasn't been in an accident. She and her husband are invited to a variety of business functions and parties at night, but they've long since stopped accepting invitations. Too often they were called away after 15 minutes by a baby-sitter unable to cope with their hysterical son.

"We had no life," yet another mother once told me. "I turned down every invitation. My son couldn't go to birthday parties. It was too frightening for him. All those people! And what if there was a clown?"

Parents who haven't experienced SAD may find the concessions that these parents make, the way they change their lives to accommodate a child, almost unbelievable. Even parents who see their children suffering can't always believe there's something really wrong. Many kids with SAD don't voluntarily share their fears, so parents find it hard, if not impossible, to understand their child's behavior. The word "manipulative" is often used—when a child has a stomachache before school but feels fine when his parents suggest a ballgame or when he seems to play one parent against another, shadowing and clinging to Mom but behaving normally around Dad. The latter situation is quite common, and the typical scenario shows an overindulgent mom giving in more easily than a tough dad. Again typically, fathers become furious and blame mothers for coddling their kids; mothers in turn get angry and accuse fathers of not being sufficiently involved.

Parents' emotions are often tempered by personal experience too, of course. If one of the parents has had SAD, the reaction can go one of two ways. It's either "Oh, I remember. It was so horrible, and my parents were so strict with me. I would never do that to my own kid. I won't make my child suffer the way I did" or "I'm not going to give in to this. I won't let this affect my child the way it did me." Complicating matters further is the guilt that many parents feel as they see a child asking for nothing more than to be with them. They see a child in pain and are led to think that by being available they can make that pain go away. It's not surprising that many parents find it difficult to turn away from a needy child.

Family members don't always help. In fact, I've talked to many parents who find it easier to avoid family gatherings altogether than to put up with the disapproving looks or critical comments they receive from friends and relatives when their child misbehaves. One mother said that family gatherings were the occasions she dreaded most: "We hated holidays, but we were expected to attend, even though they all knew that Jon had problems. We would go, but we were so anxious, so on edge about Jon that we never sat down to chat with the family or eat a meal. We had to be with him every minute, or else he'd make a scene and tear the place apart. I think they all thought, '*That's* why Jon's crazy. They never leave that poor kid alone.' I know they blamed us."

I suspect that this mother is not imagining her relatives' reactions. The world is full of people eager to express baseless, ill-considered opinions. One faction says, "This kid's a brat. The mother should be firmer, harder with this kid. What do you mean, he has a stomachache? There's nothing wrong with his stomach." The other side's take is different: "Why are you being so hard on the poor kid? The kid has a stomachache. All he wants is to be with you. That should make you feel wanted. If he doesn't want to go, he shouldn't have to."

Parents sometimes receive less than useful advice from other sources as well. I once saw a four-year-old girl, Kim, who developed SAD when she started nursery school. A lot of mothers stay with their children in nursery school for a couple of weeks, but Kim's mom stayed for four months. At that point Kim's father stepped in and said to his wife, "You can't do this anymore. You've *got* to stop." The next morning, a snowy February day, the mother told Kim that she would be going to school on her own, and Kim got hysterical. When the car pool pulled up in front of the house, Mom took Kim outside, at which point the little girl took off all her clothes and started screaming. It must have made quite a picture: snow falling, driver honking, and a stark-naked child shrieking loud enough to shatter glass. Not surprisingly, her parents decided to seek professional help.

Unfortunately their problems didn't end there. The therapist told Kim's parents that Kim was acting out because of the recent birth of her baby sister and that all Kim really needed to get her through this difficult period was to be babied. "Give her a bottle and some dolls, hug her a lot more," the therapist said. By the time I saw Kim she could barely let her mother out of her sight without hysterics. After six weeks of behavioral therapy and a low daily dose of Zoloft she was attending school—fully clothed—without a problem.

Some aspects of the treatment of SAD are subject to debate, but everyone agrees on one thing: kids *have* to go to school. Missing school is one of the few true psychological emergencies for a child, a major danger sign. The longer a child is out of school, the harder it is to get him back. Home tutoring is sometimes recommended, even by some school officials (who should know better), but I'm completely opposed to it. Having a tutor may relieve anxiety over the short term, but in the long term it makes things worse. The sooner a child returns to school the better, and parents who enlist the aid of the school in the process will get the best results.

If a child has been out of school for a long time, it's unfair to make him go for a whole day right away, so the teacher and principal should be notified that a child is going to need a more flexible schedule for a while. One mother I advised went to the principal and said, "Here's the deal. I want my kid back in school, but it's going to take time. The doctor says it's important to get him back slowly. The first week he's only going to stay an hour a day. For that hour I'd like him to stay in the library. The next week he'll stay for two hours a day, maybe with the guidance counselor or the school psychologist. After that I'd like him to go back to his class." The principal agreed to help.

A child can be reintroduced to school even more gradually than that. Another little boy I treated took two weeks to get back to his regular classroom. The first day all he did was walk in the front door of the building without his mother. Then he turned around and left. Each day he got a little closer. Again, the principal was more than eager to cooperate and made sure that the boy had the work he was missing to take home with him every day. It is the rare school official who takes a hard line about attendance when SAD has been diagnosed, although once in a great while a principal may insist that a child be "in or out." If that happens and simple reason doesn't prevail, the child's doctor should be able to help parents clear any hurdles erected by the school authorities.

In any successful treatment of SAD parents must be co-therapists, and that takes commitment, patience, and a structured plan. It's rarely easy. Checking on a child every 10 minutes in the evening after a full day's work is no parent's idea of fun, but the knowledge that next week it will be every 15 minutes and the week after that once every half-hour should provide some comfort. So should the prospect of going out to a movie or *not* sharing a bed with a five-year-old every night. Efforts made today will pay dividends later, in the form of a healthy, well-rounded, happy child.

CHAPTER 10

Social Phobia/Shyness

The day I first met Rebecca, 16 years old and just coming to the end of her junior year of high school, she had made herself so small that it looked as if she were trying to disappear into the woodwork of my office. I greeted her and asked her how she was feeling. There was no response. I tried again, but she said nothing. Finally, after I asked a third time, I got an answer. "I don't have any friends," she said in the softest voice I've ever heard, barely a whisper. "I can't talk to people." For Rebecca, that statement was practically the Gettysburg Address. As I discovered, she almost never talked to anyone. She didn't answer her teachers' questions in class or chat with her classmates. When she used the school bathroom, she had to be alone; her one friend stood guard in the hallway outside the door to assure her complete privacy. She ate by herself in the school cafeteria. If someone joined her, she moved to another table and scattered papers and books around to discourage others. Then she hid behind a notebook while she ate. Rebecca had a number of other anxieties as well, each of which has an element of social concern. She worried that teachers would call on her in class. Any kind of social interaction forced her anxiety level through the roof.

• • •

Ten-year-old Eric is in fifth grade. He's been in therapy since he was five, with three different therapists. The first diagnosis was separation anxiety disorder, because Eric was afraid to leave his house in the morning. Every day since kindergarten his parents had had a battle royal on their hands when they tried to get him ready for school. Extremely bright, Eric did well academically once he got to school, but socially he was having problems. He didn't have a single friend. If another kid tried to start up a conversation with him, Eric responded in monosyllables and retreated to a corner somewhere. The teachers tried to involve him in activities, but he was having none of it. He would talk to his teacher but only one-on-one, never in a classroom setting. Eric was terrified that he was going to say or do something so stupid that it would make everybody hate him. If he stayed home, he reasoned, that wouldn't happen. By the time I met Eric, I had to make a house call. When I got there, he was hiding under his bed.

BEYOND SHYNESS

"I was really shy as a kid. I was one of those youngsters who'd hide behind my mother's leg when my aunts came to visit."

"I'm okay in most social situations, but I don't really like them. I really have to push myself to talk to people."

"I *hate* parties. I never know what to say. I couldn't do it at all without a glass of wine."

Everybody is shy some of the time. Meeting strangers, making a speech, being the guest of honor at a surprise party—those are not situations that most people consider relaxing. Some years ago it was reported that the three greatest fears of the American people are death, heights, and speaking in public. (In fact, speaking in public ranked higher than death!) Of course, some are more shy than others; they're usually the ones standing behind the potted plant hoping no one will spot them or over by the bar having a third cocktail to loosen their tongue. Many people outgrow their shyness—by the time they're too big to hide behind Mom's leg when the aunts come to call, they don't feel the need to do it anymore—but others continue to be uneasy in specific situations. Shyness is a perfectly natural response to events, especially in children and adolescents. As long as it isn't excessive, as long as it doesn't seriously interfere with a child's ability to function, shyness is nothing to be particularly concerned about.

Obviously, Rebecca and Eric are *not* functioning very well. Both children are suffering from social phobia, an anxiety disorder characterized by the persistent fear of being scrutinized and judged by others and of doing or saying something that will be humiliating or embarrassing.

Some children become so concerned that people will be critical of them that they become unable to speak, drink, or eat in front of other people. Others are afraid to use public toilets, not because they worry about hygiene but because they worry about doing something that will make them look bad.

The key to this brain disorder is intense self-consciousness. Children with social phobia are basically afraid that they're going to do something the wrong way and consequently look foolish to others. They don't speak in class because they're afraid they'll get the answer wrong or say it in a voice that will sound strange. They don't eat in public because they might spill their food or choke. They have trouble urinating in a public toilet if anyone is around. Children with social phobia believe that all these things (and many more) will make them seem stupid. They're afraid that people will mock them for their inadequacies.

Children and adolescents with social phobia have not lost touch with reality. When confronted with the force of logic, these kids will readily acknowledge that their fears and anxieties don't make a whole lot of sense. They know that they're being "silly," but they just can't help themselves.

The numbers on garden-variety shyness are astronomically high, but true social phobia is thought to be uncommon among young people, affecting about 1 percent of the child and adolescent population. (Recent studies have found that social phobia affects as many as 12 percent of all adults.) The symptoms of social phobia are usually noticed in adolescence, especially the mid-teens, but we have good reason to think that adolescence is not when the symptoms actually begin. Teenagers with social phobia often report a long history of painful shyness or social inhibition, but until their teens, they were able to cope. With the increased demands and expectations of adolescence—part-time jobs, interviews for college, dating, and other social pressures—come the distress and dysfunction that bring these kids to psychiatrists' offices. Even perfectly normal teenagers usually go through a patch of greater-than-average self-consciousness. Teenagers with social phobia go off the charts during these years.

Social phobia in very young children often is seen as a closely related disorder: selective mutism.

SELECTIVE MUTISM

Lydia was an enchanting child—pretty, beautifully dressed, exceptionally bright. At the age of five she was already reading quite well. Her parents brought her to see me because most of the time Lydia did not speak. She *could* speak. She talked to her parents and to her brother a little, and once in a while she spoke to her grandparents. She read aloud. But otherwise she didn't talk—even to respond to direct questions—and she never participated in sharing or "show and tell" at school. Neighbors, relatives, schoolmates, and teachers had been expressing their concern and their irritation. Her teacher was worried about passing her on from kindergarten to first grade.

At nine years old Alice had been going to school for several years, but she hardly ever talked. She had one friend to whom she'd occasionally whisper. When she had no other choice but to speak to her teacher, she would get up close and speak softly into her ear. Alice's parents had been taking her for therapy for a couple of years. Every week for two years she'd go in and whisper to her therapist. The week before I saw Alice, the school had sent a letter home to the parents: "There's a real problem with Alice," it read. "We can't really evaluate what she knows and what she doesn't know. What's even more important is that Alice is incredibly uncomfortable all of the time."

A child's failure to speak—called selective mutism—has many possible explanations. It could be perfectly normal shyness; many five-year-old kids aren't crazy about chatting with strangers. It could be the result of a traumatic experience, such as physical or sexual abuse, but that connection is very rare. It might be caused by a problem with language; there is a higher than average incidence of selective mutism among children of non-English-speaking parents and among kids who have a developmental speech delay or a learning disability. Children who stutter sometimes decide not even to try to speak.

The most common cause of a child's failure to speak is anxiety. Children who are selectively mute are, quite simply, too anxious and nervous to talk in front of others. For that and other reasons selective mutism (sometimes called *elective mutism*) may be regarded as a symptom, or at least a first cousin, of social phobia.

THE SYMPTOMS

Social phobia is divided into two general types. Type one is *generalized,* an anxiety marked by the avoidance of most daily social interactions. Eric, the child hiding under his bed, described at the beginning of this chapter, has the symptoms of generalized social phobia. Just about anything that involves other people makes Eric anxious.

Type two social phobia is characterized by discomfort in and the avoidance of *specific* situations, such as speaking in public, using public lavatories, and eating, writing, or speaking in front of others. (This is a form of pathological performance anxiety.) With type two, the phobia isn't generalized; in fact, there may be just one situation that brings on anxiety. A college student I treated a few years ago was normal except for his terrible fear of using a public bathroom. He eventually had to move out of the dorm and into his own apartment because of it. When we talked about it, all he could say by way of explanation was: "I'm afraid someone will walk in on me." A junior high school girl was fine too except for her fear of being called on in class. "I have the feeling that I won't know the answer and I'll say something stupid," she told me. She would rather take a zero in class participation than respond to her teacher.

Communicating with some of these troubled children, especially the young ones, can be quite a problem. The difficulties with the kids who are selectively mute are obvious; we're lucky to get them to speak at all. I've interviewed a five-year-old who did nothing but grunt and moan in response to my questions. One of my colleagues is treating a little girl through her father; the father does all her talking for her. It's not at all unusual for these youngsters to have appointments and not show up. When the time comes to interact with a new person, they just can't do it. What's more, the very young children who *do* show up and *do* speak are not skilled at articulating the distress and dysfunction associated with social phobia. We're not likely to hear, for instance, any version of, "Doctor, I'm afraid to answer questions in class because I'll be embarrassed and humiliated by my peers" from a child with social phobia until he's well into adolescence, if then.

Even when the kids are in their teens and very smart, talking to them is often like pulling teeth. I was treating a 16-year-old boy who was on the cusp of being a genius. He had a very high IQ, and he was a whiz at math and computers. Socially, however, he was completely lost; the only people he could converse with were his sister and his mother.

When kids are capable of communicating, they may not be willing to communicate; they're reluctant to acknowledge, let alone describe the nature of, their symptoms. Many of them will dismiss symptoms as being nothing to worry about. An 18-year-old boy named Eugene was virtually dragged in to see me by his mother. He was finishing the first semester of his freshman year away at college, and his mother thought—correctly in my estimation—that he was having some serious problems. He'd been quiet and withdrawn his whole life, she told me in front of her son, but this year he'd gotten worse. All alone in his new school, Eugene hadn't spoken to a soul in over a month.

For the first half-hour I couldn't get any response out of Eugene at all. Eventually he told me, haltingly and with no eye contact: "I don't know why my mother's making such a big deal out of this. So I don't speak in class. So I don't talk to people. I just don't have anything to say."

Children later diagnosed with social phobia come to see me for three main reasons: they don't speak, they don't go to school, and they have no friends. In many cases these problems have existed for quite some time, but something has happened to make the situation intolerable. For example, one young woman's social phobia caused her to drop out of college. First she dropped an American history class because she was asked to make an oral report. The moment she stood in front of the class, she started sweating and felt light-headed. After reading only three lines of her report she had to sit down; she was sure she was going to faint. Then she dropped biology because of the lab work; it meant interacting with other people, and she just couldn't deal with it. She finally got so anxious that she dropped out of school completely. Other adolescents who have been suffering for some time may be brought in by their parents because they've started using drugs and alcohol to ease their anxiety. By the time they reach me, many young people with social phobia show symptoms of other related disorders. Studies show that some 50 percent of people with social phobia will have other anxiety disorders, and many others will eventually require treatment for depression.

THE DIAGNOSIS

Making a diagnosis of generalized social phobia is not always easy. Sifting through the underbrush of family troubles, extraneous symptoms, and other facts that occasionally clutter up the diagnostic landscape can be quite challenging, particularly if the child has been sick for some time. Penny, a 16-year-old high school senior, came to me because her home-room teacher told the parents that there was a problem. Penny was acting strange in class—a little "nutty," her parents called it. According to the teacher, she almost never spoke in class, but she would often giggle uncontrollably, sometimes so much that she disrupted the class. (It's not unusual to hear complaints about the behavior or the attitude of children with social phobia. Many of them, especially the young ones, come off as rude and defiant.)

As I learned during our first visit, Penny had other symptoms as well: frequent urination, depressive complaints, and some anxieties. There were some conflicts at home too. Penny's parents were in the process of getting a divorce, and her sister was quite ill. It took me some time to explore the issues of anxiety with Penny, distracted as I was by the family crises. But when I did get her to talk about what she was worried about, I discovered that she was a mass of fears and anxieties. Even getting on the school bus every morning scared her. "I'm nervous about saying hello to the bus driver," she told me. "I might say it wrong and sound really stupid."

Symptoms related to social phobia must be carefully assessed before a diagnosis is made. Taking a history from the child himself is only the beginning. Besides, we can't always count on what the youngsters report, because they're usually nervous about making a bad impression—one of the key factors in social phobia. We make it a point to get a detailed history from the child's parents and teachers. Teachers are not always ideal sources of information either. Some children with social phobia are completely ignored by teachers. After all, they sit quietly—*very* quietly —in the back of the classroom, not bothering anybody. They appear shy or withdrawn, as if they're watching the scene rather than participating in it. Sometimes they're perceived as being stuck up or judgmental, but it's fear that keeps them from taking part in the action. They don't want to say or do anything that will get them into trouble. The disruptive disorders are the ones that usually get a teacher's attention.

In making a diagnosis for social phobia we have to rule out other diseases with similar symptoms, especially separation anxiety disorder (described in Chapter 9), obsessive compulsive disorder (Chapter 8), and generalized anxiety disorder (Chapter 11). Schizoid disorder must be ruled out as well. A teenager sits at the table at a large family holiday dinner. She doesn't socialize with her cousins or the other guests and leaves the table as quickly as possible. The behavior could be that of an adolescent with schizoid disorder, a chronic condition that may start in late adolescence and is characterized by detachment and limited interest in others, or these could be the actions of someone with schizophrenia (Chapter 16). If the girl is silent and withdrawn because she's convinced that she will say something stupid, she has social phobia. It's important to note that people with schizoid disorder are not uncomfortable or anxious in social situations; they just have peculiar interactions. In the case of schizophrenia the youngster will be anxious and nonresponsive with everyone, while the girl with social phobia may be a chatterbox with her parents once the dinner guests go home.

Another important distinction is in the patient's desire to get well. People with social phobia aren't comfortable with their disorder; they want to go to school, speak out in class, and play with their friends. They'd like to go to a birthday party without being terrified of looking silly. They know they're in pain, and they want to feel better.

Psychiatrists look for—and frequently find—signs of depression (see Chapter 14) associated with social phobia. In the course of a recent study of adolescent depression it was discovered that 47 percent of the children with depression also had an anxiety disorder, most often either separation anxiety disorder or social phobia. Of those adolescents 84 percent had the anxiety disorder *before* the depression. What the study did not say was whether the connection between anxiety disorders and depression is biological—that is, dictated by brain chemistry—or causal. Perhaps social phobia, and the social isolation it usually brings, contribute to depression.

Social phobia is underdiagnosed and undertreated. Parents often wait a long time—too long—before seeking professional help for their kids with social phobia. "He's just shy. He'll outgrow it," is their perfectly reasonable response. They resist going to a child psychologist or psychiatrist because they're afraid, quite naturally, to find out that their child's behavior is not quite normal. "We've waited six months. Let's wait a year." "We've waited a year. Let's wait another six months." So goes the typical reaction of parents who are faced with a child who is not getting better.

I encountered some parents who said exactly that for nearly three years while their daughter got progressively sicker. Rita was seven when I first saw her. For two years and nine months the only people Rita had spoken to were her mother, her grandmother, and two of her four siblings. She had barely said a word to her teacher or to any of her classmates since the first day of nursery school, but she'd recently started mouthing words to her teacher. In fact, this concerned teacher was the reason Rita finally made it to my office. At a recent parent-teacher conference she sat the mother and father down and told them to take Rita to see a professional or else. "We're very worried. You have to deal with this. You are neglecting your daughter," she said sternly. Mom brought Rita to see me, of course, but she didn't accept the teacher's assessment of the situation. "Rita's really *much* better," said the mother. "She's mouthing words to her teacher now. And last week I think she whispered something to her cousin." Parents, feeling protective of their child, become defensive and may have a hard time accepting negative reports from the school.

THE BRAIN CHEMISTRY

Certain children are born with a genetic predisposition for social phobia. In plain English: excessive shyness runs in families. Supporting this theory is the fact that if one twin has social phobia, the other is more likely also to have it if he or she is an identical twin (with the same genetic makeup) rather than fraternal (with similar but not identical genes)— even if the twins are raised apart. Children adopted at an early age show a great similarity to their biological mothers on ratings of shyness. Parents of behaviorally inhibited children, kids who are fearful or withdrawn in new or unfamiliar situations are much more likely to have social phobia or to have had the disorder as children than are parents of normal or uninhibited youngsters.

What specific brain chemistry do children with social phobia have? As always, we can't be sure, but we can make an educated guess. Most probably the brain has too much norepinephrine and not enough serotonin. Certainly the effective medication for this disorder supports that theory. The medications that are most useful in the treatment of social phobia are the MAOIs (monamine oxidase inhibitors) and the SSRIs (selective serotonin reuptake inhibitors), both of which have an impact on norepinephrine and serotonin. TCAs (tricyclic antidepressants) have no effect on this disorder.

The animal model adds support to the argument. Studies done with rhesus monkeys have been able to identify two different behavioral styles —laid-back or uptight—and to determine that the uptight monkeys have a different brain chemistry from those who are laid-back. When given an SSRI, the uptight monkeys become more sociable and more comfortable, more like their laid-back fellow monkeys.

There's some evidence that with social phobia "nurture" plays a part as well as "nature." The basic assumption is that infants come into the world with a predisposition for anxiety. After that, any of several scenarios are possible. For example, a temperamentally inhibited infant is very reactive and hard to comfort, and a parent may find this distressing and be less attentive. The lack of attention affects the parent-child relationship, of course, and it may make the child insecure and less inclined later on to participate in other social contacts. To take another example, a shy mother or father with a shy infant is less likely to expose that child to social situations, so the child never learns to be comfortable socially. His parent, not wanting to cause the child discomfort, continues to "protect" him from the outside world. In both of these examples the children, with limited social experience, become even more anxious.

THE TREATMENT

A five-year-old boy being treated for selective mutism is making progress, but it's slow, very slow. So far the treatment has consisted only of behavioral therapy, mostly directed toward modifying the boy's behavior in school. His teacher is working with us on a program by which the child is rewarded with stars and stickers for communicating. The first step was a yes or no answer to a direct question. Step two required more than one word as an answer. Now, three months after the treatment began, there are lots of stars and plenty of stickers but no qualitative gains. The child is still uncomfortable and largely dysfunctional; his teacher said he looks pained all the time.

We give the boy a small dose of Prozac, much smaller than the customary dose—about an quarter of a teaspoon, or 5 milligrams, in liquid form from a dropper each day—and continue the therapy. Within a month the boy is communicating easily with everyone. "He became a different person almost immediately," his mother said. "He's talkative, he's friendly, and he feels at ease." Six months later we discontinued the Prozac, and the boy continued to be fine.

There's no such thing as a "good" brain disorder, but if there were, social phobia would be it. With active treatment social phobia can be cured. Behavioral therapy is an effective and necessary part of the treatment of social phobia, but because of the nature of the disorder—the patient is afraid to interact with and be judged by other people, including psychiatrists and psychologists—it is almost always a good idea for the child to be medicated as well. (Sometimes medication is all that a child with this disorder needs. I've seen it happen many times.) Medicine alleviates a child's anxiety so that he can benefit from the behavioral therapy. Most of the children we treat for selective mutism and social phobia simply couldn't do the work without the medication.

The first line of medication treatment used for children with social phobia and selective mutism is the SSRIs, specifically Prozac and Zoloft. With their minimal and infrequent side effects (occasional nausea, weight loss, restlessness, drowsiness, moodiness, and insomnia), these medicines are the drugs of choice. Also effective are the antianxiety agents, such as Klonopin, Xanax, and BuSpar. Klonopin and Xanax work fast and are quite effective in reducing the anxiety children experience before certain events. The most common side effect is drowsiness.

The MAOIs, especially Nardil, have been proven effective in treating adults with social phobia, but there are serious dietary restrictions attached to the MAOIs. When people taking MAOIs eat foods containing tyramine, a chemical found in aged cheese, red wine, beer, smoked fish, and aged meats, they may develop high blood pressure. Because of the difficulty in monitoring the diets of children and adolescents, this category of medication is rarely prescribed for them.

The category of medication most commonly prescribed for type two social phobia (pathological performance anxiety and anxiety in specific situations) is the beta blockers, especially Inderal and Tenormin. Beta blockers, which were originally developed for the treatment of high blood pressure, block the peripheral physical symptoms of anxiety, such as palpitations, tremors, and sweating. Teenagers with severe test anxiety have been treated very successfully with Inderal. One child I treated, David, age 12, hated tests. He had headaches for a few days before an exam and would awake with a terrible stomachache on the morning of the test. During the test his hands would sweat and his heart would race, but his thoughts were sluggish. He said his mind would just go blank sometimes. David's IQ was above average, and he knew the material, but he was nonetheless convinced that his teacher thought he was stupid. He just couldn't control his thoughts when he sat down in front of a test. On a low dose of Inderal he was able to take tests comfortably.

Beta blockers are usually taken an hour before any "performance," including tests, and only on an as-needed basis. Few side effects are experienced by youngsters taking these medicines, but a child's heart rate and blood pressure should be measured and an electrocardiogram done before he takes any beta blocker for the first time.

Certain medicines work well for particular kinds of anxiety but not for others. For instance, Xanax tends to relieve anticipatory anxiety—it keeps a patient from worrying in advance—but it's not recommended for performance anxiety, because it does tend to take away the edge that many performers say they need to do their best work. ("I *want* that sharpness," a musician told me. "I want to be very clear-headed. I don't want any cloudiness when I'm onstage.") On the other hand, a small dose of Inderal can work wonders for performance anxiety. I treated a nine-year-old boy, a talented musician who could not perform. He'd get backstage and just freeze with panic. He'd sweat and feel light-headed. Eventually he developed a tremor. On a very low dose of Inderal taken an hour before a performance he became anxiety-free and was able to get up on stage and play, completely clear-headed. Not only does he feel less anxious, his teacher says he's also playing better than ever.

If a child begins a careful program of behavioral therapy at the same time he takes medication, there is a good chance that he won't have to take the medicine for very long. A 12-year-old boy I treated took 20 milligrams of Prozac a day for only six weeks, during which time he worked hard with a psychologist on improving his social skills. We started the treatment in late May. By July 1 he was ready to go away to camp, without his medication. He needed a lot of encouragement and a fair amount of coaching, but he did it. What's more, his mother told me proudly, he made two friends the first day of camp.

While we're on the subject of medication, I should say that one of the major pitfalls associated with social phobia in adolescents is *self-medication;* these adolescents drink and take drugs to make themselves feel better. Many of them say that the only time they don't feel horrible is when they drink or smoke marijuana. However, when they sober up, they feel even worse than before. What's more, this self-medication inevitably escalates; as time passes, it takes more alcohol and more marijuana to get that loose, relaxed feeling.

Behavior modification—learning how to act even after the medicine has been taken away—is the ultimate goal here. The social and coping skills that come naturally to most people must be consciously learned by children with social phobia, a process that requires time and a lot of effort. Most therapists begin by teaching the child some basic relaxation techniques to combat anxiety, especially deep breathing and progressive muscle relaxation. Visual imagery, the process by which a child pictures himself in a situation that scares him and then creates an image of himself working through it, is another basic treatment technique.

Children being treated for social phobia are given assignments for behavioral changes, starting very small and working up to the big challenges. Parents are indispensable co-therapists in these efforts. "Okay. Talk to one person today. Just say hello," a mother might say to her daughter on Monday morning. On Tuesday it would be, "That was great. Now today I want you to talk to two people. And smile when you say hello." The assignments escalate, and the child is gradually exposed to more social situations and made to feel more confident. Small rewards for completed assignments will increase motivation. Stars, stickers, check marks on a calendar—all of these signs of success can be traded in for comic books, video rentals, half hours of television, or any other token or activity the child holds dear.

Assignments are great, but it's not enough to pat a child with social phobia on the head and send him out to have random conversations with the kids at school or the relatives at a family get-together. After all, children don't have a lot of experience with idle chit-chat. Kids need to be coached, and they need to rehearse. *"But what will I say? What should I talk about?"* a child will want to know. Those are good questions. All of us, not just kids with social phobia, feel more relaxed if we know what's coming next and what we're supposed to do.

I remember helping Henry, a six-year-old who had been in treatment for social phobia for a couple of months, get ready for a day he was truly dreading: Thanksgiving dinner with his large extended family. He had no idea what he was going to say to these people, and he was scared to death. I asked the parents to find out who would be sitting on either side of Henry. Then we came up with three questions he could ask each of his dinner partners. His assignment for the day was to ask those six questions and to answer any questions that were put to him. We even worked on answers to some of the more obvious questions: How is school? How old are you now? What do you want to be when you grow up? And finally, we rehearsed Henry's good-bye and thanks to his grandmother. The little boy came through it beautifully. In fact, to hear his parents tell it, Henry's social skills were a lot better than those of his aunts and uncles.

It doesn't always go that smoothly, of course. Henry wasn't a terribly tough case. Children with especially severe social phobia will have to work long and hard before they dazzle the family over the turkey at Thanksgiving. Some never quite get there. It's not unusual for kids to freeze when the moment of truth arrives. "I knew I was supposed to say something, but I couldn't remember what," one little girl said sadly. "It all just went out of my head." But practice *does* make perfect, and with the right medication combined with good coaching and rehearsal, reasonable assignments, and a lot of parental support, a child will make progress. A change of scenery can make a big difference too. Kids with social phobia may be labeled at school or at camp or even at family gatherings—singled out as that "shy kid" or the one who "never says anything"—and labels are hard for anyone, especially children, to shake.

Not surprisingly, group therapy sessions can be very useful for teaching social skills, since they replicate the social experience more closely than individual sessions do. One of the most interesting groups I know of was assembled by one of my colleagues, a psychologist. She invited three 11-year-old girls with social phobia to her office with the intention of doing some tests. What happened instead is that the girls somehow clicked. One of the girls was carrying a *Baby-Sitters Club* book, and the other two said they liked the series too. The next thing my colleague knew, they were talking among themselves, three preteens with social phobia. After discussion of the *Baby-Sitters Club* had been exhausted (none of them thought that the TV show was as good as the books), they needed coaching from the therapist. "Why don't you tell us about what happened when you went horseback riding?" she said to one. "Tell us about the new dress you got for your birthday," she told another. "What kind of costume will you be wearing for Halloween?" she asked the third. The responses were quite lively, and the session went surprisingly smoothly. The girls really seemed to understand one another.

When social phobia is treated promptly and aggressively, the prognosis is excellent. Left untreated, it may get worse, and it may have a negative impact on all important aspects of a child's life: school, work, and play. In all likelihood later on it will affect his job choice and performance and will hinder his ability to have a romantic relationship. It will have a lasting effect on self-esteem and may well result in alcohol and drug abuse.

PARENTING AND SOCIAL PHOBIA

A few years ago I saw Michael, a very bright, handsome 18-year-old boy whose mother had died six months earlier after a long illness. It was a close family, and everyone took the mother's death very hard. Michael was clearly in terrible pain. Every time his mother's name up, he would start to cry, sometimes uncontrollably. The reason he finally came to me was that a few nights earlier, at a party with his friends, he got so upset that he went to the bathroom and started smashing his fist against the wall. "I was hitting the wall and crying about how much I miss my mother," he told me.

Michael had even more reason to miss his mother than his brothers and sisters did. Although it had never been diagnosed, Michael had social phobia—his symptoms were quite obvious even in our first session—and he had always been dependent on her for help in coping with the outside world. Probably without even being aware of it, the mother had coached Michael and rehearsed with him. "I used to talk to my mother about how I was nervous about going to parties, and she would give me ideas about how to act. I could tell her anything," Michael said tearfully. She made his appointments, chose his classes, and helped him schedule every detail of his life, including what he would wear to any important social occasion. The idea of life without her was devastating.

Behavior modification, with a strong emphasis on social skills training, calls for the informed assistance of the child's mother and father—or *trainers*, as I like to think of them. Ideally Mom and Dad will help their child learn social skills by making assignments, coaching, and rehearsing. Parental intervention is not always possible, however. Some parents just aren't temperamentally suited for the task of trainer. One type of parent who's likely to have a problem is the kind who's always asking kids for a progress report. "How did everything go? What did the teacher think of your paper? Did everyone like your new shirt? Did you make a lot of friends?" Those are not the sorts of questions that put a child with social phobia—who's overly concerned about being scrutinized and evaluated to begin with—at his ease. There's already far too much anxiety associated with his social performance.

Other parents become too emotionally involved with a child's social success and consequently apply more pressure than the kid can manage. The unspoken message here is that a child's inability to handle himself in a social situation is a reflection on the parents. Such mothers and fathers inevitably communicate their disappointment or disapproval, and sometimes even their anger, to their child, and that only increases the poor kid's anxiety. To be truly helpful, parents must take the matter of social skills training seriously but not so seriously that it makes the child more nervous than he already is. A parent's goal should be to make a child feel more confident and secure. That may mean putting some emotional distance between parent and child.

"You don't understand. You have no idea what it's like to be shy," one of my patients with social phobia, a 10-year-old girl named Mary Ann, said to her father in my office one day. Mary Ann had a point. Her father, an extremely outgoing family lawyer, didn't show the remotest signs of social phobia. Not even a cocktail party filled with strangers would scare this man. Of course, he wanted to understand and help his daughter, but trying to relate to a girl for whom the briefest conversation was a trial cannot have been easy for this natural extrovert. It's not necessarily easy if the parent *does* understand what it's like to be shy. I treated a little girl with selective mutism whose mother found the child's disorder completely intolerable. She had no patience with it, and the child knew it. It turned out that Mom was painfully shy herself.

No matter how empathetic parents are—and no matter how skilled at advising and coaching their kids—there are plenty of children who simply won't *let* their parents be their trainers. They'll take advice from a therapist or a teacher or a family friend, but not from their folks. There's not a great deal parents can do when they meet this kind of resistance, except to insist that the child work with *someone* who knows what he's doing. "Okay, if you don't want to rehearse with Daddy and me, you have to talk to Aunt Laurie about it," a mother might say. The child needs training, regardless of who the trainer is.

A child's school should be made aware that he's being treated for social phobia. Many teachers can be very helpful in social skills training and other elements of behavioral therapy. If a teacher knows, for instance, that a child's assignment is to speak out once a day in class, he can help the child achieve that goal—by calling on the child early in the class to get it over with, for instance, or not calling on him more than once a day until he shows marked improvement. Every little bit helps.

CHAPTER 11

Generalized Anxiety Disorder

When nine-year-old Caitlin and her parents flew in from Chicago to see me, Caitlin had already been through more than her share of experiences with doctors. She'd been suffering from headaches and terrible stomachaches every day for months, and her parents had taken her to several specialists, most recently the neurologist who referred her to me. When I asked Caitlin what kinds of things she worried about, the floodgates opened. She worried about *everything,* she said—that she wasn't playing the piano well enough, that her father was going to run out of money, that her hair didn't look right, that she wouldn't have any friends, that she wouldn't do well in school. The neurologist said that Caitlin's headaches were caused by tension.

• • •

Larry, a sweet, serious little first-grader, came home with a handwritten note attached to his first report card. "Larry is a lovely boy. I just wish he would smile more than once a semester," the teacher wrote. Larry's parents knew exactly what the teacher was talking about. At six, their son took his academic life as seriously as a third-year law school student. From the moment he came home, he'd worry about doing his homework assignment, fretting about whether it was complete and correct. One recent morning he and his parents had the following exchange:

"Where's my homework?" Larry asked Mom.

"Your homework's in your knapsack. It's all signed," she answered.

"You signed the *homework?* You're not supposed to sign my homework. You're supposed to sign my homework assignment *book!*"

"Honey, it's okay. I'm sure it will be fine."

"No, it *won't* be fine."

"Okay. I'll write a note to the teacher and explain that I didn't know I was supposed to sign the assignment book."

"No, don't write a *note*. You're not supposed to write a *note!*"

When he finally left for school, little Larry was *not* smiling.

HIGH ANXIETY

A five-year-old boy on his way to a classmate's birthday party tells his father he'd really rather not go, thank you very much. When the father questions the child, he discovers that the boy is a little nervous about going to a house he's never visited before. He also fears that the other kids might not want to play with him. The boy finally agrees to go to the party. Dad offers to stay at the party and keep his son company for a little while, but the boy turns the offer down. No, he'll be fine, he says. And after a few minutes at the party, he is.

Another sensitive five-year-old goes to a G-rated movie only to be faced with a PG-rated preview of a coming attraction: a movie with monsters. As soon as the child hears the music of the preview, she turns to her mother and says, "This is going to be scary. I'm closing my eyes." She sits with her eyes shut tight until the ominous background music stops. "I wasn't scared," the little girl said afterward, "but it was good I closed my eyes."

Both of the youngsters I have just described were experiencing anxiety that falls within normal limits. All kids worry about something at least some of the time. They're afraid of storms, animals, strangers, loud noises, the dark. They fret about wearing the wrong clothes, taking tests, getting invited to parties, and choosing a college. They're scared that other kids won't like them. All of these anxieties are to be expected in a child's normal development.

What is *not* part of normal development is the brand of anxiety that Caitlin and Larry exhibit. Both children are suffering from generalized anxiety disorder, or GAD, which is defined in the textbooks as "pathological anxiety characterized by all-consuming worry and excessive or unrealistic anxiety about a number of events or activities occurring more days than not for a period of at least six months." GAD should not be confused with a simple phobia, which is an illogical fear of a particular thing—cockroaches, snakes, pigeons, whatever. Until recently GAD had a different name in the textbooks: overanxious disorder.

Most kids worry when they have to take a test. Children with GAD worry not just before a test but before, during, and after a test. Normal kids study, get nervous, take the test, and wait to get their grades. Children with GAD study, take the test, and then replay it over and over again in their minds, convinced that their performance wasn't good enough. They're the ones who are always asking in class, "What did you put for number 6?" or "I'm sure I failed."

Kids with GAD usually are incapable of evaluating their own performance on a test or anything else; they're just too anxious. Logic has nothing to do with how they feel about themselves. Even when they consistently pass or they always get straight A's, the worry is always there. I treated a 12-year-old boy who played the violin beautifully but was never satisfied with his performance. Even though his parents, his teachers, and the audiences at his recitals praised him to the skies, he never pleased his toughest critic: himself. He spent hours replaying and second-guessing the performance, saying, "I should have done this. I shouldn't have done that." His performances always went without a hitch, but that didn't matter to him. They were never good enough.

For these kids there's no such thing as "I've gotten 100 percent on every spelling test so far this year, so I'll do okay on this one too" or "I really know the material, so I don't have to study." And even if everything goes perfectly, they derive no real pleasure from an accomplishment. They're already worried about something else.

When a child suffers from GAD, the intensity, frequency, and duration of his anxieties are completely inappropriate to the worry itself. What's more, kids with GAD are always finding new, unexpected things to be anxious about. Here's a conversation a mother had with her six-year-old son, Jerry:

"Did the school mail my report card?" asked Jerry.

"I guess they did, honey. I don't know," she answered.

"Shouldn't it be here by now?"

"I'm not sure, honey. Are you worried about it?"

"Yes. I think it should be here by now."

"Are you worried about your grades?"

"No. I just can't remember if I was supposed to bring a report card home or if they're going to send it. Was I supposed to do something so

I get a report card? Maybe I didn't do what I'm supposed to do to get my report card."

The poor kid is worried sick about his report card, and he hasn't even seen it yet.

A certain anxiety level in a child is acceptable provided it doesn't interfere with performance or peace of mind; again, distress and dysfunction must be gauged carefully. Having some difficulty falling asleep the night before a big, important event is one thing. Lying sleepless for hours obsessing about a book report that has already been handed in or a test that has been taken is quite another.

Generalized anxiety disorder is relatively uncommon in children and adolescents—and only 3 percent of the general adult population have it, 55 to 60 percent of them female—but I've always felt that there are many more cases out there than we see in our psychiatric clinics or our private practices. After all, GAD can be a productive disorder. Children who are constantly saying, "I have to get my homework done" or "I have to study *harder*" or "I have to make sure my clothes are all set for school tomorrow" may not be perceived immediately as having any real problems. They may come across simply as conscientious.

Many of the cases of GAD I've encountered involve precocious, bright kids, especially young ones. I recently talked to a six-year-old who said to me, "You know, they have way too many nuclear weapons in Korea now. I'm very concerned about that. I'm also worried about global warming. Did you see how hot it was last week?" I've come across a third-grader who, when told to write a five-page report, turned in twenty pages instead.

Naturally, this kind of "overachiever" behavior is not necessarily alarming to parents; in fact, many parents and teachers welcome and reinforce it. Only when a child's anxieties obviously get out of hand— and they usually do at some point—do parents consider the possibility that something is not as it should be. For one set of parents it came when their daughter Annie was constantly after them to let her take a course to prepare her for the SATs. She wanted to get a high SAT score so that she could be accepted into a good college. Mother and Father said yes, of course, she could take an SAT course, when the time came. Annie kept nagging, asking them daily which course she should choose and when she could start going. Annie was in third grade at the time.

THE SYMPTOMS

Children with generalized anxiety disorder often make their way to a mental health professional's office because they have physical symptoms —headaches, stomachaches, diarrhea, restlessness, sleep disturbance, fatigue—that cannot be explained. They've had the CAT scans, the barium enemas, and all the rest of the tests, and there are still no answers. It's not that the physical ailments are not real; those pains in the head and the stomach are very real indeed. It's just that they don't have an organic explanation. There's no tumor in the brain or bacteria in the colon. These kids are having a physical reaction to anxiety, and the symptoms may range from very mild to quite severe. The most extreme anxiety symptom I ever witnessed was in a young college student, who was so nervous about her finals that she literally couldn't turn her head; the muscles in her neck had tightened up too much.

On the other hand, a child with GAD may have only the mildest physical symptoms; the real telltale signs of GAD are behavioral. Most kids with GAD will be perfectionists, conforming and unsure of themselves. They may appear tense and uptight, but they can also be quiet, compliant, and eager to please. They worry constantly about their competence and the quality of their performance and often require repeated reassurance that they're doing things the right way. Even so, assessments by others matter hardly at all to these kids; children with GAD worry about their performance regardless of what others think.

Anthony, a second-grader I treated for GAD, would walk to his teacher's desk several times during the day and ask, "Am I doing this right?" "Yes, you are doing it right," she'd reply. Anthony was an outstanding student, and the teacher often told him so. "Okay," answered Anthony. A half-hour later the conversation was inevitably repeated. Anthony didn't want to keep bothering his teacher—he tried to control himself —but his overanxiousness surfaced many times throughout the day. Anthony worried about everything. "I worry about how I'm doing in school, whether people will like me, what college I'll go to, and whether I'll do well in soccer," he told me. It was his teacher who finally noticed that Anthony needed help.

Other kids with GAD react not by demanding their teachers' attention but by being restless and on edge. They often appear (and they often are) tired; sleepless nights can do that to a child. Sometimes they're perceived to be difficult and demanding, because they're never satisfied. These kids are frequently overcautious in social and academic settings and not always very pleasant to be around.

Sometimes a child's GAD symptoms are obvious to everyone but the people closest to him, his parents. It took the grandparents of a little eight-year-old girl, Sally, to get her into my office. Lots of kids want to do well in school, but Sally was more of a perfectionist about her schoolwork than any child I've ever met. In the morning Sally would announce her study goals and schedule for the day to her mother and father. After school she would come home immediately—she refused all invitations to play with her friends, because they interfered with her plans—play the piano for 40 minutes, and then hit the books. Her dinner conversation was always about her performance: how many goals she got in soccer that day, what test she had the following day, and how she thought she did in art class. When she came to see me, Sally had frequent headaches and what her parents called a "nervous stomach."

Her parents knew that Sally's behavior wasn't normal, but it took the no-nonsense older generation, Sally's grandparents, to mobilize them at last. "Are you *crazy?*" Grandma asked delicately. "I love this child, but she acts older than I do. I don't think she knows how to relax. She's such a worrier! If Sally has a spelling test, you have to test her five times even though she got all the words right the first time." Grandpa added his two cents: "She takes more Tylenol than I do for her headaches, and every time I see her she has a stomachache. She needs to see someone."

THE DIAGNOSIS

"Gil was always a worrier. That didn't bother us. He was always nervous. That was okay too. But now he's complaining about being sick all the time and missing a lot of school. That's *not* okay."

When Gil's parents brought him in, they'd done a little research, and they thought that their 10-year-old son had a classic case of school phobia. However, after I took his history and did a thorough evaluation —interviewing parents, teachers, and, most usefully, Gil himself—I learned that Gil was afraid of a lot more than just going to school. Here, I discovered, was a kid who was worried seven days a week. He loved sports but avoided joining a team because he thought he was never good enough. He constantly worried about his future, especially his career. Watching television frightened him, especially the news, because he might see something scary or bad. He was especially terrified of nuclear war. He had trouble falling asleep and was tired and jittery much of the time.

Diagnosing GAD can be a tricky business. First of all, it's an *internalized disorder,* which means that its key symptoms have to do with thoughts and feelings. Teachers and parents are not always useful in giving a history when it comes to GAD. They usually know what the kids in their care *do,* but they don't know how the children *feel.* Parents are wonderful at rationalizing too. Seven-year-old Megan came home from school crying and told her parents that the other kids were making fun of her all the time. "They don't like me. They say, 'All you talk about is school. Why do you always talk about school?' " Megan told Mom and Dad tearfully. Megan's parents were quick to reassure their daughter. "Oh, those other kids are just jealous because they're not as smart as you are," they told Megan. "You're fine just the way you are."

Cindy's parents likewise were fooled about their daughter. "Cindy is a wonderful student," they told me. "She comes home from school and she immediately does her homework and then she always practices the violin. Before dinner she gets her clothes ready for the next day. She's absolutely perfect." What they neglected to mention is that Cindy's social life is a lot less than perfect—she spends almost no time playing with her peers—or that even though her music teacher has recommended Cindy for a special program, the child is convinced she has no musical talent. Although her parents seem to have missed the signs, an objective observer can see quite easily that there's an overanxious quality about Cindy, even when she is supposedly relaxed. She is never truly loose or at ease. The diagnosis: GAD.

GAD has symptoms that are similar to several other disorders. Restlessness and difficulty in concentrating are symptoms of attention deficit hyperactivity disorder (see Chapter 7); anxiety related to school may suggest separation anxiety disorder (see Chapter 9); and obsessive attitudes and compulsive behaviors about work may raise suspicions of obsessive compulsive disorder (see Chapter 8). In the case of pathological performance anxiety, the diagnosis can be either GAD or social phobia (see Chapter 10). Severe performance anxiety is a symptom of social phobia if the performer is worried about what people are thinking about him. However, if the feeling is, "I haven't prepared enough for this recital" and then, after a standing ovation, "I should have played the piece louder and faster and better," then it's more likely to be GAD. Of course, there is also the distinct possibility that a child has more than one disorder. In adults GAD co-occurs with depression about 80 percent of the time, with the anxiety disorder developing first.

One case of GAD I treated, a six-year-old girl in first grade, started with what seemed to be *acrophobia,* a fear of high places. Her parents told me that their daughter, Elena, who was usually quite obedient, had refused to go out for recess on the school's third-floor rooftop playground. Elena loved the playground in the park and played there often, but she wouldn't set foot on the rooftop despite the efforts of her parents and teacher. When I interviewed Elena, she told me how much she had enjoyed visits to the Empire State Building in Manhattan and the Hancock Building in Chicago, so I knew in short order that she wasn't afraid of heights. After much discussion, Elena explained her fear of going on the roof; a gust of wind might demolish the fence, she told me, and she would be blown off the roof. We treated her for GAD.

THE BRAIN CHEMISTRY

The most recent studies related to GAD—all done on adults rather than children and adolescents, unfortunately—indicate that this disorder is related to a regulation problem in the brain of the neurotransmitter norepinephrine, the brain chemical that affects concentration and attention. Specifically, people with GAD tend to have too much norepinephrine. This theory is supported by the fact that an increase in norepinephrine has several physical consequences, among them increased heart rate, increased sweating, and decreased ability to concentrate. Obviously all three areas have an impact on a person's cognitive abilities and his ability to perform so far. Studies of whether or not GAD runs in families have been inconclusive.

THE TREATMENT

The recommended treatment for GAD is behavioral therapy combined with medication. Behavior-oriented psychotherapy is effective in the treatment of GAD, but the results are even more dramatic when medication is prescribed along with it. In many cases we suggest that a child be given a small dose of antianxiety medication as he begins behavioral therapy. The medicine takes the edge off the symptoms, making it easier for the child to work on changing his behavior. Once the child is functioning and the therapy is underway, we might well take him off the antianxiety medicine or decrease the dosage.

GAD can be treated with benzodiazepines, a group of antianxiety drugs. The ones most often prescribed are Klonopin, Valium, and Xanax. These medicines may occasionally cause lack of inhibition (giddiness, impulsivity, and agitation) in children, but the side effects disappear when the dose is lowered or the drug discontinued. These medicines work fast and need to be stopped slowly; as the child gradually discontinues the medicine, he should be watched carefully for a return of the anxiety symptoms. BuSpar, a new type of antianxiety medicine, has had a positive effect on children and adolescents with GAD. BuSpar takes one to two weeks to be fully effective, and the side effects are mild and transient. When youngsters with GAD don't respond to BuSpar or the benzodiazepines, we often look to Prozac, which can take almost six weeks to get a positive effect.

The behavioral approach to treating GAD is target-oriented: quite simply, the goal is to identify the problem—find out what's bothering the child—and work with the child to make the worry go away. There's nothing passive about this treatment; a kid doesn't just sit around while various medical professionals have their way with him. This treatment is *active*. A child needs to be very much involved. He has to think about his fears, confront them, and work on ways to make them disappear. None of these things comes easily to a child, let alone an overanxious one.

A behavioral therapist treating GAD will teach kids techniques that help them to relax and settle down. The techniques are simple, but they can have a profound impact on a child's behavior, especially his ability to calm his nerves. An overanxious child, who can't "just relax," is helped immeasurably by being able to call upon these techniques when he needs them. The two relaxation techniques most often relied upon are *deep breathing exercises,* which even very young children can master, and *visual imagery.* The two techniques are almost always used together.

For example, in helping a girl who's afraid to sleep because of excessive anxiety, the therapist would first teach relaxation, have the child practice it, and then use visual imagery to maintain and reinforce the child's relaxed state. For example, the therapist would paint a verbal picture of the setting as a little girl prepares for sleep. The child would be asked for details of the bedroom, until the scene is completely set: wallpaper, pictures on the wall, dolls on the shelf, everything. Then the therapist would ask the child to picture going to sleep in a dark room. Again there would be many details, and the girl would participate actively. She would "practice" this behavior in the comfort of the therapist's office a few times, and then she'd be sent home to try the real thing. Sleeping alone in a dark room would be the little girl's assignment for the week.

Setting goals is critical to the successful treatment of GAD, and the more specific the goal, the better. A seven-year-old boy with GAD was terrified of taking tests in school. The therapist took him through a series of relaxation techniques and then actually went with him to school, to the very room where he took the tests he feared so much. The therapist got the child to relax again and then to focus on the room. Together they picked a spot on the wall that he would stare at if he became anxious. It was agreed that whenever he looked at that spot, he would stop worrying.

Another child fretted about taking a field trip with his class and used visual imagery to help himself through it. At the suggestion of the therapist, he and his parents got out a map and traced the journey every evening for a week before the trip, talking about the trip in detail. The boy was especially worried about the bridges he would have to cross— he was afraid they'd collapse—so they worked out in advance what he would do when he got to a bridge. His parents suggested he take out his crossword puzzle book and work on a puzzle while crossing the first bridge. When he got to the second bridge, he would talk to his friend.

Kids really need their parents' help in working through the symptoms of GAD. For parents, that sometimes means going against their own natural instincts. That was certainly true in the case of Ryan, a 10-year-old boy with a clear case of GAD. An excellent student, good at sports, and popular with his peers, Ryan was a mass of worries. He didn't think he could do anything right. When I first saw him, he was suffering from severe headaches and stomachaches. Ryan's parents had always taken a healthy interest in his activities, deriving satisfaction from his accomplishments and supporting all of his efforts. They applauded him for his good grades and celebrated with him when his team won. I made them change their ways.

For the six months we treated Ryan for GAD his folks were asked not to discuss performance with him. If they talked about his soccer game, it was not to inquire, "Who won?" but to ask, "Did you have fun?" There was to be no talk about winning or losing, good grades or bad. Ryan's teachers were asked to hold on to his test papers until the end of the week, so that Ryan got his grades only on Friday. If he tried to talk to his parents about his test grades, all they'd say is that they were sure he did his best. It wasn't always easy, for Ryan or his parents—in the early stages of the treatment Mom and Dad actually used cue cards to remind themselves of what they were supposed to say—but in six months Ryan's headaches and stomachaches had disappeared.

In virtually any behavioral therapy for GAD there almost always comes a time when the child is made anxious, sometimes *very* anxious. It's part of the basic process: before a child can be desensitized, he must usually be made to feel discomfort. With children the therapeutic process is usually gradual; kids confront their fears slowly, with lots of positive reinforcement (in the form of rewards and praise) and reassurance from parents and therapist. At times, mild negative consequences, such as loss of TV or play time or other privileges, are also used to "punish" a child's opposition to reasonable expectations. Both rewards and punishments are meted out for effort, not achievement.

One of the most effective techniques of getting a child over the fears and anxieties associated with GAD involves *extended exposure,* or *flooding,* in which a child is put in the very situation—either in reality or in his imagination—that causes distress for an extended period of time. He is then made to understand that the fear is irrational. This method relies upon a biological fact: the body can't maintain a high level of anxiety for more than about 90 minutes; the anxiety "burns itself out." When a child sees that what he fears has not happened, the anxiety will dissipate. If the child is to alter his thoughts as well as his behavior—the *cognitive* component of the therapy—it's essential that he know what is going on every step of the way. Children must describe their fears and then become aware that those fears are groundless.

In the case of Sally, the little girl with the impatient grandparents and the intense worries about her performance at school, here's how a flooding might go.

"Sally, I want you to imagine that you're getting ready for school," the therapist might say. "All your homework is done. But just as you're packing your bookbag, you notice that your math paper is crinkled and smudged. Just then the bus pulls up outside, and the driver beeps her horn twice. You have to rush to get on the bus, and the driver doesn't smile at you. You're afraid that you did something to make her mad. You can't stop thinking about your math paper. Your stomach starts to hurt, and you feel sick, as if you have to go to the bathroom. When the teacher asks you to hand in your math homework, you feel even sicker. You think maybe she'll tell your parents. Maybe you'll get an F."

After the flooding, the therapist would guide the child through her deep breathing exercises and reassure her that her feelings of distress and anxiety will soon pass. Once the child has made it safely through the scene, it's time to help her learn from the experience.

"So you heard the story of a really terrible day and you got through it?" the therapist might ask.

"Right," Sally would say.

"How do you feel?"

"Okay, I guess."

"Did anything bad happen?"

"I guess not."

"You were worried, right?" asks the therapist.

"Yeah."

"Did anything bad happen to you? Did your toes fall off?"

"No." Sally starts to smile.

"Are you sure your toes didn't fall off? Maybe we'd better check to make sure. Why don't you take off your shoes so we can have a look?"

At this point Sally is at ease. The crisis, or at least *this* crisis, is over.

As productive a disorder as GAD may sometimes appear to be, it is critical that a child with GAD symptoms be treated promptly. Left untreated, GAD may result in stress-related physical ailments, even something as serious as heart disease, as well as other psychological disorders, especially depression. The disorder may also interfere with a child's ability to reach his academic potential and prevent him from making friends. These children are so anxious all the time, so fearful about their competence and performance, so worried about not being liked, that they're often *not* very well liked by their peers. It's not surprising, really. The symptoms associated with GAD are not likely to make a child the most popular kid in his class. Of course, not being liked then leads to loss of self-esteem, not to mention a whole list of new things for a child to worry about.

PARENTING AND GAD

At a dinner party recently I overheard two women talking about the new teacher that their third-grade sons have in school this year. From what I was able to make out, the new guy doesn't believe in taking it easy on the kids when it comes to homework.

"What do you think about the homework assignments this year?" asked one mother.

"They're pretty heavy," said the other. "I feel sorry for Hugh sometimes."

"Chris comes home every day, and he's a wreck," said the first. "He throws himself on the bed and screams, 'How am I going to do this? It's too much. What am I going to do?' I mean, he's hysterical about it."

At this point I was convinced that this kid needed some help. However, as I continued to eavesdrop, I realized that his mother was handling her son's anxiety effectively in her own way.

"What I do is I go in there, and I say, 'Chris, let's look at the assignment and break it down into 20-minute segments. Why don't you take 20 minutes and do one part?' Then we go on to the next segment. He always gets the homework done, and the tears don't usually last very long."

What Chris's mother is doing is basically a behavioral intervention, and I don't think a therapist could have done it any better. My guess is that Chris has generalized anxiety disorder, but his is a mild case. At the moment, at least, his distress and dysfunction are modified by having the right mom.

Alas, not every child, diagnosed with GAD or not, has the right mom or dad. I have seen many parents, particularly high-powered, successful professionals, unwittingly put pressure on their overanxious kids. "I manage a large firm, and I pride myself on getting the most out of my staff," the father of a 10-year-old boy with GAD told me. "But my son practically falls apart if I put any pressure on him or make suggestions. If I criticize him, there are bound to be tears. I'm only trying to help him, but I seem to make him *less* productive."

Behavioral therapy methods can be made to work on nearly all symptoms associated with GAD, but it isn't always easy for parents to put their children through the discomfort that is involved. Some parents aren't comfortable doing what's necessary to help a child with GAD get his life in order. When a child throws a temper tantrum, these parents will say, "I can't put him through this." They might think, "I'm harming my child. I'm doing something bad to my child. Look at the distress he or she is going through." I don't blame parents who have a hard time dealing with the symptoms of GAD; after all, it's a parent's natural instinct to reduce a child's pain, not add to it, even temporarily.

While they are perfectly understandable, such feelings are counterproductive in treating an overanxious child. Parents have to be able to say, "You've got to stick it out. You've got to take that math exam" or "We have to take a plane to visit Aunt Judy. It won't be easy, but you have to get over this. We're going to help you."

While it's important for parents to be supportive, mothers and fathers should try to remain unemotional and detached to the greatest extent possible. Sometimes it helps to regard the new behavior being reinforced as an assignment, as in: "Look, it's important for you to try to do this. You've got some nice rewards coming if you fulfill these tasks, but if you don't try, there will be consequences. You're going to lose some television."

It's also a parent's job to make sure that the school is part of the solution when it comes to treating a child with GAD. Teachers need to be educated about GAD. In particular, they have to be made to understand that they need to tread lightly when they lay down the law to these children. A policy of "Absences other than for illness will not be excused" will greatly upset a child with GAD whose parents keep him out of school for a special family event. Most kids who hear the standard motivational speeches—"How you do in middle school is very important. It will predict your high school and college performance"— don't give the warning much thought, but children with GAD take the message, and all messages, very much to heart.

These kids have enough worries without being given new ones at school, so finding the right teacher for a child with GAD is critical. If there's a choice between a tough teacher and one who's more nurturing, parents would do well to place a child with GAD in the class of the nurturer. A good teacher-student match can make life a lot easier for these youngsters.

CHAPTER 12

Enuresis/Bedwetting

Glen was a terrific kid—smart, confident, personable, a good athlete. He was about to go into the sixth grade. When I met him, his parents had just brought him home from summer camp, and he was desperately unhappy. His fellow campers had come up with a new nickname for him there: "Diapers." At 12 years of age Glen still wet his bed almost every night, and despite his best efforts and those of the camp counselors to keep his bedwetting a secret all summer, the other boys had found out. The last week of camp had been sheer torture.

• • •

Six-year-old Victor was having a lot of difficulties in school, academically and socially. His speech hadn't developed according to the normal guidelines, and he was inattentive, occasionally disruptive, in class. His social skills were similarly undeveloped, and the other kids in school often made fun of him. His parents suspected that Victor had a learning disability, and one of the teachers told them it might be attention deficit hyperactivity disorder; this is what finally brought them to my office. It was only after I had seen Victor a couple of times that I found out that he regularly wet his bed at night and sometimes wet himself during the day. The parents were well and truly disgusted with their son and made no effort to hide their negative feelings. When he came to see me, Victor was so downhearted that he spoke barely above a whisper.

THE BEDWETTING DEBATE

Most children stop wetting their beds at night by the age of three, or five at the latest, but some—estimates put it at five to seven million kids— have trouble with this task. Those children suffer from enuresis, often referred to as bedwetting. According to the textbook, enuresis is the involuntary passage of urine at least twice a week for a period of three months in children over the age of five. It may occur at night or during the day.

The disorder affects twice as many boys as girls. At age five the breakdown is 7 percent male versus 3 percent female. At age 10 it drops to 3 percent boys and 2 percent girls. Enuresis is rare in people older than 18: only 1 percent of all males and about half as many females continue to be bedwetters after age 18.

There are two basic categories of enuresis: primary and secondary. A child who has never been fully trained—that is, a child who has never achieved a six-month period of dryness at night—falls into the primary enuresis group, the more common of the two. A diagnosis of secondary enuresis applies to kids who have been dry for up to a year and then start wetting again. Secondary enuresis usually occurs between the ages of five and eight. (A sub-category of secondary enuresis is transient, or tempo- rary, enuresis. This condition is brought on by trauma or stress, such as a divorce in the family, and may last anywhere from a couple of weeks to several months.)

There's a high spontaneous recovery rate with enuresis; that is, the problem goes away all by itself. Some sources put it as high as 15 percent, lower with boys than with girls. It's not difficult to understand, then, why many pediatricians send concerned parents who seek their advice about a child with enuresis away with a cavalier, "Oh, he'll outgrow it." There's a good chance the child *will* outgrow his problem, but there's also the distinct possibility that he won't.

Experts, by whom I mean pediatricians, urologists, psychiatrists, and psychologists, disagree about the age at which a child should be diag- nosed with enuresis. The *Diagnostic and Statistical Manual of Mental Disorders* declares that five years old is the cutoff point, but some pedia- tricians feel that it's better to wait until a child is seven or eight before diagnosing enuresis. Why spend time and money, they ask, treating a child who's going to get better all by himself? There's a major flaw in that argument, however: a large percentage of the children who are wet at age five will still be wet at age seven, two years later, and *the longer a child has this symptom, the more likely he is to experience negative social consequences,* including serious family conflict. Furthermore, a child is entitled not to be uncomfortable.

Controversy or no, if a child is five years old and enuresis persists for three months or more, I believe that something should be done about it. Parents should consult as many health professionals as it takes to satisfy themselves that their child is all right. If they don't, that child could end up with a nickname that will haunt him for a long long time.

THE SYMPTOMS

Most younger children with enuresis, age five and six, aren't especially bothered by their condition. True, they probably don't enjoy waking up in wet sheets or seeing their parents get annoyed at them every morning, but the level of distress and dysfunction in these kids is generally quite low. As children get older and become more interested in having an active social life, enuresis begins to interfere more seriously in their lifestyles. Sleepover dates, summer camp, slumber parties—all these things are huge obstacles for the child with enuresis. (I treated a 13-year-old girl who used to stay up all night at pajama parties, even when everyone else was sound asleep. She was terrified that she'd have an accident in front of all her friends. Once, unable to keep her eyes open a moment longer, she spent a few hours dozing in the bathtub behind a locked door.) If a kid has a problem with wetting during the day, even going to school can be a trial. I've comforted more than one child who has been brought to tears when his classmates made fun of him because of the telltale odor of his wet pants.

THE DIAGNOSIS

It is estimated that two thirds of all bedwetters never even make it into a pediatrician's office. Of those who do get to a pediatrician a sizable percentage are sent home with instructions to watch and wait. The kids who are referred to psychologists and psychiatrists are nearly always sent there because they have other behavioral problems, such as ADHD, learning disabilities, or aggression. Kids who have enuresis generally will show signs of other maturational delays, including speech lags and learning difficulties. Enuresis may also be a symptom of a power struggle between a parent and child.

Diane was a 10-year-old girl who was referred to me because of attention deficit disorder (see Chapter 7). There was no hyperactivity associated with Diane's disorder. In fact, Diane had a kind of dreamy, otherworldly quality, as if she were in some kind of trance. The little girl was an incredibly heavy sleeper, and she wet her bed nearly every night without even waking up.

Her parents told me that some nights Diane would be watching television, and, sitting on the sofa with the rest of the family, she would just urinate. To hear Diane tell it, she knew she needed to go, but she didn't want to get up. Other times she'd just sort of forget about it until it was too late. Everyone in her family was furious with her, naturally, but Diane really didn't understand why they were making such a big deal out of it.

Interviews with children who have enuresis are not usually very fruitful. Most children find it hard to explain their behavior.

"I don't know why I do it," one child might say. "It just slips out while I'm sleeping. I don't even know it's happening."

"I don't want to wet my bed. Sometimes I try to stay awake all night just to keep from doing it," says another.

"I think I was dreaming about going to the bathroom," says a third kid.

"Sometimes I'm too tired to get up and go to the toilet. I'd rather sleep," says a fourth.

The same few themes run through all the experiences of these children: I was playing with my friends and didn't notice that I had to go to the bathroom until it was too late; I was sleeping so hard I didn't even realize I had to go; I knew I had to go, but I couldn't wake up in time. Each one is a clear indication of enuresis.

THE BRAIN CHEMISTRY

There are many theories about what causes enuresis. The most widely held is that the primary cause of enuresis is a maturational lag. Some of the systems in these kids, including the bladder and the brain, are not maturing as quickly as is to be expected in normal development.

There are experts who put all the blame on a child's bladder. Many kids with enuresis do, in fact, have a lower functional bladder volume than children without enuresis; this means that a child with enuresis will urinate as much as a normal child over a 24-hour period in terms of volume, but he will need to urinate more frequently in order to put out that same volume. The problem with this theory is that there are many people in the general population who have low functional bladder volume but do *not* have enuresis.

Obviously, bladder function is not the only cause of enuresis. Regardless of the size of his bladder, the reason a child is wetting his bed is, ultimately, in his brain. His brain is not adequately reading the signal that his bladder is sending. His bladder tells his brain that it's full, but the brain just doesn't get the message, at least not in time.

A possible cause of enuresis is an abnormal regulation of a brain hormone called ADH (antidiuretic hormone), which determines the way that water is retained in the body. In some children with enuresis too little ADH is released at night, so that their bodies produce more urine than the bladder can handle. Another commonly held theory is that children with enuresis simply sleep more deeply than those who stay dry at night. Treatment with medications that lighten sleep have been effective in some cases.

Primary enuresis is genetic; what's more, a recent study has located the general site of a gene linked to primary enuresis. The gene is believed to be *dominant,* which means that if one parent has enuresis, the child is likely to have the disorder too. Studies show that 75 percent of all children with enuresis have a primary relative—a mother or, more probably, a father—who also had the disorder. (As one of my colleagues said to me, only half-joking, "It's almost always the parent who *doesn't* come to the appointment.") If one identical twin has enuresis, 68 percent of the time the other twin will have it—an extraordinarily high rate. If one fraternal twin has enuresis, the other twin will have it only 36 percent of the time. I nearly always discuss the genetic influences in the cause of enuresis with both parents and children, and I usually get a mixed reaction. Parents are embarrassed, and kids are relieved and surprised. Many children don't realize until then that anybody else in the world has this problem, let alone someone in the family.

THE TREATMENT

Virtually every child diagnosed with enuresis, either primary or secondary, receives behavioral treatment. Depending on the severity of the case and the effectiveness of the treatment, a child may benefit from medication as well. The goal in any treatment for enuresis is, of course, to change the child's behavior.

By the time a child comes to see me about this problem, there's a good chance his parents have already tried a few home remedies—not letting a child have any liquids after supper, for example, or restricting caffeine and sugar. Many routinely wake the child and escort him to the bathroom several times during the night, starting with the time the parents themselves turn in. I've known parents who set an alarm for every few hours all night so that they can wake their child. ("It takes me back to our two o'clock feeding days," one mother said.) Still others set alarm clocks for their kids.

All of these efforts can pay off sometimes. If a child is caught at exactly the right time and he empties his bladder, he may well wake up in a dry bed the next morning. (A lot of kids with enuresis tend to wet during the first two or three hours of sleep.) Of course, none of these remedies teaches a child new behavior—he doesn't learn to respond to an internal signal—so any improvements are likely to be temporary. What's more, these activities don't usually do much to improve family harmony. Parents don't take any pleasure in getting up several times a night to wake their kids, and kids positively hate having their sleep interrupted and being dragged to the bathroom. In some instances children become downright defiant, and the problem gets even worse.

The more formal treatment for enuresis isn't exactly fun either, but it does get excellent results—about an 85 percent success rate after six months. The first thing I ask parents who consult me to do is to keep a dry-wet calendar. Over a period of a month parents keep track of how many nights a child was wet and how many nights he remained dry. Then we have our baseline, and we can measure how serious the problem really is. For very small children, keeping the calendar may be sufficient to solve the problem. Simply being made aware of the problem can be enough to motivate some children to fix it, especially if those dry nights are rewarded with a small token.

At the heart of nearly all enuresis treatment is a device called the *bell and pad*. There are several versions of the bell and pad, but the principle is always the same: somewhere in the bed—under the sheet or perhaps even attached to a child's pajamas—there is a pad with a sensor that detects wetness. At the very first sign of wetness that sensor causes a bell to ring, waking the child. The child then gets up, runs to the bathroom, and urinates in the toilet. There are different kinds of pads and sensors and variations on the theme of a bell too. Some alarms are worn on the wrist. Others get attached to the collar of a child's pajamas right near his ear. Still others are made to go under a pillow or sit on a night table. Since children with enuresis are notoriously heavy sleepers, these alarms sometimes fall on deaf ears, especially if the kids become experts at hiding them. The rest of the family wakes up to the alarm, but the child in treatment sleeps right through it. One mother solved this problem by keeping the bell in a coffee can, so that the ringing sound reverberated. *Nobody* could sleep through that.

The bell and pad treatment takes time, but it does work if it is used consistently. A child probably will have occasional relapses, but "booster" sessions with the bell and pad will usually put him back on track when that happens. Care must also be taken not to stop the treatments too soon. For instance, a child who is wetting seven nights a week when he starts using the bell and pad may quickly work his way down to wetting five, then four, three, even two nights a week. After several weeks he may be dry for an entire week, and eventually he'll get to the point where he spends two consecutive weeks completely dry. Some parents (and children) are eager to toss out the bell and pad at this point. But we recommend a more gradual withdrawal.

The first week the child may sleep without the bell and pad for one night, the second week he can go without it for two nights, and so on. (This is also a good time for parents to put a child's new habits to a real test by letting him drink a pint of liquid before going to bed. By this time his bladder should be able to detect the sensation of fullness, and he should be able to wake up in time to get to the bathroom.) By the seventh week he'll be weaned off it entirely, and he's less likely to have a relapse than if he'd kicked the bell and pad cold turkey. No one wants the child to fail and have to go through the whole process over again.

The bell and pad treatment works, but it's not always easy, especially at the beginning. It takes enormous patience and commitment on the part of parents. It's tempting for parents to give up easily, and I've met many who did. "We tried the alarm and it didn't work," a mother might say after a week. "He sleeps right through it." In the first two weeks a child literally has to be taught to wake up when he hears the sound of an alarm, not the sound or the nudges of his parents. That means letting the alarm sound until the child is awake and out of bed, not turning it off when it gets to be too annoying. It also means that if a child doesn't hear the alarm, the parents have to figure out a way to make it louder. Where there's a will there's definitely a way.

The bell and pad treatment can be made even more effective if it is combined with a system of positive and negative reinforcement. If a child is dry, he gets a small reward, something as little as a gold star or perhaps a sticker. A certain number of stars or stickers may be traded in for a prize a child values, such as playing a video game or buying a comic book. If a child is not dry, he gets something taken away. We're not suggesting actual punishment; parents should take away privileges and treats—television time, snacks, that sort of thing—that the child doesn't really need anyway. Making fun of a child, striking him, or otherwise abusing him for this behavior doesn't help, and it will damage him further. Kids, especially older ones, are humiliated enough by their problem without having the situation made worse by frustrated, irritated family members with a short fuse. Parents should let their children know that undesirable behavior has consequences, but they shouldn't add to the child's distress.

We strongly suggest including another element in the behavioral treatment of enuresis: *cleanliness training.* When a child wakes up wet in the middle of the night, he has to help strip the bed of its wet sheets, take them to the laundry hamper, and put clean sheets on the bed. He also has to take his underwear and pajamas to the hamper and choose dry clothes. This increases a child's motivation to jump out of bed the moment he hears the bell and not just lie there thinking about it. The faster a child reacts to the bell, the less work there is to be done. Participating in the cleanup makes the child more conscious, more awake during the process. Few kids can change their sheets when they're half asleep. Getting involved in this way also forces children to take more responsibility for their actions. Finally, sharing the burden of housework may keep some parents from blowing their stacks.

Everybody with a problem, any problem, wants quick results, of course, but the mother who contacted me last year about her son with enuresis deserves some sort of prize in that category. The call came on June 15. "Look, Keith is going away to camp at the end of the month for two weeks," she told me. "I really need him to be dry by then."

In fact, there is a "quick fix" for enuresis. It's called Desmopressin nasal spray, a synthetic antidiuretic hormone that decreases the number of a child's wetting episodes in one to three nights. Desmopressin has no effect on a child's long-term behavior, but it does help to keep children dry. The spray can be indispensable in the early stages of the bell and pad treatment. I've also used it on kids in special circumstances—such as sleepaway camp—and when there's special distress, especially for children being physically abused by their parents for wetting their beds. As medications go, Desmopressin is quite safe for children. Mild nasal irritation and headache are infrequent side effects. Desmopressin may lower the seizure threshold, so caution must be exercised in giving it to a child with a seizure disorder. Otherwise children tolerate the drug very well.

Before we had Desmopressin spray, the standard medication used in the treatment of enuresis was one of the TCAs (tricyclic antidepressants), especially Tofranil, which is often prescribed for separation anxiety disorder in children and depression in adults. No one is sure precisely why the tricyclics have an effect on this disorder. They may change a child's sleep patterns, so that he doesn't spend so much time in the deep stages of sleep. They seem to have an effect on the sphincter (the muscle that holds the bladder closed), and because they affect the brain's level of norepinephrine, they may increase functional bladder volume. There are many side effects associated with Tofranil. One of the less disturbing of those side effects is dryness: dryness of the mouth, dryness of the eyes, and urinary retention. Of course, for a kid who regularly wets his bed, a little dryness can be a wonderful thing. The more serious cardiac side effects of Tofranil are rare at the low doses prescribed in the treatment of enuresis.

Tofranil can play an important part in the treatment of enuresis, but it is no cure by itself. Without behavioral treatment, such as the bell and pad, the problem will come back the moment the medication is stopped. Tofranil should be used sparingly and only in conjunction with the bell and pad. Ideally, as soon as a child starts to respond to the bell and pad, his Tofranil dose should be gradually lowered. The child may start to wet a little bit as he is weaned off the medication, but by then he should be waking up when he hears the bell.

There are other medications that have been tried, sometimes with success, in the treatment of enuresis. Dexedrine prescribed with the bell and pad can sometimes speed up the training process, simply because the medicine lightens a child's sleep. It's easier to train a child with the bell and pad if he's not too deeply asleep.

At the end of the day, however, the best treatment of enuresis is behavioral, and that means the bell and pad. Medication may physically decrease a child's urine output or keep him awake or allow him to focus better on the task at hand, but the only thing that is going to make his problem go away and stay away is learning a new way to behave. His brain has to learn to listen to and hear the message coming from his bladder.

PARENTING AND ENURESIS

The sad truth about enuresis is that many parents of children with this disorder are embarrassed and even repulsed by their children's behavior. Emotions run extraordinarily high. "I just can't believe that he can just lie there and do that every night," one squeamish mother said to me. "The sheets are so disgusting I practically get sick to my stomach every morning."

Other parents get angry, convinced that the child is wetting his bed on purpose. "How come he doesn't wet the bed when he spends the night at his grandmother's house?" one father demanded. "He's just doing it to make us crazy." As difficult as it may be for some mothers and dads to believe, enuresis is not volitional. Children do *not* wet their beds on purpose. If they're dry when they spend a night away from the family home, it's probably because they are not sleeping as soundly there are they do in their own beds.

One of the most important reasons that this disorder is so emotionally charged is that in three out of four cases the parent—usually Dad—used to wet the bed as well, and most parents aren't too happy to take that particular trip down Memory Lane. Someone who went through a traumatic experience himself can find it extremely upsetting to watch his child go through it, and his attempts at empathy may misfire. In talking to parents I try to "de-emotionalize" the issue, to keep it as unconnected to the emotions as possible, especially on the part of the parents. Behavioral treatment won't work very well if everyone is upset all the time.

The treatment also won't work unless everyone is motivated. I've seen plenty of cases in which the parents think that enuresis is a problem, but the kids couldn't care less. A five-year-old named Alex was brought in by his mother. Alex was wetting his bed nearly every night, and several days a week he returned home from kindergarten in fresh clothes, having had an accident in the ones he was wearing that morning. The teacher hadn't complained, but the mother, quite sensibly, thought she'd better make sure nothing was wrong with Alex.

As the three of us discussed Alex's problem, it became clear that the mother was experiencing some distress, but Alex was just fine about it. When I asked Alex directly how he felt, he was quite cheerful: "Oh, I just don't like getting up in the middle of the night. I'd rather sleep." What about wetting himself at school? Well, the kids didn't make fun of him and the teacher didn't scold him, so he didn't really mind.

Obviously a child like Alex has to be made to understand and appreciate that he *has* a problem before he can be effectively treated for it. One way to do that is to promise a reward for good behavior ("You will get a star for every dry night and your favorite ice cream for every three stars") and/or a punishment for continued undesirable behavior ("You have to try to stop wetting your bed. For every wet night, you will lose an hour of television"). In reality, however, neither of these strategies works very well unless the child is experiencing some distress. When I see someone like Alex, I'm tempted to tell the parents, "Why don't you come back in six months or when your kid wants to do something about his problem?" Without the child's participation the process is probably doomed.

On the other hand I've also seen situations in which the child cares more about solving the problem of enuresis than his parents do. I worked with 12-year-old Brendan and his parents with the bell and pad for about three months. The parents never really got the hang of what they were supposed to do; it was obvious they found the whole thing distasteful and didn't want to be involved. But Brendan was desperate to stop wetting his bed, so he persuaded his parents to let him work with me directly. Brendan used to call me on the phone himself whenever he needed help working with the bell and pad. All his parents had to do was to keep their end of the bargain. For every week Brendan was dry, they took him to a movie on the weekend.

It's not easy to be a parent of a child with enuresis. There are a lot of tears involved, not to mention a great deal of extra laundry. The behavioral treatment we recommend takes time and patience, and even if everything goes well, parents most likely will lose sleep over it, literally and figuratively. But the treatment does work, and the results—more friends, increased confidence, greater self-esteem—will make an enormous difference in a child's life.

CHAPTER 13

Tourette Syndrome

Becky, 10 years old, had always been bothered by little tics. First came the blinking, which she did nearly all the time. Next were the shoulder shrugs. Recently she had started clearing her throat all the time, usually quite loudly, slapping her thighs, and bending her arm behind her. When people asked her why she did those things, she always came up with an explanation. The sunlight was making her blink or she was coming down with a cold or she needed to scratch her back.

• • •

I met 12-year-old Kevin two days after he set fire to his grandmother's house. Kevin was no stranger to doctors; he'd been treated for severe asthma since he was five. (He announced, quite proudly, that he had been hospitalized 35 times.) His parents, who brought him to my office because of the fire, were used to Kevin's not being like other kids in the neighborhood—he'd always been a "little odd," they told me—but arson was more than they could handle. Besides, he didn't seem to be able to concentrate in class, and his grades were dropping. What his parents didn't tell me was that Kevin had tics, lots of tics. He blinked his eyes, cleared his throat, and grimaced almost constantly. He repeated himself often. When I asked Kevin's mom and dad about the tics, they seemed surprised, as if they hadn't really noticed them before. They did recall that their son used to bang his head at the age of two. They thought he'd been blinking since about six.

"TWITCH AND SHOUT"

When I was a kid, I used to love talking to my best friend's father, partly because he was a terrific guy but also because he did what I thought was a great imitation of a turtle—craning his neck and bobbing his head all the time. He was constantly in motion, and quite noisy too; I'll always associate the sound of keys and money jangling in a pocket with my childhood and Mr. Knepper. Sometimes the sound was so loud I couldn't hear his voice, especially since he was always clearing his throat. My parents told me that Mr. Knepper was "a very tense man." My guess is that my pal's dad had a mild case of Tourette syndrome.

Over the last several years Tourette syndrome (TS), a relatively rare brain disorder characterized by *involuntary motor and vocal tics* that begin before the age of 21 and last for at least a year, has been getting a lot of attention, in fact and fiction. A story line of the hit TV show *LA Law* had one of the Mackenzie, Brackman attorneys defending the rights of a man who'd been fired because of Tourette syndrome. Oliver Sacks wrote *An Anthropologist on Mars,* a book about Dr. Carl Bennett, a Canadian surgeon diagnosed with TS at age 37. The subject even made a couple of appearances on the sports pages, when Phillies outfielder Jim Eisenreich and Denver Nuggets guard Mahmoud Abdul-Rauf went public with the news that they have TS. In the spring of 1995 a documentary about Tourette syndrome—called *Twitch and Shout*—won critical acclaim.

The TS numbers aren't very large. It is estimated that some 200,000 Americans have full-blown Tourette syndrome and that another 1.8 million have some tics. Only about 1 in 2000 schoolchildren have the disorder, but as many as 15 percent have transient tics, ones that come and go. TS is much more commonly diagnosed in males; some studies say that the ratio of males to females is 3 to 1, while others put it at 5 to 1.

It often takes some time for tics to make an appearance in a child later diagnosed with TS, although very young children will sometimes rock or bang their heads. Most kids with TS were being treated by age two or three for sleep disorders, language problems, or behavioral difficulties; parents say they're restless, difficult, or oppositional—like the firebug

Kevin, described earlier in this chapter. They're easily frustrated and have frequent temper tantrums. They have more sleep disorders, especially sleepwalking, than the general population of youngsters. They usually have trouble concentrating on their studies and getting along with their peers, so teachers may think that these children have attention deficit hyperactivity disorder. By the time these kids reach my office, many of them have been examined by a battery of experts, from allergists to neurologists to ophthalmologists. The words "Tourette syndrome" probably have not come up. If the words have been spoken, there's a good chance the parents have not accepted them as gospel.

It's only at around age six or seven that children with TS start getting simple motor tics; the vocal tics begin at about nine. Typically the symptoms increase as a child matures, and TS is usually at its most severe during adolescence. Their symptoms may decrease, or even disappear, as kids reach their twenties, but some will continue having severe TS symptoms as adults. The worst tic I ever witnessed was in a 30-year-old man with a whole body tic; he would arch his entire body and throw himself backward.

Motor tics seem to follow a head-to-toe progression. Someone who has had TS for a number of years will usually say that it all started with a facial tic—the eyes or nose or mouth—and then moved, in turn, to the shoulders, arms, and legs. As the disease progresses, the tics also become more complex; tics wax and wane and change form. Motor tics do not automatically indicate TS. A diagnosis of TS requires both motor and vocal tics. That's why the documentary is called *Twitch* and *Shout*.

THE SYMPTOMS

The motor and vocal (also called *phonic*) tics associated with TS may be simple or complex. The most common simple motor tics are blinking, shrugging, grimacing, and nose twitching. The complex motor tics are slower and may appear purposeful: kissing, pinching, sticking out the tongue, touching, gyrating, throwing things, making obscene gestures (called copropraxia), and imitating the gestures of others (echopraxia). Simple vocal tics are meaningless sounds and noises, including grunting, tongue-clicking, hooting, and clearing of the throat. Complex vocal tics are words that have some meaning even if they make no sense: "But!

But!" or "Oh, boy!" for example. The best known complex vocal tic associated with TS is actually the least common: coprolalia, or outbursts of foul language. (Not surprisingly, the *LA Law* character with TS had this symptom. That's show biz.) Only about 15 percent of those diagnosed with TS have such outbursts. Somewhat more common is echolalia, the mimicking of the words of others.

There's a lot of shame connected with TS; after all, the symptoms can seem pretty strange. When kids are very young, with only minor tics, they're usually not too anxious about it, but when the teasing starts— and it nearly always does—a child quickly loses confidence and self-esteem. Adolescence can be brutal, as a child's symptoms typically worsen and peers become relentless in their criticism. One teenage girl I treated for tics was called a "retard" and a "mutant" by her classmates at school. That was on the good days.

It's easy to understand, therefore, why some children are not always forthcoming or honest about their symptoms. In fact, their imaginations sometimes work overtime as they try to invent plausible explanations for inexplicable behavior. A little boy told me he clears his throat all the time because he's got a tickle in his throat. "Maybe it's postnasal drip," he said. A child who is obviously involved in an involuntary action will sometimes try to make it seem voluntary, converting a shoulder shrug into a stretch, for instance. Jessica, an 11-year-old girl I treated last year, had so many body tics she practically tied herself in knots trying to hide them. Between the energy used up by the tics themselves and the additional energy expended to camouflage them the poor kid was completely spent.

Complicating the detection of symptoms further is the fact that in addition to waxing and waning, tics may occasionally be suppressed, either willfully or not. Suppression of tics nearly always occurs when kids are asleep or when they're engaged in an activity that requires serious concentration. I've seen children with very severe tics who are tic-free when they play Nintendo. I once watched two 13-year-old boys play a killer game of handball. The boys were evenly matched, and the competition was fierce. Both kids appeared to be completely normal. When the game was over, I noticed that one of the boys—the winner, as it happened—was a mass of tics: blinking, grimacing, and shaking his head from side to side. The other boy asked him—with all the delicacy and sensitivity for which children are famous the world over—what the *hell* he was doing. "Oh, I just do this between games," the boy with the tics replied.

It's not uncommon for a parent to notice TS symptoms while a teacher is unaware of them. If they can manage it, many kids hide their tics while they're at school. A child will be mild-mannered and well behaved all day in class and a total mess the minute he gets home. "He'd open the door, and his books would just go flying," said the mother of a 13-year-old boy who kept his tics under control all day at school. "One day he walked in, twitching like mad, and called me a bitch. Keeping everything bottled up all day just made everything worse. He literally couldn't control himself for another minute. He had to let it out." I had occasion to see this same boy at school one day. Laughing with his friends, who obviously found him very good company, he seemed like a normal all-American boy.

THE DIAGNOSIS

Motor and vocal tics are the essential symptoms of Tourette syndrome, but it's rare to find a child who has just a tic disorder. Some 40 percent of all kids with TS also have attention deficit hyperactivity disorder (see Chapter 7), and even more of them—perhaps as many as 80 percent— have symptoms of obsessive compulsive disorder (Chapter 8). Many children have all three disorders at once, a situation that can, of course, cloud a diagnosis and make treatment quite complicated. The diagnosis of Tourette syndrome comes only after taking a history from the child, the child's parents, and, whenever possible, the child's teachers.

Ron, 10 years old, was referred to me after being diagnosed with severe ADHD and some serious language problems. During our first visit I didn't notice that he had tics, although it was obvious he had a number of compulsive symptoms. For example, he had to touch every- thing in my office five times; I could hear him counting the touches under his breath. The following week I was talking to Ron's mother while Ron waited outside, and I heard a barking noise. The sound was repeated several times. "That's Ron," his mother said finally. "You know, he does this all the time." His vocal tic was later confirmed by his teachers, and it became clear that he had some motor tics as well. His family history was full of language disorders, stuttering, and tics. In addition to ADHD and OCD Ron obviously had Tourette syndrome.

Janis's parents brought her in for an examination because her teachers had been complaining about her behavior in school. Mom and Dad suspected ADHD. Janis, nine years old when I first saw her, had had what her parents called "crazy fears" nearly all her life. Her earliest fear was of ducks. Lately she was terrified to go anywhere in the car because she thought people in the other cars were looking at her. Vans in particular sent her into a tailspin. (Janis knew, by the way, that her fears had no basis in reality, but they still caused her great distress.) This time I noticed a tic right away, since Janis had echolalia; she repeated just about everything anybody said, often many times over. Again there was a family history of tics, and Janis's parents, when questioned directly about it, remembered that their daughter had had both vocal and motor tics in the past that had since disappeared. I diagnosed TS.

Parents are not likely to welcome the news that a child has TS, but in my experience children are relieved to learn that what is wrong with them has, finally, a name. "What you have is called Tourette syndrome. About 200,000 other people have it too, and this is what we're going to do to make you feel better" feels a lot more comforting to a kid than the notion that he can't control his own body. "I can't keep my leg from moving," a third grader said to me with tears in her eyes. "I can't stop blinking," said another, equally distressed. Almost without exception kids are reassured to know that there's a real problem and that help is on the way.

THE BRAIN CHEMISTRY

There's a great deal of evidence to suggest that dopamine is the neurotransmitter that is most strongly affected in Tourette syndrome, but norepinephrine and serotonin seem to play major roles as well. (Neurotransmitters in the brain do not act independently; they all interact.) Basically, a child with TS has too much dopamine and too little norepinephrine and serotonin. We know that medications that block dopamine and medications that increase norepinephrine are helpful in the treatment of TS. We also know that dopamine-enhancing agents make tics worse. Neuroimaging techniques, such as CAT and PET scans, have demonstrated differences in the size and activity level of certain parts of the brains of patients with TS.

Tourette syndrome runs in families, but it's not always a simple matter to detect the disorder. While TS is genetically transmitted, having the gene makes a person a "carrier"; it doesn't necessarily mean he will have the symptoms of the disease. It's extremely important to obtain a comprehensive family history when we suspect TS. Of course, not all parents realize that they have a history of tics in the family. Every child and adolescent psychiatrist has stories about parents who are less than candid in their responses, either because they're hiding something or because they're ignorant, blissfully or otherwise.

Many parents who see tics in their children don't recognize their own tics or identify them as such; they're just harmless "habits." One of my favorite experiences in that category came a few years ago. I was evaluating a little boy with the symptoms of TS, and I asked his parents the standard question: "Is there anyone in the family who has tics?" Both replied with an emphatic no. The problem was, at the time Dad was twitching and shrugging so much he was making the chair shake, and Mom was constantly clearing her throat.

THE TREATMENT

I'll never forget the day I told Barry, a nine-year-old boy with a sweet smile and a wonderful disposition, that he had a tic disorder. "A tic disorder?" he said. "Does that mean I have to wear a flea and tick collar?"

Nothing would have made me happier than to say yes. All doctors fantasize about a magic cure for disease. Why not a tic collar for treating Tourette syndrome? Unfortunately, however, there is no cure, magic or other, for TS. The best we can do is to control the disorder, and there are two basic methods of doing this. The first is relaxation techniques, especially self-hypnosis. The more tense and anxious a child is, the more severe his TS symptoms will be. If we can relieve stress, we can decrease symptoms. Even if the first element of the TS treatment is effective, we will almost always need the second part as well: medication. The recommended drugs for the treatment of TS fall into two major categories, *neuroleptics* and *antihypertensives*. Both offer good news and bad news.

The neuroleptics work, but the side effects associated with them are often troublesome, so the first-line drugs for TS are the antihypertensives, especially Catapres. After a 12-week trial of Catapres most children with tics are 60 percent improved and experience limited, harmless side effects

—mostly drowsiness (usually only during the early stages of treatment) and dry mouth. The Catapres doesn't interfere with learning or general functions. Another antihypertensive that is prescribed for TS is Tenex. Klonopin, an antianxiety agent, has also been effective in suppressing tics in some kids with TS.

The *neuroleptics,* most notably Haldol, Orap, and Prolixin, are better than Catapres at getting rid of tics—studies have shown 70 to 80 percent improvement in kids—but the side effects can be numerous and unpleasant: drowsiness, weight gain, decreased concentration, and sometimes impaired memory. Long-term use of neuroleptics may lead to tardive dyskinesia—involuntary muscle movement—in adults, but this effect of the neuroleptics on children has not been documented. I prescribe neuroleptics only when tics are causing great distress and dysfunction.

Many children diagnosed with TS also are being treated for ADHD and OCD. Attention deficit hyperactivity disorder usually calls for a psychostimulant, such as Ritalin; and OCD is ordinarily treated with an antidepressant, such as Anafranil or Prozac. All these medications have possible nuisance side effects. Anafranil may cause dry mouth, drowsiness, low blood pressure, dizziness, and constipation. Prozac may cause sleepiness or lack of inhibition. Ritalin may cause tics to increase. Because of all these variables, the child's treatment package here must be monitored especially carefully.

It is estimated that 20 to 30 percent of all children with TS outgrow the disorder naturally in their teens or early twenties. I know of a couple of cases in which the tics just disappeared, as if by magic. One of those children has been tic-free for more than five years now. However, it would be a grave mistake for any parent to count on or even hope for a spontaneous remission. The treatment for Tourette syndrome is not ideal, but it is essential. There are risks attached to the medication, but leaving TS untreated poses a much greater risk to a child's health and well-being.

TS can be a very debilitating disorder, hard on the body as well as the mind. I've never seen a 14-year-old look as tired as Wendy. She came in with a severe blinking problem. It started when she was seven years old, but it's gotten a lot worse lately, so bad, in fact, that it's interfering with her ability to study. A straight-A student since first grade, she was having trouble academically. As I talked to Wendy about her problem, I discovered that blinking was just the tip of the iceberg. Many other tics were filling her day. She's been barking, shrugging her shoulders, and twisting her upper body, sometimes hundreds of times a day. Embarrassed and ashamed about her tics, she's been avoiding school; that is why her grades have dropped. These tics take a tremendous amount of concentration and energy. As anyone who saw the dark circles under this teenager's eyes could easily tell, Wendy was exhausted.

Children with TS who don't receive prompt treatment will suffer in other ways too. They'll probably be alienated by their peer group and find it difficult to function socially. TS will affect their ability to date, to marry, to go out and get a job. Not surprisingly, a tic disorder can have a devastating effect on a child's self-esteem. Left untreated, it may contribute to depression. The worst case I've come across was an 18-year-old boy who, I learned, had untreated tics since he was in the first grade. By the time I saw him, he was demoralized, hopeless, even suicidal. "I'm not living. I'm just surviving," he said in desperation. "Wouldn't it be great not to be alive at all? Then I wouldn't have to worry about doing all these crazy things anymore."

Tourette syndrome cannot be cured, true, but it can and must be brought under control with medication. With the right treatment children and adolescents with TS can lead well-rounded, productive, happy lives. Some of them even make it to the major leagues.

PARENTING AND TS

"We have three children, but one of them, Bradley, takes up 90 percent of our time. Brad runs all our lives. The family can't function because we have to concentrate on making sure he's all right all the time. When he was young, he was afraid of everything. Now that he's older, he's angry all of the time, always having tantrums. Every small thing in life gets blown up to a huge thing. He feels as if everyone is judging him. My husband and I have to think about him 24 hours a day. We don't even have time to feel guilty about neglecting the other two kids."

Even in the best of times, parenting is a precarious balancing act—nurture and support on one side, control on the other. Maintaining the correct balance between the two is a goal that every parent takes very seriously. When a child is sick, the rules of parenting sometimes have to be revised, if not rewritten, and accommodations must be made. Still, balance—between protecting a child and helping him to get well—remains something to strive for, tics or no tics.

Some parents find that the best response to a crisis in the family is action. One mother of a 13-year-old boy I'm treating for TS is constantly looking out for her son, clearing the path in front of him, but she is careful to stay behind the scenes, where her son can't see her.

"The day before school opened, I went to the principal's office and checked Philip's schedule. I noticed some problems and asked the principal to make some changes. He said to me, 'Oh, don't worry. Phil can change it tomorrow.' I said, 'No. You don't understand. Phil can't change things. When he sees these mistakes on his schedule, he'll be too upset.' I sat there until all the changes were made. The principal was great about it."

Not all principals are great, of course, but this enterprising mother is politely unstoppable. Here's more.

"Phil was going through a terrible time in sixth grade, so I wanted him to have a teacher who wouldn't put too much pressure on him. I worked it out with the school in advance, but when he got to class on the first day of school, he had the wrong teacher, one I knew would be horrible for him. I marched in to talk to the principal, but they told me he couldn't see anyone for two weeks. I said, very politely, 'That's okay. I'll just sit here and wait.' And I did. He had no choice but to see me, and he did what I asked. I'm not an aggressive person; you can ask my husband. But my kid is too important for me not to go the extra mile. I mean, if my kid has to give a speech in class, he's a nervous wreck until he's called on and gets it over with. What's wrong with asking a teacher to call on him first?"

As far as I can tell, there's nothing wrong with the kinds of things that Phil's mother routinely does behind the scenes. I'm in favor of parents' protecting their children, of not putting a child in a position that will cause distress. For example, I advised another set of parents not to give their soon-to-be-13-year-old son, who had fairly serious TS, a traditional bar mitzvah celebration. The ceremony and the party afterward are stress-provoking for the most stalwart and brave boys; for this boy it would all be too much. Much to his relief—and theirs, I'm sure—the parents took the boy on a short trip instead.

Parents should be careful not to expect too much from their children, but they shouldn't expect too little either. Children, even ones with a serious disorder like TS, have to make their way in the world, and that means learning to fit in and follow the rules. There are certain symptoms that a child with TS can't control, even when he is appropriately medicated, but there are others that can be reined in. Like any child, a youngster with TS must understand that there are limits. It's the parents' job to set and enforce these limits, to help a child to function in polite society. Allowing a child to behave badly does him no service whatsoever.

Out there in the real world people may not enjoy looking at facial tics or listening to throat-clearing, but those behaviors are tolerable in society. What people can't and won't tolerate is someone who shouts obscenities or touches everyone's food at the dinner table. A child must be told what will and will not be permitted. For example, a child who misbehaves in a restaurant should know that his actions have consequences.

"Look, this behavior is really unacceptable," a parent might say. "You have to stop arguing with us and cursing when we go out to a restaurant."

"Well, I have no control over it," the child might answer.

"Your mother and I think you *can* control it. If you feel you are going to yell and can't control it, we think you should leave the table. If you can't control yourself, you won't be able to go out with us to dinner anymore."

"But I can't help it."

"We think you can, and the doctor thinks so too. Here's an idea: if you feel the need to scream, excuse yourself from the dinner table and go wait in the bathroom until the feeling goes away."

I've spoken to parents who worry about punishing a child for behavior he can't control, and I sympathize with their concerns. But there's nothing punitive or even unreasonable about that exchange. A child is not being threatened with punishment because he can't stop blinking or sniffing. He's being asked to modify behavior that he *can* control. By the way, this process of setting limits should be honored by the extended family, including close friends and doting grandparents. No one should be permitted to sabotage the parents' efforts. Everybody should know and abide by the rules.

Psychotherapy is not part of the standard treatment package for Tourette syndrome, but parent counseling or family therapy can be extremely beneficial for all concerned as a family tries to invent ways to cope with a disturbing, sometimes all-absorbing brain disorder. Parents of kids with TS need all the education and support they can get, and many find it by joining parent support groups or patient support groups, such as the Tourette Syndrome Association. The organization keeps its members up to date about the treatment of TS, publishes a regular newsletter, and sponsors various activities that bring together people whose lives are touched by TS. Once in a while they even arrange a movie screening. Their latest? *Twitch and Shout,* of course.

CHAPTER 14

Major Depressive Disorder

Until a month before I met her, Claire, 15 years old, had always been the life of the party. Attractive, bubbly, and smart, she made excellent grades, held down a job at a drugstore after school, and had an active social life, including a boyfriend. I first saw Claire just after the start of her junior year of high school. Her parents said that she hadn't really been herself since she returned from a summer away at camp. She'd been having trouble concentrating on her studies, she quit her job at the drugstore, and her boyfriend broke up with her. She'd been having a lot of trouble sleeping. Her parents said she was snappish and short with them and spent most of the day in her room. "Everything is an effort. I don't enjoy anything," Claire told me when we first met.

• • •

Charlie, also 15, was reading aloud in English class one day, and right in the middle of *A Separate Peace* he burst into tears. When the teacher took him to see the guidance counselor, Charlie was inconsolable, and his parents had to be called to pick him up. Everyone who knew the boy was baffled by what had happened. He seemed to have everything going for him—he was nice-looking, a talented musician, a good athlete, and a nearly straight-A student—but when he came to see me, he was sleeping all the time. For the past two months he'd been eating very little, and his weight was plummeting. He had stopped playing baseball. He said that he woke up every morning thinking that life wasn't worth living.

MOOD DISORDERS

Until about 15 years ago—the year that Charlie and Claire were born—it was generally accepted that children couldn't *be* depressed, not clinically at least. The thinking was that the egos of children were not sufficiently developed to be affected by mood disorders. Today we know better. There is irrefutable evidence that major depressive disorder, or MDD, does exist in children and adolescents. In prepubescent children it's quite rare, affecting only 1 to 2.5 percent of the population under the age of 12 and 2 to 8 percent of the population between the ages of 12 and 18. Among children it seems to affect boys and girls equally, but in the adolescent population females are more likely to have it.

Depression is the most common brain disorder in America; each year some 8 to 14 million Americans are recognized as suffering from clinical depression. One survey found that 19 percent of all adolescents had experienced an episode of MDD.

"It's been raining all weekend. I'm so depressed."

"That movie was *so* depressing."

"I had such a depressing day at work today."

"I can't believe the Yankees lost again. I'm incredibly depressed!"

We've all heard comments like those. Most of us have made them ourselves. *Depression* is an overused word these days, describing our reaction to everything from a train crash to a failed soufflé. Of course, true clinical depression—MDD—is a lot more serious than a bad day at the office. It's a serious mood disorder with very specific symptoms, and it requires prompt, active treatment.

MDD may come and go, with occasional flare-ups; kids with MDD have their "ups and downs." For example, Charlie, described earlier in this chapter, had his first depressive episode back in the first grade. His mother says she knew there was something wrong, but she had no idea what it was. Then Charlie got better and stayed that way until fifth grade, when he went through a month-long period of being agitated and all but impossible to live with. That too passed, and he was fine until that frightening incident in tenth-grade English class, the one that led his parents to my office. MDD doesn't spring up overnight, although it may seem that way sometimes. Like a volcano, it simply lies dormant until some sort of crisis triggers the first episode.

Other children and adolescents suffer from *dysthymia,* a milder, more chronic form of depression, which should be distinguished from MDD. If MDD is like a full-blown infection, dysthymia is like a chronic virus —with a low-grade fever, some aches and pains, perhaps a mild headache. Kids with dysthymia get the "downs," but they rarely experience any "ups." One child who fits this description perfectly is Dominick, 16 years old. To hear his mother tell it, Dominick is a child who never seemed to get any joy out of life. He was the best student in his class and the star of the football team, but none of it seemed to make him happy. Getting an A on a test was incredibly important to him—he was completely focused and driven in his efforts—but when he got the A, there was no pleasure attached to the accomplishment. Dominick wasn't morose, but he had no zest for life. "He never cries, but I don't think I've ever seen him smile either," his mother said. Recent studies show that dysthymia may well be a stepping-stone to MDD. Dominick is a likely candidate for clinical depression.

THE SYMPTOMS

Major depressive disorder in children and adolescents is characterized by at least two weeks of a nearly constant depressed mood severe enough to cause distress and dysfunction. (We look for the so-called *depressed triad:* feelings of hopelessness, helplessness, and worthlessness.) The two-week minimum requirement for symptoms rules out the many unpleasant events and situations that can and do cause people to be unhappy and even temporarily depressed, such as a divorce, a medical emergency, a family financial crisis, or any of a dozen other problems. (An important exception is bereavement. The period of mourning considered normal for a death in the family is two months.) If the depressed mood is not a result of MDD, it will wax and wane; it won't be predominant for two weeks.

In addition to the two weeks of depression, a child or adolescent with MDD will have at least four of the following symptoms: inability to concentrate, irritability and anger, marked fatigue, feelings of worthlessness, sleep problems, appetite disturbance, social withdrawal, restlessness, and decrease in libido. One final symptom of MDD that may be present is *anhedonia:* the inability to experience pleasure. Most youngsters have had their symptoms much longer than two weeks by the time they receive professional help.

MDD manifests itself differently in children and adolescents. Very young children may not necessarily look or act sad, although some will have downcast eyes or a blank expression. In fact, many children with MDD will seem more oppositional than depressed. They'll be irritable and cranky; *everything* bothers these kids. Behavior disturbances such as hyperactivity, temper tantrums, and absence of normal play are not unusual. A small number of children, perhaps as many as a third, will have thoughts of suicide. They also often complain about various aches and pains—headaches, stomachaches, even back troubles. Typically a depressed youngster will see his pediatrician or some other physician before finally making his way to a child and adolescent psychiatrist's office.

In teenagers the symptoms of MDD tend to be a little different, more like those of depressed adults. Depressed mood, diminished ability to concentrate, sleep, and appetite disturbance, sensitivity to rejection, a feeling of being weighed down, and thoughts of suicide are common symptoms. Depressed adults often undereat and undersleep; teenagers are more likely to overeat and oversleep. A lot of depressed adolescents sleep in the middle of the day, coming home from school and taking a nap. Then they wake up at seven or eight o'clock in the evening, grumpy and irritable. After having something to eat—probably not with their parents and the rest of the family—they're wide awake until three o'clock in the morning and have trouble waking up the next day for school. Sleep disturbance is a vicious circle.

Depressed teenagers often have an additional symptom: *mood reactivity.* These youngsters are able to cheer up when they are in a positive interaction or environment. Chad, a 16-year-old boy I treated for MDD, was chronically irritable. He didn't eat much, showed no interest in television, and couldn't concentrate on his schoolwork. That was when he was home alone or with his family. When his friends came over, his mood would brighten; sometimes he seemed almost happy. His father was baffled and angry. "He must be doing this on purpose," he said. "How can he be so pleasant when his friends come and so miserable the rest of the time?"

Depressed teenagers may also be very sensitive to rejection and may have a tendency to be histrionic, with extreme reactions to real or imagined slights. One 16-year-old girl with MDD whose boyfriend broke a date with her went up on the roof of her house and threatened to jump off. She stayed up there for hours, feeling completely despondent. She told her mother and father that life wasn't worth living if her boyfriend didn't love her. The fact that he had canceled their date because he had to study for a test made no difference.

The irritability associated with MDD can lead to very erratic, even violent behavior. A 14-year-old boy named Gerard was brought in to see me after pulling a knife on his father. Gerard had been having problems at school—skipping classes on a regular basis and behaving badly when he did attend. On the days he didn't go to school, he would just lie in bed all day, mostly sleeping but occasionally watching television. He hardly ate at all. He had no social life, no friends. One evening his father lost patience with Gerard and told him he had to go to school or else, and Gerard became enraged. That's when he reached for the knife, after pounding on and then overturning the kitchen table. When I interviewed him, Gerard wasn't forthcoming about his symptoms at first except to say he was tired all the time. All he would tell me about the episode with the knife was: "My father made me mad."

THE DIAGNOSIS

It is highly unlikely that anyone watching Gerard turn over that table and grab that kitchen knife would describe him as depressed. The word *depressed* summons up images of a weepy, withdrawn child. By the same token, when a child or an adolescent does look unhappy or withdrawn or demonstrates any of the other symptoms associated with clinical depression, there are many possible explanations besides MDD. Before making a diagnosis of major depressive disorder, a child and adolescent psychiatrist must take a detailed history by interviewing the child, the parents, and the teachers. Then he must systematically consider and rule out all the other possibilities, bearing in mind that co-occurent conditions are very common with MDD.

It's not uncommon for kids with MDD also to have an anxiety disorder, especially separation anxiety disorder (discussed in Chapter 9) and social phobia (Chapter 10). Studies have shown that nearly half of the children diagnosed with MDD will have an anxiety disorder as well. Leonard, a 16-year-old boy I treated for MDD, was originally diagnosed with social phobia. When I first met him, Leonard told me that he had been feeling unhappy for five years. The other kids think he's weird, and he's afraid to talk to people at school, he told me. He would like to have friends, but he doesn't know how. Leonard's mom and dad have their own theories. Dad says that the problem is that Leonard has always had low self-esteem. Mom says it all started because Leonard is the smallest kid in his class, and that makes him feel inadequate. One thing I learned during that first visit was that lately Leonard has been having a lot of trouble sleeping. He's been suffering from both *initial insomnia* (trouble falling asleep) and *middle insomnia* (waking up in the middle of the night). Both sleep disturbances are common symptoms of MDD.

Major depressive disorder may sometimes look a lot like attention deficit hyperactivity disorder too (see Chapter 7). Not too long ago I saw a little eight-year-old boy who was sent to me by a neurologist because of his disruptive behavior at home. He behaved himself at school well enough, but after school he would bang on the walls of his bedroom until he made holes in them. Almost anything would set him off. He was agitated and cranky all the time, and he had many physical complaints. Nothing gave him pleasure. When his parents didn't give him his way, he went ballistic. My eventual diagnosis was MDD.

Yet another relative of MDD is CD: conduct disorder (Chapter 18). Jamie, a 16-year-old boy, came in because he was irritable, fresh, and always getting into trouble both at home and out in the world. He was terrific at sports and a very good artist, but his academic achievement left a lot to be desired. He frequently cut classes and had lots of fights after school. A psychologist had given Jamie's parents the diagnosis of CD, and there was no question that Jamie had it. It turned out that he also had MDD. (Depressed kids are often regarded as oppositional because of their irritability.) It took me a few weeks to find out that Jamie was also feeling, in his words, empty. "I felt like nothing. I felt like: Why move? Why get out of my chair?" he told me. It's important to remember that teenagers Jamie's age, and particularly those considerably younger than Jamie, don't necessarily speak the language of MDD. They don't say they're depressed or blue or gloomy or morose or any of the many words an adult might choose. *Empty* was the closest Jamie could get.

Another disorder that must be ruled out is schizophrenia (see Chapter 16). This can be a tricky business sometimes, because children and teenagers with MDD may have delusions and other psychotic symptoms. The key here is that the delusions and hallucinations are all mood-congruent—consistent with the mood of the youngster—and, in their own way, logical. For instance, kids with MDD will be depressed because they think they're dying, or they may hear voices that criticize them. When I met Franklin, I was all but certain that he had schizophrenia. He had just dropped out of college, and he had all sorts of symptoms: obsessions, compulsions, anxieties, the works. He thought his eyes were burning, so he had to look down at the floor all the time. He also constantly inspected his hair and his clothes. He told me he felt sad all the time, and he couldn't sleep. After a lifetime of accomplishments—he had good grades in high school, and he was a varsity basketball player—Franklin had zero confidence in his abilities. "I feel as if I've lost myself," he told me. "When I lie in bed, I have to keep checking to see if my heart is still beating. I'm sure I have a tumor in my chest." Franklin's delusions sounded like schizophrenia, but further investigation pointed toward MDD.

Chronic fatigue syndrome is another disguise in which major depressive disorder may appear. That's what everyone thought was wrong with 14-year-old Nellie, who came to see me after she had been sick for over a year. Nellie had always done well in school, but friends didn't come easily, even back in elementary school. The other kids teased her a little back then because she was so shy and awkward. By the seventh grade she had no friends to speak of, but no one really knew why. At the beginning of the ninth grade Nellie had mononucleosis, which basically put her out of commission for a couple of months. She was better by Christmas, but in February she had a relapse. She was tired all the time. In March her pediatrician diagnosed chronic fatigue syndrome and sent her to school with a note saying she should take a nap every afternoon.

Fatigue was just the beginning of Nellie's symptoms. Before that school year was over, her list of complaints was quite long. She couldn't concentrate; she cried all the time; and for the first time ever, she didn't make the honor roll. Her appetite was terrible, and although she went to sleep every night at nine and got up at six, she woke up several times during the night. The reason I didn't have the opportunity to see her—and diagnose her MDD—for nearly a year is that her parents and everyone else around her thought that all her new symptoms were simply an offshoot of her chronic fatigue syndrome. They thought Nellie was just tired from her illness and overwhelmed by the workload of a regular teenager.

In the process of making this very elusive diagnosis of major depressive disorder, the child and adolescent psychiatrist must eliminate one last disorder, the one most closely related to major depressive disorder: bipolar disorder. As will be explained in Chapter 15, bipolar disorder combines depression and mania, a sustained "high." With major depressive disorder (occasionally referred to as unipolar disorder) there is depression but no mania.

The best way of diagnosing major depressive disorder in children and adolescents is to come face to face with the troubled child. The essence of the diagnosis for MDD is hearing the youngster's responses and getting a feel for his mood.

THE BRAIN CHEMISTRY

When I was growing up, everybody thought that acne was caused by eating chocolate: if we ate chocolate, we'd get pimples. Of course, lots of kids ate chocolate and didn't get pimples. Some ate chocolate and got a few now and then. And then there were the poor kids who didn't eat any chocolate but had terrible skin anyway. Today we know that chocolate isn't the culprit; some people are just vulnerable to acne. Certain external factors may bring on acne and make it worse, to be sure, but the vulnerability has to be there first.

It's a lot like that with MDD. There are internal and external events that may bring on a depressive episode, but the vulnerability—in this case a neurochemical vulnerability—has to be there first. Demoralizing or tragic events don't make everyone depressed; some people are born invulnerable. Given sufficient stress, both physical and psychological, nearly everyone has some sort of physical reaction; asthma, high blood pressure, ulcers, colitis, migraines, and even cold sores can be brought on by stress. In some people it's the brain that's affected, and a depressive episode is the result. It's important to remember, however, that it wasn't the death in the family, the breakup with a boyfriend, or the five straight days of rain that caused the depression. The cause of MDD arises in the brain.

The chemistry of a child's brain is what determines his vulnerability to MDD. A child inherits brain chemistry from his parents, so, not surprisingly, depression runs in families. Children whose parents have

MDD have a greater than average chance of having MDD themselves; the relatives of youngsters with MDD are more than twice as likely to have the disorder than the relatives of normal kids. Abnormal responses have been reported in depressed adolescents during challenge testing of their endocrine system. These tests are not diagnostic, but they lend support to a biological basis for MDD.

The neurotransmitters that improve our mood or keep it stable are dopamine, norepinephrine, and serotonin. Any imbalance in these three neurotransmitters may account for an onset of MDD, but it is generally thought that underactivity of either serotonin or norepinephrine is largely responsible. In addition to those neurotransmitters the brain also produces endorphins, the chemicals that give people satisfaction or a sense of joy. Both internal and external stressors can have a strong effect on all of the brain's chemical components. In an effort to "fix" what is causing their child pain, parents often spend too much time and effort trying to puzzle out what might have caused a child's depressive episode and not enough time and effort seeking treatment. To treat the disease, it's not necessary to know what causes depression. Saying, "Oh, his parents are getting a divorce. That's why he's depressed" is a typical response. MDD can't just be explained away. It can't be willed away either, although there are many people who would like to think so. "If she would just pull herself together" and "If she would just stop feeling sorry for herself" are typical reactions to depression in both children and adults. Years ago I met a woman who had MDD episodes after the birth of each of her children. For the first five kids she didn't seek help, and no one encouraged her to do so. She figured she just needed to pull herself out of it; seeing a psychiatrist was a sign of weakness. After the birth of her sixth child she ended up in the hospital, psychotically depressed. Even then she was reluctant to talk about her symptoms. She felt guilty and ashamed. "Having babies is the most natural thing in the world," she said. "What's wrong with me?"

THE TREATMENT

The best treatment for MDD is a combination of pharmacotherapy (antidepressants), psychotherapy, and family intervention. The medications that are the most effective and most commonly prescribed for

MDD are the SSRIs (selective serotonin reuptake inhibitors), especially Prozac but also Zoloft, Paxil, and Luvox. The side effects, which are mild and infrequent, are diarrhea, nausea, and sleeplessness. Parents and children are amazed at how fast the SSRIs work sometimes. The parents of a severely depressed 10-year-old girl for whom I had prescribed Prozac reported that her symptoms began to disappear in only three weeks.

Another group of antidepressants used in treating children and adolescents with MDD are TCAs (tricyclic antidepressants): Tofranil, Pamelor, Elavil, and Norpramin. These medicines take longer to work than the SSRIs; they require four to six weeks for a clinical response. The nuisance side effects of the TCAs are dry mouth, constipation, and drowsiness, but they may also have an effect on the cardiovascular system. Before the medication is started and before the dose is increased, a youngster should have his blood pressure and pulse measured and he should have an electrocardiogram. These medicines need to be monitored carefully, since an overdose can be lethal. There have been several reports of sudden death of children taking Norpramin, but there is no proof that the Norpramin caused the deaths. When a child's MDD is severe and other medications have not been effective, Norpramin may still be the answer. The nuisance side effects of Norpramin are minimal, and it *does* work.

Also occasionally prescribed for MDD are the atypical antidepressants, especially Wellbutrin and Trazadone. Wellbutrin has been used in patients who have not responded to either the SSRIs or the TCAs. Side effects of Wellbutrin are agitation, restlessness, and irritability, but they are infrequent, and they nearly always disappear over time or with a lower dose. Trazadone is usually given in addition to another antidepressant. The most common side effects—sedation, increased blood pressure, dizziness, and nausea—are mild and transient. A rare but serious side effect of Trazadone is priapism, a prolonged erection without sexual stimulation. For obvious reasons, Trazadone should not be prescribed for adolescent males.

A group of antidepressants that have been used in adolescents with MDD who have not responded to other antidepressants are the MAOIs (monamine oxidase inhibitors): Nardil, Parnate and Marplan. Dietary restrictions are required with these medications. Foods that are rich in tyramine, such as aged cheese, beer, red wine, smoked fish, and aged meats, interact with MAOIs to produce a hypertensive reaction: severe headache, palpitations, neck stiffness, nausea, and sweating. Because of the difficulty of monitoring the diet of a child or adolescent, we usually stay away from the MAOIs.

Synthetic thyroid hormones have been used to increase the effectiveness of antidepressant medications, especially in adolescents with MDD who have responded partially or not at all to antidepressants. The hormones most frequently used are T3, Cytomel; and T4, Synthroid. The side effects are weight loss and nervousness, but they are unusual.

Parents whose children are taking medicine worry about a lot of things. When the child or teenager is being treated for MDD, we often hear parents voicing concern, even fear, that the child will become addicted to the drug. Some drugs that alleviate depression *are* addictive—cocaine and speed are two of the best known—but these drugs are different from the medicines we prescribe. When the effects of cocaine and speed wear off, there is a "crash" and a strong desire for more of the drug. The antidepressants aren't like that. A child may well *need* to take this medication in order to rid himself of the MDD symptoms that are causing distress and dysfunction, but he will not become addicted.

An adolescent diagnosed with major depressive disorder may benefit from this medicine for a long time. Even with the medication, however, he may have an occasional relapse, usually brought on by stress. About 50 percent of all depressed children will have a second depressive episode within five years of the first.

The most significant problem associated with prescribing medication for MDD is that kids often take themselves off the medication, even though the beneficial effects of the medicine are nearly always quite obvious. I prescribed Tofranil for Wesley, a 17-year-old boy who was almost completely dysfunctional when he came to see me. He didn't go to school or see friends. He barely left his bed. After a few weeks of the medication he was going to school every day and holding down a part-time job in his father's store. He didn't have any friends yet, and he still felt, in his own words, "lousy." He decided that the medicine wasn't doing him any good—he wasn't *happy*, after all—so he stopped taking it. Shortly after that Wesley took to his bed again, until we got him back on the medication.

Lynn, a 14-year-old girl I treated for MDD, had a long-standing love-hate relationship with her medication. A bright girl with normal intelligence, she had a strong family history of MDD. Her older brother had attempted suicide a year earlier, and she herself had seriously considered taking her own life. Lynn responded well to Prozac, and cognitive behavioral therapy with a psychologist was progressing nicely. She was, she told me, "feeling pretty good." The problem was that she didn't like the idea of taking medication even if it did make her feel better. Her mother wasn't happy about the medicine either and made no effort to disguise her feelings. Lynn was constantly asking to be taken off the medicine. "I'm feeling so much better now. I'm sure I'll be fine," she said. When I told her she needed more time with the medicine, she took herself off it anyway. Her depression got worse almost immediately; she stayed in bed all day, crying and overeating. Her thoughts of suicide returned. Even in her severely depressed state Lynn knew that she needed to start taking the medication again.

Parents will have to monitor a child's medication, but the more involved a child is in the treatment process, the better the results will be. A youngster who understands that something is wrong with him and accepts the fact that this little pill is helping him to feel better is more likely to thrive than one who is kept in the dark about what's going on or someone who is terribly resistant to the medication. Adolescents—Wesley and Lynn, for example—should be encouraged to take the initiative in their own treatment, especially since mothers and dads don't typically have a great deal of power or influence over them anyway.

I find that making an adolescent take responsibility for treating his own illness may serve as a kind of wake-up call. "Okay. Why don't you try yourself without medication for the next two weeks and we'll see how it goes?" I said to one of my teenage patients recently. "But I want you to call me next week and report in about your symptoms. And that means *you*. I don't want your mother to call me. And I don't want to have to call you. This is your job now. You have to tell me what's going on." With the right kid, that strategy can work miracles.

Medication is an indispensable part of the treatment for MDD, but therapy, especially symptom-oriented therapy, also plays a vital part. Cognitive psychotherapy helps a child or adolescent to change the negative thinking that is symptomatic of MDD and work on improving his social skills so that he can make friends. Like children with social phobia, kids with MDD have to learn how to meet people and talk to them, and this requires preparation and rehearsal. Children with MDD have to learn how *not* to be depressed, and that takes practice and informed instruction. Professionals can be an immense help.

A specific treatment program for MDD, called interpersonal psychotherapy (IPT), has been helpful in the treatment of adults with milder forms of MDD, and recently it has been used for adolescents as well. The 16-week program, which focuses on helping the adolescent understand his illness and exploring how it affects his interpersonal relationships, can be extremely helpful in combination with the right medication.

Family intervention is often very beneficial as well. It helps the child, the parents, and the rest of the family to understand the nature of MDD as well as the treatment process. Parent counseling may provide insights about making changes in the child's environment and resolving school and family problems that may have contributed to the depression in the first place.

Often regarded as a last resort, electroconvulsive therapy (ECT) has been effective in treating severely depressed adolescents who have been unresponsive to any other treatment. ECT induces a seizure in the patient while he is under anesthesia. A series of eight to twelve sessions is usually required. Although widely misunderstood and almost as widely maligned, ECT has been shown to be a safe procedure that can produce wonderful results with no long-term side effects.

Prompt treatment makes a big difference in the prognosis of this disorder. The earlier MDD is treated, the shorter and less severe any subsequent depressive episode is likely to be. Left untreated, MDD will get worse; the episodes will last longer and be much more serious.

PARENTING AND DEPRESSION

"I can't remember a time when there wasn't something wrong with Aaron," recalled the mother of a teenager who was diagnosed with MDD nearly ten years earlier. "He has always been moody and irritable. When he was three years old, he'd get angry at us and stalk off and slam the door. He was hard on himself too. From the beginning my husband thought we should get some help, but I just couldn't face the idea that such a little boy could need a psychiatrist. By the time he was five, he was talking about death all the time. That's not something you expect in a small child. Everyone suspected that he was depressed. On his sixth birthday we took Aaron to see his first psychiatrist."

Aaron's mother is not alone in her reluctance to accept the fact that she has a clinically depressed child. Emotions run very high with this disorder, and it is the rare parent who doesn't react with strong feelings to the behavior of a child with MDD. Anger and frustration are especially common, since these kids are usually sullen and difficult to manage. Generally speaking, children with MDD are not very pleasant to be around, and it's not unusual to discover that their parents don't like them all that much. "I feel terrible about this, but I actually dislike my own daughter," said the father of a 10-year-old. I've heard that comment, or some variation thereof, dozens of times.

Teenagers with MDD can be particularly annoying to their parents because it seems that they often have enough energy to do certain things, such as go out with their friends, but not others, such as their homework. They're pleasant enough when they're in the outside world and save their sullenness and their lethargy for the folks at home. There are occasions too in which a child is unpleasant with one parent but not the other. As difficult as it is to manage sometimes, parents have to realize that the behavior of a child with MDD is not willful. He's not being impossible on purpose.

Most parents of kids diagnosed with MDD feel more than a little guilty too. After all, it is a parent's job to make his child happy. Being happy is a basic essential of life. If a kid is depressed, the thinking goes, it must mean that the mother and father are doing something wrong. None of this is true, of course, but even parents who know better sometimes consider themselves dismal failures. The feelings of parental guilt associated with this disorder are very strong, particularly when a child tries to commit suicide. One of the many reasons we recommend parent counseling is that it helps parents understand that *no one*—not the parents, not the child—is to blame for this disease. There's no reason for a parent to feel guilt or shame.

Another way in which parent counseling can be useful is to help parents redefine and come to terms with their special role as the mother and father of a child with major depressive disorder. Being the parent of a child or adolescent with MDD isn't easy, to say the least. There are all sorts of unexpected questions that may arise, especially as a child moves through adolescence to adulthood.

"I never know how much slack to cut her," said the mother of a 15-year-old girl diagnosed with MDD. "I know I have a right to expect things from her, but it takes so much effort for her to do the easiest things. I don't want to ask her to do too much and put a lot of unnecessary pressure on her. On the other hand, I don't want to let her off the hook about everything just because she's sick." This mother makes an excellent point. Sooner or later her daughter will have to take her place out in the world, and it's her parents' job to prepare her for that day. Parent counseling will bring these issues out into the open.

Even when a teenager is diagnosed with MDD, parents have to learn to let go a little and encourage a child to be independent. Allowing a child to make his own decisions is difficult for any parent; when a child's decision-making abilities are impaired by major depressive disorder, it can be nearly impossible.

"I've always been a little overprotective; I admit it," said one mother. "My older daughter is 21 years old and perfectly normal, and I still interfere in her life too much. My 19-year-old is the one who's depressed, and I have to remind myself constantly not to take over her life. I'm tempted to ask her every day if she's taking her medication and to call the doctor to see if she's showing up for her appointments, but I don't. I know that would be wrong."

Yes, that would be wrong, but the impulse is perfectly understandable. Knowing when to get involved and when to step back and let it happen is a real skill for any parent. Here's how yet another mother, whose 22-year-old clinically depressed son has just moved into his own apartment for the first time, expresses the conflict: "Part of me wants to let him go completely—say, 'It's your life and your problem.' But then I think, 'Wait. If my son had a broken leg, I wouldn't just point to the stairs and wish him the best of luck getting to the top. I'd get him a crutch or let him lean on me. Together we'd work out a way for him to get to the second floor.' "

CHAPTER 15

Bipolar Disorder/
Manic Depressive Illness

A ccording to his parents, Leo, nearly 14 years old, had been perfectly normal until about a year before he came to my office for the first time. At the age of 13 the boy had been doing well in school, and he'd had a full social life as well, with plenty of friends and activities. But then things started to change. Leo became rambunctious and difficult to deal with. He was very sad at times, becoming tearful and even crying quite often, and his judgment was poorer than it used to be. He dyed his hair bright red and then streaked it with purple. Then he got himself a small tattoo. Mom and Dad thought it was a rebellious teenager phase at first. Then Leo's behavior became even more worrisome. He overslept often and virtually had to be forced to go to school. He complained of headaches, neck discomfort, and other assorted pains. He was totally enervated one day and so energetic the next that he claimed he didn't need sleep. Instead he'd stay up all night practicing the guitar. When I talked to Leo about his music, he told me, in the most matter-of-fact way, that he needed to practice. He was going to be a *huge* rock star.

• • •

For the last few months Molly had been talking to herself a great deal, but her mother figured that her daughter was just rehearsing for the school play. At 16, Molly was quite passionate about acting. For the three weeks before I met Molly, the girl had been "blue," as her mother put it—withdrawn and isolated from her friends and family, unable to concentrate on her studies. Then, two days before Molly came to see me, she came out of her funk with a vengeance. She was yelling and screaming incoherently and talking nonstop even when no one was around. She would eat only when forced to do so and hardly slept at all. By the time I saw Molly—and checked her into the hospital for a short stay—she was out of control, talking incessantly (mostly about Madonna) and singing songs from *The Sound of Music*. Her first night in the hospital she took off all her clothes and danced in the bathroom. The nurses said that Molly appeared to be having the time of her life.

HIGHS AND LOWS

Adolescents are moody. That's an indisputable fact, like the sun rising in the east. Parents of teenagers expect erratic behavior from their kids, and so they should. Adolescence is a time for change of all sorts, and hormones tell only part of the story. Kids also go through some important developmental stages at this point in their lives, the most significant of which are separating from Mom and Dad and coming to grips with their sexuality. Normal, healthy teenagers will accomplish these tasks without too many casualties, although there will probably be some serious power struggles along the way. Rebellion and moodiness come with the territory.

The territory occupied by bipolar disorder—also called *manic-depressive illness*—is characterized by a very different, much more serious brand of moodiness. This disorder involves intense, persistent moods that are clearly different from and much more intense than the child's usual demeanor and are extremely inappropriate to the event and the environment. The mood swings must be severe enough to cause distress and dysfunction.

The word *bipolar* refers to the two poles of this very serious disease: mania and depression. (Chapter 14 covered major depressive disorder, or *unipolar* disorder.) A child with bipolar disorder will have had at least one episode of mania—or *hypomania*, a milder, less intense version of mania. The symptoms of mania are distractibility, irritability, grandiosity, racing thoughts, a decreased need for sleep, an increased speed of speech, poor judgment, increased risk-taking behavior, and a break in reality testing, usually characterized by delusions and hallucinations. An adolescent having a manic episode, which may last anywhere from several days to a few months, typically will feel hypersexual and expansive, will have unrealistic expectations about his performance, and will make rash decisions and spend money recklessly. A 16-year-old girl I treated once took her mother's credit card and bought a plane ticket to Boston to see a rock concert. Another time she was caught shoplifting. "I'm a movie star," she told the security guard. "My agent will pay for this stuff."

"Having Rory around is like watching an episode of *Lifestyles of the Rich and Famous*," said a fed-up father of a 17-year-old boy in the middle of a manic episode. "He likes only the finest things—the best watches and the best luggage and the best clothing. One day he charged a $500 ski parka, a $300 pair of alligator shoes, and two Armani sweaters and had it all sent home by Federal Express. Of course, he put everything on *my* credit card."

To be diagnosed with bipolar disorder adolescents must also have had a depressive episode, which lasts anywhere from two weeks to several months. Its symptoms are loss of concentration, sleep disturbance, change in appetite, fatigue or decreased energy, agitation, lethargy, a feeling of worthlessness, and an inability to experience pleasure.

The incidence of bipolar disorder in children and adolescents is not known. The lifetime risk of bipolar disorder is about 1 percent among the general population—affecting men and women just about equally—but it can be much higher in families in which other members have mood disorders. The condition is very rare in children under the age of 12, although there have been reports of bipolar disorder in children as young as four.

Bipolar disorder often starts in adolescence, but is not recognized and diagnosed until much later, when kids become older and display classic adult symptoms. A survey conducted by the National Depressive and Manic-Depressive Association found that 59 percent of those surveyed reported suffering their first symptoms of bipolar disorder during childhood or adolescence. The age of onset of bipolar disorder is most frequently between 15 and 19.

THE SYMPTOMS

The distress and dysfunction associated with bipolar disorder can vary greatly, depending on the severity of the illness and which of the two poles—mania or depression—is "in charge." When adolescents with bipolar disorder are in the depression stage of this condition, they're usually pretty miserable. (The elements of the "depressed triad" say it all: feelings of hopelessness, helplessness, and worthlessness.) Mania is something else again. "You don't know what you're missing, Doc," one of my patients told me, describing what it's like when he's manic. "There's really nothing like it. I feel great. I look handsome. I'm brilliant. There's nothing I can't do." Patients in a hypomanic phase are often productive and very pleased with themselves. As long as they are in that state, their heads are filled with ideas, and they have the energy to act on them.

Most of the kids eventually diagnosed with bipolar disorder come to my office complaining about depression. I've had only one patient who complained about mania, a shy, soft-spoken, extremely religious 16-year-old girl. She told me that what bothers her most about her illness is her conviction that she's better than everybody else. "I don't want to be better than everybody else. I don't want to feel this way. It's a sin," she told me.

Patients in the *mixed state*—described by some experts as being trapped between depression and mania but not quite in either one—are usually in a lot of pain. The combination of feeling sad and worthless and weighed down and, at the same time, having racing thoughts and delusions of grandeur is incredibly exhausting and upsetting to adults; it can be devastating to a child or an adolescent. Many of the patients I've treated say they feel out of control, all revved up but depressed and crying at the same time. It's in this mixed state that distress and dysfunction are often most severe.

One final term to address is *rapid cycling*. Officially defined as four or more distinct mood episodes in one year, rapid cycling may involve even more abrupt and frequent mood swings: up one day and down the next sometimes. Rapid cycling is relatively rare, however. Only about 20 percent of all patients with bipolar disorder have it, and most of them experience it relatively late in the illness. It is much more typical to hear the cycle described the way the mother of one of my young patients put it: "She's not up and down, up and down, up and down. She's down and then she's normal. Then she has an episode where she's really up, and we worry about her doing something dangerous and foolish. Then there's a long period of time when things are okay again. Then she's down again."

Bruce, who turned 15 just a few days before I first met him, was a classic case of rapid cycling bipolar disorder. His parents said that Bruce had been having troubles for about three months. He was withdrawn and somewhat irritable, and his sleep/wake cycle was reversed; he was sleeping in the daytime and staying awake almost all night. He would go on sleeping binges, staying in bed for days on end, and then he wouldn't sleep for 48 to 60 hours straight. All night long he would sit at his computer, totally absorbed in the intricacies of the Internet and communicating with people all over the world. When he finally got bored with his computer bulletin boards, he turned to the Home Shopping Network and ordered hundreds of dollars worth of merchandise. When I talked to Bruce, he was sweating profusely and talking a mile a minute. The topic he liked most was himself. He couldn't decide whether he should be president of the United States or play center for the New York Knicks.

Benjamin, 15 years old when I started treating him, had a full-blown manic episode during the two weeks he was away at camp last summer. According to the camp counselors, Benjamin was withdrawn and almost morose when he arrived at the camp, but over the course of that first week he became increasingly euphoric and irritable. He would talk very fast, sometimes so fast that no one could make sense of what he was saying. As the week wore on, he stopped sleeping and started masturbating several times a day. He also began to spend large amounts of money on inconsequential items for himself and everybody else in the cabin. He found a Bible and read it all the time, sometimes aloud to his bunkmates. I later learned that Benjamin was reading the Bible for a specific reason: he thought that he'd been chosen by God for a special purpose.

The reason behind a symptom can often be instructive in identifying any disorder. Ann-Marie, a 16-year-old girl I treated quite recently, had a couple of symptoms with especially significant explanations. Her father brought her in because her teachers and the principal of her school told Ann-Marie's parents that something was seriously wrong with their daughter. "I've been going to these parent-teacher conferences ever since she was in kindergarten," he told me. "This is the first time I've ever heard any complaints." The teacher told the father that Ann-Marie had taken to getting up in the middle of class, walking around the room, giggling, and talking back to the teacher. She was looking strange too, dirty and unkempt and often dressed in odd color combinations. Her handwriting, once so tidy and precise, had become very flamboyant. She refused to make eye contact, they said. Ann-Marie's parents told me that her behavior at home was a little strange too. She had been talking to herself, and she became terribly upset whenever the television was on. Every time anyone turned on the set, Ann-Marie would rush to switch it off.

I later learned that there were very specific reasons for Ann-Marie's lack of eye contact and her hatred of the TV. Ann-Marie didn't want to look anyone in the eye because she was convinced she had special powers. She thought that if she looked directly at anyone, she would cause that person harm. In fact, she wouldn't even look in the mirror when she combed her hair, so frightened was she of what she might do. Her powers were so great they terrified her. She avoided the television because special messages were being broadcast to her through the TV. These facts combined with Ann-Marie's other symptoms led me to a diagnosis of bipolar disorder.

THE DIAGNOSIS

"Are you *sure* this is manic-depressive illness?" a mother asked me. "Maybe I just have the world's most obnoxious teenager."

Bipolar disorder is a difficult diagnosis to accept. It's also not easy to make. There is no blood test or brain scan to aid the process. Furthermore, a lot of these troubled adolescents start medicating themselves— with alcohol, cocaine, marijuana, or Quaaludes. Drug and alcohol use clouds the diagnostic picture even more. In making a diagnosis we conduct a physical examination to rule out thyroid problems or drug abuse. Then we take a detailed history from the youngster, his parents, his teachers, and anyone else who knows him well. Along the way we look long and hard for a family history of depression, mania, schizophrenia, alcoholism, or drug addiction.

Bipolar disorder is especially difficult to diagnose in young children. Even very young children can have sleep disturbances, loud speech, and most of the other symptoms associated with bipolar disorder, and they might also become suddenly oppositional. Of course, they're not likely to go on spending sprees or fly off to rock concerts. Their manic phase will probably look different from that of teenagers.

The most common symptoms of bipolar disorder in the very young are irritability, moodiness, talkativeness, hyperactivity, and distractibility

—all symptoms for attention deficit hyperactivity disorder as well. A six-year-old child who is acting uncharacteristically silly or giddy may be doing so for any one of many reasons. The typical scenario is this: a first-grader who is sitting still in class, concentrating on what the teacher is saying, suddenly jumps up out of her chair and starts giggling, pulling her dress up, and talking animatedly to everybody in the class. Clearly she's out of control. Her behavior could be interpreted as ADHD, but she may also be showing signs of bipolar disorder. Children with bipolar disorder are more moody than kids with ADHD, and their activity is more focused. Furthermore, children with bipolar disorder may have hallucinations and delusions.

Nick, a 12-year-old boy who had been diagnosed (incorrectly) with ADHD, came to see me when his parents decided that his behavior was becoming more and more bizarre. The last straw was the hole he punched in his bedroom wall. Nick had been having problems at school for some time, refusing to study and often creating problems in class. Lately he's been agitated, unmanageable, and out of control both at school and at home. His appetite has decreased. He's been provocative and verbally abusive to his parents. When I met Nick, he told me that he hasn't been sleeping very well, and he's been having some crying spells. At night when he can't sleep he plays with a Ouija board, and he's convinced that he has powers that make the board talk to him. I diagnosed bipolar disorder and explained to the parents why their child didn't have ADHD. To begin with, Nick had not had any symptoms before the age of 12. The signs of ADHD must show up in early childhood.

Even when the child has reached adolescence, the diagnosis of bipolar disorder frequently comes via a long, circuitous route. Several related disorders must be ruled out along the way. One of the possible candidates is conduct disorder (described in Chapter 18). Another is major depressive disorder, which is, of course, frequently one of the "poles" of bipolar disorder. Studies show that someone who experiences his first episode of depression in adolescence carries a 20 percent risk of developing a manic episode within three to four years. It is not uncommon to diagnose major depressive disorder and then, when the first manic episode finally occurs, to revise that diagnosis to bipolar disorder.

With teenagers the biggest diagnostic challenge is differentiating between bipolar disorder and schizophrenia (Chapter 16). The two illnesses have many characteristics in common. Like schizophrenia, bipolar disorder may be accompanied by psychosis. Kids with either of these diseases may lose touch with reality and have hallucinations and delusions. However, with bipolar disorder the delusion is usually a grandiose one, whereas with schizophrenia it is more likely to be simply bizarre. Debbie, a lovely, charming 17-year-old girl I treated for bipolar disorder, introduced herself at our first session as a famous supermodel and told me she had her own exercise show on television. When Debbie did her exercises in front of the mirror at home, she explained to me, her performance was transmitted through the mirror to a recording studio, which broadcast it on MTV. Schizophrenia was the first thing that came to mind when I heard Debbie's story, but once I focused on the grandiose nature of the delusion and the "coherence" of her story, I was inclined to go the other way.

Another difference between the two diseases is that bipolar disorder has mood swings—from mania to a normal mood or depression and back again—but schizophrenia doesn't. What's more, people with schizophrenia don't usually have a lot of energy or talk rapidly. Adolescents with bipolar disorder, unlike those with schizophrenia, have *flight of ideas;* their thoughts and comments may be rapid and seemingly all over the place, but close examination will reveal that there is a connection between one thought and the next. (The lightning-fast comic routines of Robin Williams come to mind.) The thoughts associated with schizophrenia are random and often disjointed—this is called *looseness of associations.* Despite all these differences, plus many more, distinguishing the two disorders is a real challenge.

THE BRAIN CHEMISTRY

Bipolar disorder is genetic. Hardly a month goes by without a report in the scientific literature that the specific gene for this disorder is about to be identified. More than half of all people diagnosed with bipolar disorder have a relative who has either bipolar disorder or depression. If an identical twin has bipolar disease, the other will also have it 65 percent of the time; this occurs only 14 percent of the time with fraternal twins. Adoption studies add support to the genetic theory behind bipolar disorder; a child whose biological mother has bipolar disorder has a 31 percent chance of having the disorder even if he is adopted at birth; if his biological mother does not have bipolar disorder but his adoptive mother does, we're down to 2 percent.

Neuroimaging techniques have been performed on only a small number of youngsters with bipolar disorder, but preliminary findings suggest that the left and right sides of their brains are different in very specific ways. Neurotransmitter regulation is also believed to be abnormal in people with bipolar disorder. Excess dopamine and the disregulation of norepinephrine may cause manic episodes. Lithium, the medication most commonly prescribed for bipolar disorder, affects both dopamine and norepinephrine.

THE TREATMENT

There is no known cure for bipolar disorder, but there is a fairly effective treatment: medication combined with supportive psychotherapy. The medicine of choice is Lithium, a natural salt that acts as a mood stabilizer. Lithium, which is occasionally used in children to treat aggressive outbursts, works in two ways: it treats a current episode of mania or depression, and, in 70 to 80 percent of all patients, it decreases the frequency and severity of future episodes.

For many people Lithium is an honest-to-goodness miracle drug; it gives them back their lives. Of course, not everyone responds so dramatically to Lithium. I've had patients with bipolar disorder who take their Lithium faithfully, never missing a dose, and still have problems once in a while. Still others do just fine for a time and then have a "breakthrough" episode—the illness basically breaks through the Lithium. When that happens, we either adjust the dose of Lithium or recommend an additional medication.

Lithium treatment requires monitoring, especially in the first few months after the medication is prescribed. It is especially important to check people on Lithium when the temperature is high; hot weather and strenuous activity lead to dehydration, which increases the concentration of Lithium in the blood and may produce unpleasant side effects. Lithium may also suppress thyroid functioning, so we check the thyroid on a regular basis with a simple blood test. If thyroid functioning is being affected, it's easily treatable by adding a synthetic hormone. Lithium is so beneficial that most people prefer to take the additional synthetic thyroid hormone rather than discontinue the Lithium.

There are many potential side effects associated with Lithium. The most common are acne, weight gain, increased thirst, frequent urination, nausea, and hand tremor. Having witnessed the side effects of many different drugs, my colleagues and I regard these as relatively benign— we call them "nuisance" side effects—but most adolescents would disagree. I've been put in my place more than once by an irate teenager who told me in no uncertain terms that having bad skin or being overweight *is* a big deal. The hand tremor can be upsetting to these kids too, since it makes them look odd, something no child or teenager relishes. A 16-year-old patient of mine quit her job as a cashier after one day because the customers noticed that her hand was shaking as she gave them their change. All of these side effects can be minimized by adjusting the dose of Lithium, adding another medication that addresses the specific side effects, or both.

Another medication-related difficulty for teenagers is the inadvisability of drinking alcohol or taking drugs when being treated for a mood disorder. To my patients with bipolar disorder I strongly recommend moderation when it comes to alcohol and abstention from illicit drugs.

Because of the nature of Lithium—it is a mood stabilizer—kids and especially their parents often express concern about the effect the medication will have on the child's personality. "We want our son to be well, but we don't want to *lose* him," one mother said to me. "Will he still have that spark?" They worry that a child's emotions will be chemically regulated and that he'll end up bland and boring. That's not what happens. Lithium doesn't change the personality; it just prevents those undesirable extremes—mania and depression—from happening. A child on Lithium will still be upset if something bad happens and extremely joyful when there's something to be happy about. One of my colleagues likens the role of Lithium to regulating a thermostat. Most of the time the thermostat that controls our mood works just fine, but every now and then there's a little glitch and we go up too high or down too low. This salt, Lithium, helps our thermostat to function better.

Lithium is not the only medication recommended for the treatment of bipolar disorder. An anticonvulsant called Tegretol, another mood stabilizer, has also been used to good effect. A patient taking Tegretol has to be monitored too; we particularly look for a drop in the white blood cells, which fight infection, and an effect on the liver. (These side effects are uncommon but serious.)

Depakote, another anticonvulsant, is also often prescribed for bipolar disorder. There are fewer side effects with this medicine than with either Lithium or Tegretol. The "nuisance" side effects are stomachache and nausea, but the major problem—which seems to occur only in very young children—is liver toxicity. Liver function should be checked regularly, particularly in the first six months a child or teenager takes the medication.

Not surprisingly, treating the two poles of this disorder—mania and depression—can be quite complicated, especially since antidepressants have been known to bring on a manic episode. That happened with a teenage girl I recently treated for major depressive disorder. The Zoloft she had been taking for her depression for nearly two years eventually brought on a manic episode. It's very important to remember that the antidepressant didn't *cause* her mania; that was there to begin with, and the episode was bound to happen some time. The medication just pushed her into the manic phase. (What's more, the mania didn't go away when the medication was stopped.) Some people with bipolar disorder require not just one medication but several working at once. For instance, antipsychotic agents such as Haldol may be given in conjunction with the mood stabilizer during the onset of the manic episode.

The biggest problem associated with the treatment of bipolar disorder is getting kids to take their medication. Studies show that one-third of all adolescents stopped taking their Lithium within a year of its being prescribed. Patients never run out of reasons to stop taking their medicine. They start to feel normal, and they forget that it's the Lithium that's making the difference. Or they'll start to pine for that great feeling they used to have in the manic phase and decide to go for it again. Many kids deny that they are sick, so they stop taking the medicine to prove their point. Unfortunately, relapse rates are very high, and sometimes kids do not respond as fast or as well the second time medication is tried as they did the first time.

When it comes to the problem of noncompliance with medication, parents don't always help either. They mean well when they say things like, "There's nothing wrong with her. Maybe she shouldn't be taking medication" or "Let's experiment. Take him off the Lithium," but their refusal to accept the fact that it's the medicine that's making their kids better only makes the problem worse. It's hard to think of a youngster taking a mood stabilizer for a lifetime after only a single episode, I know, but parents need to understand that a serious disease—which bipolar disorder most assuredly is—calls for serious treatment. Bipolar disorder is a treatable illness, but the only way the medicine can work is if the child takes it. Moms and dads who have doubts should know that more than 90 percent of adolescent manic patients who discontinue treatment for bipolar disorder will have a recurrence of the disease within 18 months.

In addition to medication we recommend psychotherapy for youngsters with bipolar disorder, and we encourage their families to join them. Therapy can help everyone concerned to understand the nature of this complicated illness and deal with the strong emotions that it brings to the surface. One patient with bipolar disorder I have been treating is a 16-year-old girl who blames her father, who also has bipolar disorder, for her disease. "He's never been any good, and now he's passed on his lousy genes to me so I have to suffer," she said. The therapist can help her and her father understand the truth about the disease.

A therapist will help families deal with practical as well as emotional issues. They'll learn how to cope with the medication, how to detect the early signs of a relapse, and how to identify the stressors that might trigger an episode. For instance, a college student with bipolar disorder should know that pulling all-nighters to study can be dangerous, since a lack of sleep can precipitate a manic episode. Drinking and taking drugs may also act as triggers.

Bipolar disorder calls for prompt, active treatment. Severe mood changes and high-risk behaviors during a child's formative years may have lasting effects on his development. Left untreated, this dangerous disorder may lead to alcohol and drug abuse and even suicide. The suicide statistics for this disorder are staggering; some 15 percent of all patients with bipolar disorder commit suicide.

PARENTING AND BIPOLAR DISORDER

Parents of children with bipolar disorder have their work cut out for them, and some are better at it than others. One set of parents I know nearly drove themselves to distraction looking for early signs that their son was having a relapse. They were constantly hovering, on the lookout for signs of mania. "One of us is always watching Lee. I'm afraid to go out at night any more. What if he goes haywire while I'm at the movies?" the mother said to me. The parents were obviously passing along their anxiety to their son. Lee called me one afternoon without telling his mother and father. "I can't take it. I'd rather go back to the hospital," he told me. "If I laugh two seconds longer than anybody else, they think I'm manic. If I'm upset because I got a bad grade, they're worried I'm going to fall into a depression." It is important for parents to be knowledgeable about the disease and watchful for signs of a relapse, but it's equally important to keep surveillance efforts under control.

With bipolar disorder there are times when hospitalization is necessary. Kids who are *very* distressed and *very* dysfunctional may need the around-the-clock medical care and attention that only a hospital can provide. When a kid is not taking care of himself—not bathing or eating or sleeping—and he's in a severe state of mania, he needs medication and intensive supervision until he gets back on track.

Many parents have difficulty accepting the behavior associated with bipolar disorder as a real illness. Sharon's parents had always been very proud of their teenage daughter. Smart, outgoing, and funny, she had many friends, and all the parents in the neighborhood used to enjoy her company. Sharon was constantly being invited to her friends' homes for dinner or a sleepover date. All of a sudden things began to change. Sharon became obstreperous, disruptive, noisy, and very disrespectful to her elders. "She's turned into a real troublemaker," one of the neighbors told Sharon's mother. "I'm sorry, but we just don't want her over here anymore."

Unfortunately, Sharon's parents were not able to recognize how severely ill their daughter was. As a matter of fact, the father thought he could solve the problem himself. Convinced that Sharon was just being willful, he decided to punish her for her behavior. Needless to say, the punishment did not improve Sharon's demeanor or her behavior; if anything, her disease grew steadily worse. Her parents, finally realizing that they couldn't fix things for their child, brought her in to see me.

Most children being treated for bipolar disorder will need help regaining their confidence and self-esteem, especially after a manic episode. There's a good chance that children who go through a manic episode are severely embarrassed by their behavior afterward, and even though they had no control over what they said or did, they may need to be forgiven by their families, their friends, their teachers, and even their doctors.

I'll never forget a girl I treated for bipolar disorder in the hospital several years ago. In the throes of a manic episode she was completely out of control, screaming curses and ethnic slurs at me and being sexually provocative. We soon got her Lithium to the right level, and she was fine. In fact, she was a lovely girl, charming and good-humored. As she was leaving the hospital, I could see that she was in tremendous pain when she said good-bye to me. With tears in her eyes she said, "I can't stop thinking about the terrible things I said to you. I called you such awful names."

I told her not to give it another thought. "That was your illness talking, not you," I explained. What I told the girl was true, of course, but that didn't make the burden that she was carrying any less heavy. Understanding, sympathetic parents can do a lot to lessen a child's load of guilt and shame.

CHAPTER 16

Schizophrenia

The first time I met Thomas, he was 15 years old, and his parents had just about given up on him. According to Mom and Dad, Thomas had been a problem child for a long time; he was always acting "kind of weird," they said. A few days before I saw him, Thomas's school bus driver said the boy had "flipped out" and refused to get off the bus when they reached the school. A couple of teachers finally had to pull him off the bus and into the building. Thomas's parents had been trying to cope with their son's behavior by themselves for several long months, but the night before our meeting, he had crossed over the line. When Thomas's father came home after work, Thomas walked up to him and, without saying a word, punched him in the face, hard. The event could have been interpreted as typical adolescent conflict gone haywire, but after spending only a few moments with Thomas I realized that there was something a lot more serious going on. Thomas was hearing voices, and those voices told him that his father was out to get him. That's why he struck his dad. He couldn't get off the school bus because he was too frightened. The lights in his homeroom emitted rays that were controlling his mind.

• • •

Sixteen-year-old Miranda was transferred to my care from the emergency room of a nearby hospital. Miranda had gone to the ER by herself after school that afternoon because she wanted to have X rays taken. Miranda was convinced that there were rats living in her stomach, and she wanted proof. When Miranda's mother and father were called, they were horrified but not really surprised. They hadn't heard about the rats before, but they knew very well that Miranda sometimes saw and heard things that weren't there. She thought that the television was talking to her, and she had been communicating regularly with Marilyn Monroe and Elvis Presley; in fact, Marilyn had recently been telling Miranda not to bathe, change her clothes, or go to school. Recently Miranda had started to use drugs and hang out with a bad crowd.

THE REALITY TEST

All children enjoy make-believe. One of the best parts of childhood is being able to pretend, to create fantasies and make up stories. Even imaginary playmates are acceptable under the right circumstances; they're part of the package of being a normal, well-adjusted kid. However, being controlled by rays from lights in the classroom and taking orders from Marilyn Monroe—these are a far cry from the enchanting world of make-believe. They are the symptoms of a extremely serious brain disorder called schizophrenia.

Schizophrenia affects about 1 percent of the country's population. According to the National Institutes of Mental Health, about a million people in this country are being treated for schizophrenia on an outpatient basis. In childhood the gender distributions of schizophrenia is marginally weighted toward boys, but by adolescence the female-male ratio is just about even. Among adults there are as many women diagnosed with schizophrenia as there are men.

Childhood onset schizophrenia—before the age of 12—is extremely uncommon. (The youngest patient I ever saw with diagnosed schizophrenia was a five-year-old girl named Deborah, who thought she had a baby caught in her throat.) The earlier the disorder shows itself, the more severe it will be. It is during adolescence, most commonly at about age 18, that schizophrenia is most often diagnosed. That's when a child is most likely to have his first *break from reality*. The break is usually dramatic, and it can sometimes be quite sudden. I've spoken to parents who describe their child as perfectly normal one day and totally off the wall and out of control the next. (These are the parents who usually show up in the emergency room.) It's more common, however, to see a gradual decline in a child's behavior before the first big break, some early signs that trouble is on the way.

Children later diagnosed with schizophrenia fall into two broad categories. The first group is the childhood asocials; these are the withdrawn kids, the ones whose behavior has always been strange. "He never seemed quite right" and "She was always a little off" are descriptions we commonly hear from the families of these children. There is a great deal of evidence to suggest that those families are correct in their not-very-scientific assessment. Some years ago an experiment was conducted with the home movies of the families of children who were eventually diagnosed with schizophrenia. In each case the families had more than one child, but only one of the kids had schizophrenia. With 100 percent accuracy the mental health professionals who viewed those old home movies could pick out the child with schizophrenia when he was only five or six years old. There was nothing specific about their findings. There was simply the sense that there was something "not quite normal" about the child in question, in the way he interacted with the other kids or with the camera. These youngsters are often aloof, not interested in socializing.

Not all children demonstrate those early signs of more serious disorders to come. The other basic group of people with schizophrenia is made up of kids who seem perfectly "normal" right up until the break. I myself had a childhood friend who belongs in this category. Mike had everything going for him; he was valedictorian of our class, all-city tennis champion, and Mr. Popularity. His life seemed absolutely perfect until the September he went off to an Ivy League college, at age 18. Three weeks later he had his first break with reality; he was convinced that his room was under surveillance and that he was being monitored 24 hours a day by Martians. He was eventually diagnosed with schizophrenia.

THE SYMPTOMS

Schizophrenia in children may be hard to recognize in its early stages. The child suffering from schizophrenia may have *delusions,* fixed beliefs that other people don't have. He may have *hallucinations,* hearing things that others don't hear and seeing things that others don't see. He may have difficulty distinguishing dreams from reality. He'll have vivid and bizarre thoughts and ideas. He'll be moody, exhibit strange behavior, and withdraw from social interactions. Often he'll think that people are out to "get" him. He'll confuse television with real life, and he'll have problems making and keeping friends. To meet the official definition of schizophrenia the symptoms must persist for a period of six months. (If the symptoms have not been present for six months, we make an initial diagnosis of *schizophreniform disorder.* The treatment for this disorder is the same as that followed for schizophrenia.)

The delusions associated with schizophrenia may take many forms. I've talked to a 15-year-old boy who thought that David Letterman was talking directly to him every night; another teenage boy who was so convinced that his parents were trying to poison him that he stopped eating; an 11-year-old girl who thought that her parents had been taken over by aliens; a 16-year-old girl who sat in the TV room of the hospital and watched her favorite soap opera, *Another World,* completely convinced that the show was being performed just for her; and a 17-year-old who thinks that it's *his* face on the dollar bill. I treated an 18-year-old teenage boy who believed the government was beaming poisonous rays down on his head that were making him bald and deaf. One day during a session with him I scratched my head, and he shouted, "I knew it! You're in on it!" It turns out that head-scratching was a sign that I was part of the government's plot against him.

All of these unfortunate children and adolescents have one important characteristic in common: they are living in a world of their own creation, and they believe in it totally, regardless of the efforts of others to bring them back to reality. The voices they hear become as real to them, and as important to them, as anything in the real world. For example, nothing anyone could do or say would persuade Miranda that rats are *not* living in her stomach. We seriously considered giving her the X rays she asked for in the emergency room but decided against it. It would be pointless to show her an X ray of her stomach—without rats, of course. She would simply say that the rats had moved to her knee or that we had given her someone else's X rays by mistake. Reasoning or arguing with kids suffering from these kinds of delusions—saying, for example, "Don't you see? This just doesn't make sense"—is fruitless at best.

Adolescents with schizophrenia at times exhibit bizarre and inappropriate behavior. One 16-year-old I talked to about his delusions (he thought that the FBI was following him) couldn't stop smiling and giggling as we talked. He seemed to be having a wonderful time.

People with schizophrenia have an explanation for everything, no matter how strange. One little girl, just starting the second grade, came to us because she heard voices that wouldn't stop. She used to walk around with her hands covering her ears, crying, "Make them stop! Make the voices stop! I can't stand it anymore." After a few weeks of Haldol the voices finally did stop, and she told us so. "Where did the voices go?" we asked her. "They went shopping," she replied.

There are two kinds of symptoms associated with schizophrenia: positive and negative. The *positive symptoms* (called positive not because they're good but because they involve excessive distortion of normal function) include the delusions and hallucinations, which are relatively easy to identify. A 16-year-old girl who thinks she's a rock star whose video runs on MTV every night at midnight exhibits a positive symptom. The most common of the *negative symptoms* (negative because they involve loss of normal function) is withdrawal, demonstrated in kids who pull back from the world. These kids seem flat and distant; they don't initiate or respond to conversations; they're detached but not really depressed. Positive symptoms are easier to treat than negative symptoms. We can give medication to an adolescent and make his hallucinations and delusions go away. What we can't do quite so easily, even with medication, is motivate kids who sit in their rooms all day and watch television while the world passes them by.

Some of the symptoms we see in examining schizophrenia may seriously endanger a child. One of the saddest cases I've come across was that of a seven-year-old boy who was admitted to our unit with severe burns on his abdomen. The little boy had been burning himself with his father's cigarette lighter. When we asked him why he did it, he said, without blinking an eye, that the voices told him he had to.

THE DIAGNOSIS

It is not particularly difficult to identify a symptom of psychosis, but identifying the symptom is not enough. To make a proper diagnosis—to find out precisely what is wrong with a child or an adolescent—we have to know more about the company that symptom keeps. Symptoms of psychosis may have many causes, including drug abuse and extreme stress. A psychotic symptom is like a headache. It can be caused by an allergy or a simple infection. Or it can be the result of something consid-

erably worse. Kids, especially teenagers, may be guarded or even decep-
tive about their symptoms, and this complicates the process of making a
diagnosis even further.

In the early stages of this disorder, just after the first or perhaps the
second episode, it can still be quite difficult to pinpoint the problem. As
the disease progresses, the symptom picture usually becomes a lot clearer,
and we can be more precise. Bipolar disorder (Chapter 15), major depressive disorder (Chapter 14), pervasive developmental disorder (Chapter 19), and obsessive compulsive disorder (Chapter 8) are just some of
the diseases that must be ruled out. Because of the serious and complicated nature of schizophrenia, it is crucial that a correct diagnosis be
made, ideally by a child and adolescent psychiatrist with experience in
dealing with severely ill youngsters.

In examining a child or an adolescent who shows symptoms associated
with schizophrenia (especially delusions and hallucinations) we have to
rule out some of the other disorders that have similar symptoms. Psychotic symptoms can be categorized as *mood congruent* or *mood incongruent.* Quite simply, the mood congruent symptoms make a little more
sense than the mood incongruent ones, because they correspond to the
mood of the patient. For instance, if the youngster has depression with
psychotic symptoms, his delusions or hallucinations will have a tone that
is consistent with being depressed. For example, he'll think he has a
terminal illness and is going to die. If he hears voices, they'll say something along the lines of, "You're no good. You've never been good. You
never will be good. You must be punished." If an adolescent is manic,
his mood congruent symptoms will echo that mood, telling him that
he's a world-famous sports hero or a millionaire with superpowers. On
the other hand, adolescents with schizophrenia will have symptoms that
are mood incongruent; they have no relationship to their mood or to
reality.

Someone with bipolar disorder will have *flight of ideas* in his speech;
he moves quickly from idea to idea, but there will be a connection
between those ideas, however tenuous. The ideas of someone with
schizophrenia are completely disjointed, characterized by "looseness of
associations." The conversation of someone with schizophrenia in its
most extreme form is incomprehensible; we call it "word salad." Words
just come spilling out, and no one can understand them. More often
than not, the patient isn't even aware that he's not making sense.

People who have schizophrenia are usually frightened and confused. I've examined kids who heard voices and had imaginary companions but weren't afraid of them or impaired by them. One boy I remember in particular, five years old, was able to exercise full control over his invisible friends. They did exactly what he told them to do. Another kid, this one age seven, had voices who helped him with his homework. He said to me: "Oh, I like this voice. He gives me the answers on my test." It's developmentally normal for kids to hear voices and have imaginary play-mates. Neither of these children was diagnosed with schizophrenia.

Adolescents with schizophrenia do *not* have that control over the voices, and they don't like them. They're the kids who say, "The voice is telling me to do something I don't want to do. If I don't do it, it's going to make me do something even worse." They are deluded, but their fear is very real. Often they're afraid to eat, to sleep, or to walk down the street. They have belief systems that are personal and often painful. They're tortured by their symptoms. Children and adolescents with schizophrenia are often in great pain.

A diagnosis of schizophrenia is not easy for a physician to give or for a parent to hear, and no one is inclined to use the term lightly. A correct diagnosis is essential. One of the most significant criteria for a diagnosis of schizophrenia is "deterioration with no return to baseline," which means that even with treatment, the patient's condition is unlikely to get better over time. In fact, as time goes on and the number of episodes increases, a youngster's level of function may become lower. In the case of childhood onset schizophrenia a child will probably fail to reach the expected developmental milestones. Adolescence is a critical period for the acquisition of vocational skills. New learning is difficult for young people with schizophrenia. An adolescent who used to be able to drive a car before the "break" will most likely be able to drive again; however, an adolescent who didn't learn to drive before the illness will find the new task very difficult indeed.

One set of parents I know refused even to say the word *schizophrenia.* They insisted on calling what was wrong with their son "an anxiety disorder" or "a psychotic problem." At 16 their son Rick had his first psychotic episode when he was away at summer camp. He thought that people were out to get him, that his food was being poisoned, that his camp counselor was interested in having sex with him. Rick became increasingly agitated at camp, and his parents were finally summoned to take him home. Rick's diagnosis was schizophrenia, and he started taking Haldol right away. It took his parents nearly a year to use the correct word.

I can't really blame those parents for their reluctance to acknowledge that their boy had schizophrenia. There's no way around the fact that schizophrenia is an extremely distressing diagnosis. Still, for all the pain and disappointment the news may bring, the sooner the diagnosis is made, the sooner the treatment can begin.

THE BRAIN CHEMISTRY

There's no doubt about it: schizophrenia is the result of a malfunction in the brain. However, what causes the brain to malfunction is still a largely unanswered question. According to the most recent studies, there are many underlying influences of schizophrenia, some of them genetic and some environmental.

We know quite a bit about the genetic influences associated with schizophrenia. For example, we know that the first-degree relatives— offspring and siblings—of people with schizophrenia have 10 times greater likelihood of developing the disorder themselves. We also know that the concordance rate of schizophrenia in identical twins is 50 percent, as opposed to 10 percent in fraternal twins. (Among identical twins reared apart from each other in separate families, the concordance rate is still extremely strong.) Other research shows that when a mother with schizophrenia adopted a child who was not genetically predisposed to the disorder, the child did not develop schizophrenia, no matter how crazy or disturbed the adoptive mother was.

Obviously, this disorder has a strong biological component, but just as obviously, schizophrenia is not always passed on from generation to generation. Plenty of cases are sporadic, and many theories have been advanced to explain them. Some say it's caused by a virus. Others say it must be the result of a genetic mutation or a neurodevelopmental delay. Evidence for the genetic mutation theory is supported by the fact that adults with schizophrenia do not reproduce as often as the general population, yet the prevalence of the disorder remains constant.

We have benefited a good deal from knowing something about what the brain of an *adult* with schizophrenia looks like. Brain scans—both

CAT scans and MRIs—of adult patients show that the brain of someone with schizophrenia looks different from that of a "normal" adult. There are several differences, but the most telling are the enlarged cerebral ventricles and the diminished activity of the prefrontal cortex in the brains of people who have schizophrenia and the fact that the overall brain volume of adults with schizophrenia is 8 percent smaller than that of normal adults. There are studies in progress now that will tell us more about the brains of children and adolescents with schizophrenia, but early findings suggest that the same kinds of brain discrepancies will be found.

These days the most widely held theory about what causes the psychotic symptoms of schizophrenia is *too much dopamine* in the brain. One of the facts supporting this case is that drugs that increase the brain's level of dopamine, such as cocaine and amphetamines, may bring on psychosis; certainly they can mimic some of the psychotic symptoms. Another reason to take this theory seriously is the fact that all the medications that reduce the symptoms of schizophrenia have some effect on the dopamine system. As usual, nothing is simple about this area of research, however. The drugs that seem to work best—especially Risperdal—affect other neurotransmitters as well, especially serotonin.

THE TREATMENT

Treatment for schizophrenia should ideally include family support and education, social skills training and other behavioral therapy, vocational rehabilitation, and, eventually, supervised housing, all of which will make the adolescent with schizophrenia and his family more comfortable and better able to cope with this serious illness. But before any of these efforts can be put into motion, the first and most effective line of treatment is *medication*. The only treatment that has any marked effect on the symptoms associated with this disorder is medicine.

The drugs traditionally prescribed for the treatment of schizophrenia are the *neuroleptics,* which are divided into two categories: high-potency neuroleptics, such as Haldol and Prolixin; and low-potency neuroleptics, of which the most commonly prescribed are Thorazine and Mellaril. The medicines are equally effective in the treatment of the symptoms of schizophrenia, but they have different side effects. The low-potency neuroleptics may cause low blood pressure, dry mouth, blurred vision, lethargy, constipation, and weight gain. The side effects of the high-potency neuroleptics sometimes cause "pseudo-Parkinsonism," restlessness, weight gain, and acute dystonic reactions (muscle spasms). Dystonic reactions may be frightening to patients and family members, but they are easily reversed with an injection of the antihistamine Benadryl.

The most disturbing side effect associated with long-term use of neuroleptics is tardive dyskinesia, in which various parts of the body—especially the tongue, the facial muscles, and the arms and legs—wriggle and writhe involuntarily. Tardive dyskinesia ranges from very mild to quite severe. The most serious concern about tardive dyskinesia is that it can be permanent. The other side effects associated with the neuroleptics will disappear quite quickly if the medication is stopped. Tardive dyskinesia doesn't always go away even if the drug is discontinued. The more neuroleptic medication the adolescent takes over time, the greater is his risk of developing tardive dyskinesia. However, if the medication is stopped too soon—because of the patient's noncompliance, for example —the likelihood of a return of the psychotic symptoms increases. This often means that the adolescent will need larger doses for each new episode, which in turn increases his chances of developing tardive dyskinesia.

In the late 1980s a new antipsychotic medicine, clozapine (brand name Clozaril), was introduced for the treatment of schizophrenia. The good news: Clozaril has proven to be very effective, even on particularly resistant, hard-to-treat cases of schizophrenia. There are fewer side effects with Clozaril than with Haldol; and Clozaril is less likely than Haldol to bring on tardive dyskinesia. The bad news is that Clozaril may cause the white blood cell count to drop, sometimes dangerously. Anyone who is taking Clozaril must have his blood monitored closely.

Another promising newcomer in the treatment of schizophrenia is the antipsychotic risperidone (brand name Risperdal). Like Clozaril, Risperdal has fewer side effects than the neuroleptics and seems less likely to cause tardive dyskinesia. Over the next few years there will undoubtedly be many other new entrants in this area of pharmacology.

Children and adolescents diagnosed with schizophrenia respond quite well to low doses of antipsychotic medication, especially if they're treated promptly. One study showed an 80 percent response rate in children between the ages of five and 12. The longer someone diagnosed with schizophrenia goes without treatment, the less likely he is to get rid of all his symptoms when help does finally come. A child who has been sick for six months is probably less likely to respond to treatment than one who has been sick for a month.

One of the most serious problems associated with schizophrenia has to do with the fact that people being treated for the disorder have a tendency to discontinue their medication. For example, a patient who hears voices will take his medicine, the voices will go away, and he'll decide that he feels fine. If he feels fine, then why, he wonders, should he bother to take his medicine anymore? So he goes off the medicine, and the voices come back.

Going on and off the medication makes the problem even worse than it already is. Studies show that this disease progresses with each psychotic episode. The more often the medication is discontinued, the less effective it is the next time it's taken. There's an 80 percent response rate in people with schizophrenia who are given medication after their first break. By the time patients have reached the fourth or fifth episode, the response rate drops to about 70 percent. With ensuing episodes, the response continues to drop. The higher the number of episodes, the worse a patient feels and the less effective the treatment becomes.

For best results someone diagnosed with schizophrenia should take his medicine without interruption. (The best way for parents to encourage their youngsters to keep taking their medication is to believe wholeheartedly, and without ambivalence, that it is the right thing to do.) Sticking with medication has become a lot easier recently, since some neuroleptics, including Haldol, now come in injectable form. One injection is good for 30 days. Unfortunately, that means that side effects last for 30 days too, so great care has to be taken with dosages. There is a good chance that people diagnosed with schizophrenia will have to take medication for the rest of their lives. Since the average age of onset of schizophrenia is about 18, that could mean 60 or more years of medication—a daunting prospect to even the most stalwart of parents. There's all the more reason, then, for families to be aware and informed about what the medication can and cannot do and what the side effects are likely to be and to make sure that their child's progress is closely monitored. An essential component of the treatment of schizophrenia is management. In recent years there have been great advances in the long-term management of this disorder, which usually includes rehabilitation and occupational therapy.

The prognosis for childhood onset schizophrenia has not been well studied, but we know something about the outlook for adults and adolescents. We know, for instance, that the earlier the onset of the disorder is, the poorer the prognosis will be. In some rare cases there is full remission, but "deterioration with no return to baseline" is the more likely prospect. What's more, most people with schizophrenia are not going to be high achievers after the disorder has struck, not even the ones who started out as valedictorians of their class. The typical person with schizophrenia is unlikely to hold a significant job or to maintain a marriage or any other successful long-term relationship. Women with schizophrenia have been more likely than men to get married and have children, but there is no question that a severe relapsing disorder impairs a person's ability to interact with others. Not surprisingly perhaps, some 25 to 50 percent of all people with schizophrenia will abuse drugs or alcohol, and there is a very high suicide rate attached to the disease, the highest of all the psychiatric disorders. According to recent studies, 35 percent of all people diagnosed with schizophrenia will attempt or will seriously consider suicide at some time. About 15 percent of all people with schizophrenia will commit suicide.

PARENTING AND SCHIZOPHRENIA

The parents of Deborah, the five-year-old girl who thought she had a baby living in her throat, thought at first that their daughter's illness was their fault. They had just had a second child, and they were sure that the new baby was upsetting their older daughter and making her feel unloved. "She wasn't ready to share the limelight. I'm sure she'll be okay if we just pay more attention to her," Deborah's mother said.

Geoffrey's parents also blamed themselves for what happened to their son. Geoffrey, a seemingly healthy, happy, overachieving young man, went off to Harvard in September. His goal: a bachelor of arts degree and then law school. By November of his freshman year he was back home with his parents, being treated for schizophrenia. "I'm sure it's because we pushed him too hard," his father told me. "He was doing fine."

"And he would have stayed fine if he'd gone to City College," his mother added. "Why did we make him go to a high-pressure university like Harvard?"

So many parents reproach themselves for things they could have done and should have done. "I should have seen this coming," they'll say. "Remember how quiet he was, even back in third grade? I should have known something was wrong. If I'd done something about it then, this never would have happened."

It's not hard to understand why Deborah's and Geoffrey's parents and just about all other parents of children with schizophrenia feel the way they do. Schizophrenia has no satisfactory explanation and a terrible prognosis, so taking the blame can be a comfort to many parents. "If it's our fault, then maybe we can fix it," the thinking goes. It's often easier to accept the blame than it is to accept the truth.

The truth, whether parents like it or not, is that it's *not* their fault their child has schizophrenia. It's nobody's fault. Having a new baby brother or matriculating at Harvard can create stress in a child or an adolescent, true, but it does not bring about a psychotic episode. Little kids have baby brothers every day and teenagers go away to college every September, and most of them get through it just fine. They don't always love or even welcome the changes in their lives. Some are even made uncomfortable by them. But discomfort is a long long way from psychosis.

It's not usually necessary to urge parents to get prompt treatment for children who have the symptoms of schizophrenia. Mothers and fathers can and often do ignore the symptoms of other brain disorders, or at least they take their time having the child looked at, but there's a certain urgency associated with schizophrenia that simply will not be ignored. When a child has a break from reality, most parents will head straight for an emergency room, and from there they're sent to a child and adolescent psychiatrist. Most of the children with schizophrenia I see are sent not by a pediatrician but from a hospital emergency room.

Of course, there are exceptions. One girl I treated had her first break at age 16, almost exactly a year before her parents brought her to see me. They had been in family therapy for most of that year, but it didn't seem to help. She continued to have paranoid delusions, mostly about people following her and thinking bad thoughts about her. When she was driving her car one day, she thought that a young man who pulled up next to her at a traffic light was planning to kill her.

I've come across parents who refused to be involved with their children with schizophrenia or even to see them after they got sick. One woman wouldn't allow her son in the house after a few particularly bizarre outbursts, and eventually she refused to see him at all. His father visits him every Sunday without his wife.

Having a sick child is never easy. When that child is diagnosed with schizophrenia, it is incredibly difficult for parents. From the moment a child is born, parents have hopes and dreams and plans for that child. In some ways they think they'd like to keep their kids small and helpless forever, but not really, of course. All parents look forward to the day that their kids become independent. They want their kids to go to college, get a job, get married, have kids, move away but not too far. They look forward to having an adult relationship with their child.

When a child has schizophrenia, those hopes and dreams will probably not be realized. A child with schizophrenia will in all likelihood not become an independent adult, capable of having an adult relationship with his parents. Even when he reaches maturity, he'll depend on his parents for many of his needs. He probably won't get a good job, marry, or have his own home. Coming to grips with these cold, hard facts is a truly heart-wrenching experience for parents. Some look for and find solace in therapy or in support groups. One of the most widely respected is the National Association for the Mentally Ill. NAMI offers a wide range of resources that have proved invaluable to parents of children and adolescents with schizophrenia.

It's natural and healthy for parents to grieve over their loss, because that's what this is. One of my colleagues describes it as "mourning the loss of what you expected from your child." After that mourning period is over, parents can get on with the new relationship they must forge with their child. The new relationship is not what Mom and Dad had in mind when the new baby was born, to be sure, but any parent-child relationship has enormous satisfactions.

Here's how one mother described her feelings about her son, now in his late twenties, who had been diagnosed with schizophrenia nearly ten years earlier. "For a long time I walked around in pain. It was as if my old son had died, and I was grieving for him. His personality and his sense of humor just weren't there anymore. His 'essence' was missing. But then I realized I had a new, different son in his place, and I started to feel better. I miss my old son—I'll probably always miss him—but I love the new one too, very much."

CHAPTER 17

Eating Disorders

Justine, 15, was warm, friendly, smart, and polite—one of the pleasantest young people I've ever met. The first time I saw her, Justine weighed 90 pounds. She was almost a skeleton, so thin that her collarbone and even the bone on her forehead stuck out. Her parents said they were almost afraid to touch her. A year earlier Justine's weight was 130, which was perfectly fine for her five-foot, five-inch frame. But then she started starving herself. She ate practically nothing, and the more her parents pleaded with her or scolded her or threatened her with punishment, the more determined she became to avoid even a scrap of food. She eventually got so weak that her parents brought her to our emergency room. Her blood pressure and pulse were alarmingly low, and she had fine white hair, just like a newborn baby's, growing on her arms and back.

• • •

By the time she reached her seventeenth birthday, Trudy—another lovely, personable girl—was bingeing and purging for nearly six hours a day. That was three years ago. Today, at 20, she's down to only a half-hour a day and well on her way to recovery. Still, she's preoccupied with taking in and getting rid of large quantities of food. Trudy says that when she walks into her house, she feels as if she's walking into a giant refrigerator. When she opens the front door, all she can think about is food, food, food.

FEAR OF FATNESS

The two most common eating disorders among adolescents, nearly all of them girls, are anorexia nervosa and bulimia nervosa. The peak age of onset for anorexia is 14, during the transition between childhood and adolescence. Bulimia's age of onset is 19, so it is associated with the transition from adolescence to young adulthood. Because the two eating disorders are so different, I'll take them one at a time.

ANOREXIA NERVOSA

Anorexia nervosa—commonly referred to as anorexia—is, quite simply, self-imposed starvation. The girl who is officially diagnosed with anorexia —more than 90 percent of these patients are female—will weigh at least 15 percent less than she should, according to the growth charts. However, the true hallmark of anorexia is *body image distortion;* no matter how much weight they lose, these girls still see themselves as fat, and being fat is what they fear most. Even 90-pound Justine, with the protruding forehead and clavicles, thought she looked fat. "Look how the fat just hangs off my arms," she'd say to her mother. About 1 percent of the school population will be diagnosed with anorexia, and some studies show that the number is growing. In the last 35 years the incidence of anorexia has increased some 30 percent every five years.

As I already said, the age of onset for anorexia is around 14, but it may take as long as a year after the symptoms begin for parents and their child to make their way to a child and adolescent psychiatrist's office. Often the parents will try to work with a child themselves for a while, assuming that a refusal to eat is just part of their daughter's rebellious teens. A neighbor, a minister, or a family friend might get involved before the pediatrician is consulted. When parents do finally get to a pediatrician's office, most doctors are quick to diagnose anorexia and refer these children to a child and adolescent psychiatrist.

By the time we see these girls, there are nearly always some secondary physical symptoms to deal with, among them low blood pressure, low pulse, and dizziness when they stand up. Their estrogen, progesterone, and cortisol levels will probably be abnormal. They will have stopped having menstrual periods. They may have baby-fine white hair on their arms, back, and neck. In all likelihood they will be anxious about their sexuality. Some girls with anorexia have boyfriends, but they are almost never sexually active. These girls are often afraid of sex and sometimes fearful of growing up. They are not ready for parties or the drugs, alcohol, and sex that are often to be found there. Many of these girls want to stay prepubescent, childlike. The typical youngster with anorexia is the good little girl who studies hard and tries her best to please everyone.

Adolescents with anorexia will be obsessive in their thoughts, always thinking, "I can't believe how much I ate! Look how fat I am," and compulsive in their actions, incorporating food-related rituals that annoy and exasperate their friends and family. They cut their food into little slices and push them around the plate for a half-hour, never actually eating anything. They hide food in their rooms, not to eat it but just to make sure it's available. When they prepare their own meals, they make a huge, time-consuming production out of even the smallest concoction. They know everything there is to know about calories and weight reduction. Girls with anorexia have very poor self-esteem. Because their interests are so restricted—they're focused entirely on food—they usually don't have many close friends.

A diagnosis of anorexia requires a comprehensive history, including an examination of the course of the symptoms and observation of the family. In taking the history we get full details from these girls on their food intake, their eating behaviors, and their thoughts about and attitudes toward food. A thorough physical examination by a pediatrician or family practitioner, including a complete blood workup and an electrocardiogram, are essential; kids with anorexia may have medical complications that have to be addressed immediately.

THE BRAIN CHEMISTRY Parents have taken a lot of heat over anorexia—people blame mothers and fathers for their child's eating disorders—but it is undeserved. There is no scientific evidence that faulty parenting or dysfunctional families cause anorexia, or bulimia either. Those theories tossed around about how forcing children to clean their plates or not allowing them to have a piece of candy between meals when they were toddlers leads to eating disorders later have no basis in fact.

The widely believed theory that a girl starves herself because she has a fear of physical and emotional maturity or that she's rebelling against her parents is still hotly debated.

Family and twin studies offer evidence to support a genetic component attached to anorexia. The families of girls with anorexia seem to have a higher than average incidence of weight problems, physical illness, depression, and alcoholism.

One biological theory that needs further study suggests that adolescents with anorexia have a physiological response to dieting that is different from that of the rest of the world. Most people feel discomfort when their calories are restricted; girls with anorexia are different. Weight loss makes them feel successful, disciplined; they aren't sensitive to the usual discomfort associated with dieting. As the girls begin to starve, there is a release of opioids (brain chemicals that long-distance runners also produce), which give them a "high." Restricting calorie intake brings genuine pleasure, and a vicious circle has begun.

THE TREATMENT In some ways the biggest problem associated with treating adolescents with anorexia is that *adolescents with anorexia don't want treatment.* They scream and cry and curse their parents for bringing them to psychiatrists' offices, accusing them of not trusting and not loving them. Then they deny having a problem at all. (Their parents see them as sick, but they feel wonderful, because they're thin!) Finally, they admit they have a problem but promise they'll eat if they can just leave the hospital and go home. The tears, denial, and recrimination are all perfectly understandable, of course. These girls know that getting "better" means putting on weight, and that's precisely what they don't want.

Even so, it is essential that these girls get the treatment they need. Anorexia is a very serious disorder. If these girls don't get better, they may die. Recent studies say that anywhere from 5 to 7 percent of all children with anorexia will die within 10 years. With treatment, about 70 percent will eventually have full medical, social, and psychiatric recovery. The sooner the disorder is treated, the more favorable the prognosis will be.

The best treatment for anorexia is cognitive behavioral therapy, often in combination with medication and family counseling. After an initial examination, including a thorough physical, children with anorexia will need at least weekly sessions with a psychiatrist; many will need to come in twice a week. They also need weekly weigh-ins and other medical follow-ups. In the past, when dysfunctional families were thought to be the cause of eating disorders, family therapy alone often was the treatment of choice. Today we rely largely on cognitive behavioral therapy, which concentrates on changing the girl's distorted perceptions about food and decreasing the significance of thinness in determining her self-worth. Family counseling can be very useful in helping parents and other close family members cope with a sick child.

Not all child and adolescent psychiatrists have experience with anorexia, and others aren't really comfortable treating these kids. Parents shouldn't be shy about getting answers to some important questions here, since finding the right physician is critical. "Do you treat kids with anorexia?" is the best place to start. "Do you believe in outpatient management?" "Do you use medication?" and "May I talk to you and be involved in the treatment?" are other questions to which a parent should receive an unqualified yes.

It's not necessary to find an eating disorders specialist for the child with anorexia or to check her into an eating disorders clinic, although there are many good ones out there. It is necessary to find a good psychiatrist who is interested in the disorder and can do the therapy, prescribe medication, and follow the child for at least a year and a half. That's about how long the outpatient therapy for anorexia will take, though severe cases will take longer, sometimes much longer. The worst case I've encountered took six years of treatment before the girl was completely well.

Many children being treated for anorexia will take some sort of medication, but the role of medicine is limited with this disorder. Antidepressants, specifically the SSRIs (selective serotonin reuptake inhibitors), such as Prozac, Zoloft, and Paxil, may help with the obsessive-compulsive symptoms and the depression that often accompany anorexia. Prozac has been effective in helping these girls maintain their weight gain and normalize their eating habits. The medicine needs to be taken for at least a year. Appetite stimulants are sometimes recommended; the one most often prescribed is Periactin, an antihistamine that has been helpful in increasing weight and maintaining weight gain. The MAOIs (monamine oxidase inhibitors), especially Nardil, have also helped girls put on weight.

Many of these girls hate taking pills, and not for the usual reason. They panic because they think the coating has too many calories. Others are terrified that the pills will make them eat, so I tell them—quite truthfully—that there is no pill that makes a person eat. "I wish there were a medicine that would make you eat, but there isn't," I say. "All this pill will do is help you not to worry so much about what you *do* eat."

When the medication and therapy described above don't work, when there is no increase in weight and no improvement in the child's overall health, hospitalization may be necessary. Hospital care offers a multidisciplinary approach to the disorder, involving dietitians, nurses, and psychologists as well as psychiatrists. Inpatient treatment can be done in any adolescent psychiatric unit or in special eating disorder units that combine both pediatric care and child and adolescent psychiatry.

BULIMIA

The young women who have bulimia (again, some 90 percent of the patients are female) don't starve themselves; they *binge,* they *purge,* they try to *fast,* and they have strange attitudes about food. Like girls with anorexia, they're afraid of getting fat, but they don't have a distorted body image. They don't see themselves as fatter than they are. They're afraid of food, but they can't help taking in a huge amount of it— anywhere from 3,000 to 20,000 calories per binge. I've talked to girls who would eat several loaves of bread and boxes of cereal at home and then go from one fast food restaurant to another, consuming an enormous amount of food in a few hours. The frequency of the binges of someone with bulimia will vary greatly, from twice a week to several times a day. A binge may last from several minutes to several hours. Young women with bulimia describe having a lack of control during the binges; some describe it as an altered state of consciousness. Unlike girls with anorexia—who are preoccupied with their success at restricting their calorie intake—young people with bulimia are not very good at dieting. They often diet, but restricting calories makes them uncomfortable and usually leads to bingeing.

After bingeing usually comes purging (some people with bulimia binge but don't purge), by vomiting or using laxatives—as many as 20 a day

—or both. Many use diuretics or diet pills. Some exercise for hours at a time. Not surprisingly, there are medical complications associated with bingeing and purging, among them low blood pressure, dehydration, low potassium and other metabolic problems, cavities, constipation, swollen cheek glands, and hormonal changes. The physical signs of bulimia are frequently pointed out by other health care professionals, especially dentists, who notice the enamel wear on a young woman's teeth as a result of the acid in the vomitus.

It's not difficult to spot a girl who has anorexia, no matter how baggy her clothes are, but people with bulimia can look completely normal. In fact, most are of normal weight or even a little heavier. Young people with bulimia are generally older than girls with anorexia too; the peak age of onset of bulimia is 19 years. The incidence of bulimia is estimated at 2 percent of the population, but some studies show that 3 to 5 percent of all college-age girls have this disorder.

Many people with bulimia have a history of anorexia or obesity. There is also a high co-occurrence with major depressive disorder, generalized anxiety disorder, social phobia, and panic disorder. Alcohol and substance abuse are also common.

THE BRAIN CHEMISTRY There is almost certainly a genetic component attached to this disorder. Twin studies of bulimia show a higher rate in identical twins than in fraternal twins, and family studies tell us that the relatives of people with bulimia have a higher incidence of the disorder than the relatives of people who don't have it. Other evidence suggests that there is a neurochemical component to bulimia, specifically a decrease in the manufacture of serotonin and a hypersensitivity to changes in serotonin levels.

THE TREATMENT Unlike kids with anorexia, young women who have bulimia will ask for treatment. The distress and dysfunction associated with this disorder are such that these girls with bulimia *want* to get better. Untreated, people with bulimia will continue to get worse over time. Their binges begin to get more and more extreme, and their distress grows. A small but significant percentage of all young people whose bulimia is left untreated will die within five years; many of them will commit suicide. With treatment about 70 percent will have a full recovery.

Again, the treatment is cognitive behavioral therapy combined with medicine. We usually recommend individual therapy with a cognitive behavioral approach. This treatment, which requires a minimum of six months, has four phases. In the first phase, we examine the problem with the girl's active participation, asking her to monitor her food intake and record her eating habits, especially binges and purging. Next we focus on changing her eating behavior, limiting food intake to three meals a day and two snacks. In the next phase we work on correcting her distorted thoughts and attitudes about calories, weight, and body image. And finally we move to relapse-prevention, in which we simulate high-risk situations and encourage the girl to practice her new behavior. Interpersonal psychotherapy (IPT), discussed in Chapter 14, has also been useful in the treatment of young women with bulimia. Group therapy can also be very helpful for these girls; discussing their eating behaviors openly tends to make them feel less isolated. College students often do well in group cognitive behavioral therapy.

Meanwhile, antidepressant medication, such as Tofranil, Desyrel, and Prozac, will help to cut down the frequency of the bingeing and vomiting cycles and alleviate the underlying depression. Tofranil may cause dry mouth and sedation, and it has effects on the heart that make cardiac monitoring necessary. The most common side effect of Desyrel is sedation, and because it may also cause nausea and vomiting, the medicine should be taken with meals. Prozac and the other SSRIs have minimal side effects. For best results, medication for bulimia should be taken for six months to a year.

PARENTING AND EATING DISORDERS

Family dinners are often the setting for conflict and disagreement in any household. It is a rare family indeed that doesn't feature a tantrum, a blowup, or some other scene at the dinner table once in a while. When there is a child in the house who has an eating disorder, every meal is a potential nightmare.

"We just sit there, day after day, watching her starve herself to death, and it's killing all of us," one desperate mother told me. "I know that the minute we go upstairs she's going to run into the downstairs bathroom and start vomiting, and there's nothing we can do about it," said another. "My husband and I are desperate."

Parents faced with their child's eating disorders *do* become desperate. They also become depressed, angry, and worried. Having a child with anorexia or bulimia has a tremendous impact on the entire family. Parents feel frustrated and helpless because they can't control their children and make them well. After all, giving a child nourishment is one of a parent's fundamental responsibilities. Normal siblings may become jealous and angry because, the way they see it, their parents are being tricked and manipulated. "I think you should just *make* her eat," they might say. "She always gets her way. She's just doing this so you'll pay attention to her."

The parents of Susannah, a 17-year-old girl who was successfully treated for an eating disorder, say now that in some ways the hardest thing about the disorder was admitting that they couldn't fix what was wrong with their daughter. For nearly a year they did everything they could to persuade Susannah to eat, but she was obviously getting worse. They finally took her to a child and adolescent psychiatrist who specializes in treating anorexia and bulimia.

"The hardest thing for us was accepting the fact that we couldn't do it alone, that we needed someone to help us. We really thought we could handle Susannah's problem ourselves. Once we did put her and ourselves into the hands of a professional, things really did get better, not just for her but for the rest of the family too. It was such a relief to talk to someone who didn't blame us for what our child was going through and who didn't hold it against us when we lost our tempers with her. And because he kind of 'took charge' of Susannah, he freed us up to spend more time thinking about our other kids. In that year before we took Susannah to see the psychiatrist, there were times we almost forgot we *had* other children. But the best thing about it is that Susannah got better. He gave us our daughter back."

CHAPTER 18

Conduct Disorder

Douglas, 12 years old, was brought into the hospital by his parents after he tried to choke his five-year-old brother. It wasn't the first time Douglas had done something terrible at home. Over the three or four years before we saw him for the first time, Douglas had set several fires. Quite recently he had soaked a whole package of firecrackers in gasoline and had lit them, basically destroying half of his family's back-yard. Douglas was odd and socially awkward, and his classmates never let him forget it. They teased him mercilessly and refused to include him in their activities. In the last year Douglas had been going through some tremendous mood swings, including lengthy periods of depression. I don't think I've ever met anyone of Douglas's age who was so socially inept.

• • •

Jared was 10 years old and in fifth grade when he first came to see me, but he had been having behavior problems ever since nursery school. At three years old he was already a "handful," his parents said, and as the years went by, Jared's behavior got worse. At school he routinely stole from his classmates. In third grade he beat up a child because the boy had "squealed" on Jared, telling the teacher that Jared cheated on his math test. He took the pet turtle from science class, threw it into boiling water, and watched as the turtle died. Jared was an unusually attractive boy, with blonde hair, blue eyes, and a dimple. He was even a little charming, despite his grisly exploits. As he told me about the things he had done, he showed no remorse whatsoever.

THE "BAD SEED"

It's the stuff of fiction: children who set fire to the living room curtains, boil their turtles, throw their baby brothers down the stairs. But it can also be fact, if a child has conduct disorder. Children with conduct disorder—CD—are physically and verbally aggressive. They routinely lie, steal, set fires, and torture animals. When they reach adolescence, they may rape and otherwise physically abuse people and terrorize the community. It's no wonder that kids with CD are featured so prominently and so often in fiction. They seem too bad to be true.

THE SYMPTOMS

All children misbehave some of the time. Children and adolescents with CD misbehave a lot of the time, in fairly serious ways. They have temper tantrums and use bad language. They do things that violate the rights of others, such as stealing or defacing property or creating a nuisance. They're physically aggressive and may even be sex offenders. They have symptoms that fall into four categories: aggression toward people and animals; destruction of property; deceitfulness and theft; and serious violation of society's rules. It is estimated that 6 percent of all children have CD, with a male-female ratio of about 4 to 1.

There are two types of CD: early-onset CD, which occurs before the age of 10 and is the most common type; and late-onset CD, which comes after age 10. The age of onset for CD is significant; there's a tremendous difference between someone who first shows the symptoms of CD at age six and someone who does so at age 15. The earlier the onset of CD is, the worse the prognosis is.

CD may show up in the very young. Children as young as three may behave aggressively, fighting with their siblings and their peers. I've seen five-year-olds who become sexually aggressive. They're too young for rape, of course. Small children are more inclined to take off all their clothes and play with their genitals or to try to touch their peers. The more violent behavior associated with CD, such as animal torture and attacks on people, occurs during the elementary school years. Rape and the other serious assaults come later, in the teenage years.

Another significant factor associated with CD is the IQ of the child. A child with CD whose IQ is 70 presents a very different picture from one with an IQ of 125. On the one hand, the child with the higher IQ will be easier to work with when it comes to treatment; on the other, he's probably more imaginative and creative in acting out his antisocial behavior to begin with. He may also be more wily in evading detection.

Many children with CD have learning disabilities and lower-than-average verbal skills. Although children with CD often seem tough and fearless, the very embodiment of the word *bravado,* they usually have very poor self-esteem. The younger children are impatient and easily frustrated, given to frequent outbursts of temper. Teenagers with CD tend to be more reckless and accident-prone.

A few years ago there was a story in the New York newspapers about a gang of girls in their early teens who were roaming the streets of Manhattan's Upper West Side, sticking unsuspecting passersby in their backsides with pins. It didn't take long for the girls to be apprehended, and when police questioned them, their ringleader explained their behavior in a way that has stayed with me ever since: "We thought it would be fun, and it was."

The leader of that girls' gang vividly illustrates one of CD's most dramatic symptoms. Children with conduct disorder do not seem to experience remorse. Quite the contrary: they enjoy their antisocial behavior and often welcome the opportunity to tell people what they've been up to. Listening to some of their stories can be positively bloodcurdling. I'll never forget the time a cherubic six-year-old told me in gruesome detail what he did to the gerbil the teacher brought to his classroom. Just about the only time these children are in any real distress is when they've been caught and are about to be punished; they show remorse to lessen the punishment. Then they become angry and upset at the system for not letting them do exactly what they want.

THE DIAGNOSIS

In making the diagnosis of CD we talk to the child, of course, but we also interview parents and teachers and look closely at school records. We take a comprehensive history, paying special attention to the youngster's development and his aggressive behavior, and examine the family history for conduct problems and criminal infractions. Before an official diagnosis of CD can be made, the symptoms of CD must be persistent—children have to have several symptoms for a period of at least one year and at least one symptom for the past six months—and the symptoms must exist in more than one setting. (We have to satisfy ourselves that the symptoms are not just reactions to a bad situation.) Finally, we look for other disorders, especially attention deficit hyperactivity disorder, separation anxiety disorder, and major depressive disorder, all of which are likely to co-exist with CD. At least 50 percent of all kids with CD also have ADHD.

THE BRAIN CHEMISTRY

Conduct disorder has not been widely studied, but the information that has been gathered indicates that certain children have a genetic vulnerability to this disorder. When that vulnerability is combined with certain high-risk environmental factors, such as poverty, parental neglect, marital discord, parental illness, parental alcoholism, and having a parent with antisocial personality disorder—the adult version of CD—the child's chances of having the disorder are even greater.

The role of genetics in CD is less than crystal-clear. We do know that a vulnerability to the disorder is inherited. The chances that a child will have CD increase if one parent has it and go up even more if both parents have it. (If either of the parents abuses drugs or alcohol as well, the chances of CD in a child are greater still.) Twin studies have shown that if one twin has CD, the other is more likely also to have it if he or she is an identical twin rather than a fraternal twin. Adoption studies show that there is an increased risk for a child to have CD if *both* his adoptive and his biological parents have this disorder, further supporting the nature-plus-nurture "double whammy" theory.

Neuropsychological testing has shown that children and adolescents with CD seem to have an impairment in the frontal lobe of the brain, the area that affects their ability to plan, to avoid harm, and to learn from negative consequences. Another study demonstrates that the serotonin levels in the brains of children and adolescents with CD were even lower than the serotonin levels in the brains of children and adolescents with obsessive compulsive disorder.

THE TREATMENT

Conduct disorder is by far the most difficult disorder to treat in all of child and adolescent psychiatry. There is no one drug of choice for all the symptoms of CD and no one therapy that has an appreciable effect except in rare cases. When treating children with conduct disorder I, like every other child and adolescent psychiatrist, hope that in addition to the CD there is another disorder that we *can* treat. If CD is co-morbid with another disorder, we treat the other disorder first; if there is evidence of ADHD, for instance (and about half the time there is), we'll prescribe Ritalin or sometimes Cylert. Dexedrine works well too, but we've found that kids with CD are more likely to *sell* their Dexedrine than to take it as prescribed. Once the symptoms of the other disorder have subsided, we're often faced with a very different child. With luck the "new" child will be more responsive to medication or behavioral therapy or both.

If the child with CD does not have ADHD, we'll probably give him Ritalin anyway, since Ritalin is effective in decreasing negative behavior (specifically aggression toward teachers and other kids) in children with CD. If Ritalin is not effective and the child is very aggressive, we may give him a trial of Lithium, which is used to reduce aggressive behavior in adult males. Also prescribed in the treatment of bipolar disorder in children and adolescents, Lithium alleviates the aggressive explosiveness that kids with CD sometimes demonstrate. (Because of the possible effect that Lithium may have on the thyroid, a youngster taking the medication will require blood monitoring.) If Lithium doesn't work, we usually try Depakote, another medication used for bipolar disorder.

In addition to medication we recommend therapy for the child, specifically a cognitive behavioral approach that helps the child learn new ways to resolve conflict. This is a very active process, employing a lot of role playing and rehearsal. A child is taken through simulated or real events that involve conflict and encouraged to forget his usual responses —aggression and other forms of antisocial behavior—and learn new, nonviolent, socially appropriate ways to react to these events. This form of behavior modification basically gives the child a whole new way to behave and to respond to conflict of any kind. Because of its strong cognitive component (that is, it requires thinking), the program usually works better with adolescents than with young children.

When the diagnosis of a child with CD is in question or when it becomes necessary to get immediate control of a very aggressive child or adolescent, hospitalization will probably be called for. An out-of-home setting provides more intensive supervision and structure than anything that can be done while the child is living at home. Once the child has made significant progress, and provided his parents are cooperative, treatment can be continued on an outpatient basis.

Early detection and treatment are vital here. Every day care center in America should be on the lookout for obviously aggressive and out-of-control three-year-olds. Nothing is to be gained by watching and waiting to see if these kids will outgrow this behavior by the time they're four or five or 10. By then their behavior will be even more sociopathic; also, they'll do badly in school and won't have any friends. Even more important, they'll probably have parents who can hardly bear to be around them. If there is any chance of turning these kids around, it must be done in the early stages of the disease, before they've "progressed" from lying and shoplifting to assault and rape. Left untreated, these kids are at high risk for substance abuse, imprisonment, and death by unnatural causes.

PARENTING AND CD

In my practice I meet a lot of unhappy, angry, embarrassed, frustrated, helpless, hopeless, and overwhelmed parents. The ones who would take first prize in all categories were the mother and father of Edward, an 13-year-old boy being treated for conduct disorder. The parents adopted Edward at birth, and they had a few good years with their son, they said. By the age of three, however, Edward was already a terror. The parents, who are conscientious to a fault, looked for help right away, and over the years they had tried everything, including trials of medication, private schools, and family therapy. Still, a week doesn't go by without an alarmed phone call from Edward's teacher, saying that he beat up one of the other kids. The neighbors call too, to report that Edward stole the barbecue grill or urinated on the front lawn. Edward's parents are at their wits' end. They don't know what to do next.

I'd like to say that I was able to give them an easy solution to their problem, but that wouldn't be true. Treating conduct disorder, which Edward clearly had, is never easy. We treated Edward with Ritalin, and we started him in therapy; at 13 the child was a good candidate for the cognitive behavioral approach. We also added yet another element of this "team" approach to the treatment of CD: parent training, in which a therapist works with parents to help them understand the disorder and gives them strategies for making the other parts of the treatment more effective. Normally this means asking parents to learn how to discourage their child's negative behavior—temper outbursts, destructiveness, refusal to follow the rules, and so on—and to reward desirable, socially acceptable behavior. Punishments are nonviolent, of course, and usually involve the loss of privileges, such as watching television or playing outside. Rewards are stars and check marks that can be traded in for something a youngster particularly values. Parents must monitor their child's behavior regularly and stand ready to intervene promptly with either positive or negative reinforcement.

This is not as easy as it might sound. Kids with conduct disorder are *tough,* and parents should be prepared for a labor-intensive, time-consuming treatment. For these mothers and fathers there's no such thing as being "off duty." Frequently these children, when faced with new rules and regulations, become even more defiant, and that makes the training program even more challenging for even the most motivated, devoted parents. And the changes usually come a lot more slowly than anyone would like. In my experience the program takes at least a year.

CHAPTER 19

Pervasive Developmental Disorder and Autism

Terry, 11 years old now and getting along quite well, has had developmental problems ever since he was two. He grunted and pointed, but he didn't speak, and his mother wasn't sure he understood what was being said to him. For a while his parents thought he was deaf, but they had him tested and discovered that his hearing was fine. He slept badly from the beginning too, and his behavior was always a little off. There were a lot of temper tantrums. When Terry wanted something, he couldn't express himself, so he'd throw things. He wasn't any good at throwing, either, even when he got older. His coordination was terrible. He couldn't run or throw a ball like the other kids. When he did eventually speak, he could barely be understood. At 11, Terry has been seeing various specialists for nearly nine years.

• • •

Clara, age three and a half, is a spectacularly beautiful little girl—big blue eyes, blonde hair, pink cheeks. The day I met her, her mother had dressed her up like a little doll. Clara didn't speak or make eye contact. According to her parents, she never did. She screamed, though. If she didn't get what she wanted right away, she would let loose the most bone-chilling shrieks, sometimes for hours at a time. Clara didn't interact with me the way a typical three- or four-year-old usually does. There was no connection between us. She wouldn't play. She didn't respond to, "Can you say hello?" or "Please pick up the doll." When I asked her to wave bye-bye, she stared right through me. I offered her a piece of candy, but she wasn't interested. Her parents say that all Clara will eat, literally, is food from McDonalds—a hamburger for breakfast, french fries for lunch, and another burger for dinner. Every morning they drive to the golden arches for Clara's daily rations.

DEVELOPMENTAL DELAYS

Most parents know a little something about the milestones of child development—when a child should walk, talk, use the toilet, and so forth. Many parents take these things for granted, not even realizing how fortunate they are to have children who are right where they should be, just like clockwork. Terry's and Clara's parents don't have the luxury of such thoughts. Their children have pervasive developmental disorder, PDD. Terry's case is relatively mild; today he is quite high-functioning, and with continued work he will probably go to college and maybe even get married. Clara's prospects are not so bright. Clara has autism, the most severe form of PDD. With treatment and a lot of hard work she may well be able to hold a job of some sort, but it's unlikely that she'll ever be independent or have a family of her own.

THE SYMPTOMS

Regardless of the severity of the disorder, all kids with PDD have serious impairments in several areas of development, especially language and communications skills and social interactions. Sometimes physical coordination will be impaired and the child will exhibit strange behavior. The development may be uneven—a child will be strong in one area and very weak in another—but overall these kids are weak in many spheres of development. That's what makes this disorder *pervasive*. Reports indicate that approximately 1 percent of the population has PDD; most people with PDD are diagnosed after the age of three.

Autism is a very rare disorder (it occurs about five times in every 10,000 live births, with a boy-girl ratio of 4 to 1) but widely studied. Some say that there are more people doing research on autism than there are people who *have* the disorder. People, not just psychiatrists and medical researchers, seem to be fascinated by this bizarre, inexplicable disease. Television shows and movies are filled with characters who have autism: a doctor's son on *St. Elsewhere,* a victim on *Law and Order,* and, of course, the movie *Rain Man.* Most of them don't exactly conform to the facts of the disease, but the true symptoms of autism don't always make for good theater.

Autism is a congenital disorder—that is, a child is born with it—characterized by severe impairment in the areas related to communication, social interaction, and the ability to use play and abstract thinking. The essence of autism is a lack of interest in people and a failure to appreciate and make use of the nuances of social interplay. Kids with autism don't respond to the subtle social cues that are obvious to most youngsters. A child with autism will know when his parents are *very* angry or *very* happy, for example, but he's not able to detect anything in between. The difference between a grimace and a friendly smile of greeting will be lost on him, and voice inflections will mean little or nothing. Children with autism understand black and white, but they don't usually understand gray. Subtleties are wasted on them.

Language deficits are a major component of this disorder. Only half of all children with autism will develop functional speech. Children with autism commonly have echolalia, which is the repeating of the words or phrases they have heard. They misuse pronouns and invent new words. The tone, pitch, accent, and cadence of their speech are abnormal. They have trouble *sequencing* (putting a story in order so that it makes sense) and *encoding* (storing information that has an emotional component). About 75 percent of all children with autism are also mentally retarded to some degree.

Children with autism may have strengths, though, especially in such skills as putting together puzzles or constructing objects. A very small number of people with autism—the Dustin Hoffman character in the movie *Rain Man,* for instance, who was fantastic with numbers and had memorized all the statistics about airline accidents—have phenomenal abilities in particular areas, such as memory, calendar calculations, and art.

Many kids with PDD and especially autism have attentional problems and exhibit repetitive behaviors. They may also be impulsive and hyperactive, often to the point of being self-destructive. I once treated a 14-year-old boy who would pick at his own skin until it bled. He'd also bang his head and his legs against brick walls until he'd break a bone or knock himself unconscious.

THE DIAGNOSIS

When PDD is suspected, we concentrate on getting as much information as possible about a child's history, his behavior, and his abilities, looking to parents, teachers, and anyone else who has spent time with the child. Long-term baby-sitters, grandparents, and other relatives can sometimes be very valuable historians. In taking a history we pay special attention to delays and deviations from normal development, especially in the child's acquisition and use of language and his social interactions. We check the family medical history, looking for a neurological disease or psychiatric disorders, particularly PDD or autism. The child's pediatrician does a complete physical, including a neurological examination. Psychological testing can help in the diagnosis by giving us an assessment of the child's social skills, language skills, and intelligence. Children with PDD will have higher performance scores than verbal scores.

An official diagnosis of autism is rarely made until a child is 18 months old, but often the disorder can be detected much earlier. Autism can appear from birth all the way up to 30 months. Babies with autism don't make eye contact and don't even want to be held. Even in the crib they may show a tendency toward repetitive actions. Other children will be fine in infancy but will start to show signs of autism later. Typically, they don't pick up language when they should. At age three or four children with autism will have significant delays in all developmental areas, especially language. They'll be unable to make distinctions between people and objects in their environment, and they won't get or give pleasure during social interactions.

What may at first seem like autism in a child may be developmental language delay; language problems often lead to problems in communication and in some social interaction. However, children with language delay, unlike those with autism, engage in imaginative play and usually have normal social interactions with their family and friends. They don't exhibit the same abnormal patterns of language as those typical among children with autism.

THE BRAIN CHEMISTRY

PDD is a complex disorder that probably involves variations in the structure of the brain; that is, the brain was not put together correctly, so there are some chemical abnormalities, ones that will probably never be repaired. As I mentioned earlier, there have been many studies of autism, so most of the information we have about the causes of PDD have to do with its most severe form.

Twin studies support the belief that autism is genetic; the concordance rate of the disorder is 91 percent in identical twins and 0 percent in fraternal twins. Family studies reveal that if one child in a family has autism, the likelihood that his brother or sister will have the disorder is increased. Studies of the brains of children with autism indicate that there is something wrong with how the brain processes certain information, especially sounds and language. Neuroimaging techniques and autopsies show that there are abnormalities in the cerebellum.

THE TREATMENT

Here's how one mother describes the treatment that Jacob, her 10-year-old child with PDD, is undergoing. "He's on Dexedrine, a little bit in the morning for his attention span. He's on Depakote twice a day for his irritability and impulsivity. He takes Paxil every night and Xanax when he needs it for anxiety.

"He sees a speech therapist who also does NDT—neurological developmental therapy. He really needs help with his articulation. He's a lot better than he used to be, but the kids still make fun of him. A few months ago he saw a behavioral therapist, and she helped him get a little more organized. I'd been trying to get him to clean up his act around here, but I wasn't getting anywhere. She made a chart with a list of things he has to do around the house. Every time he does his chores, he gets a star. When he does his homework right after school, he gets a star. She worked on table manners with him too. Eating properly is hard for him because he's so uncoordinated, but they practiced, and she figured out a reward system for dinnertime too. He trades in his stars for time playing Sega, which he loves.

"He goes to group therapy too, so he can practice his social skills. He's learning how to talk to people if he goes someplace new. He's also learning how to handle the teasing he gets at school. Kids who are different get positively brutalized by the other kids. Jacob is learning concrete ways to defuse what they say and when to ignore it. He's learning specifically what to say and do when this happens. They don't do theory there. They rehearse and practice, with role playing and everything. Group therapy has been great for Jacob."

I've offered up the details of one boy's treatment package not because Jacob's treatment is right for every child with PDD but because it illustrates two important facts about any treatment for PDD. The first is that we don't cure PDD; there is as yet no cure. We just fix as many symptoms of the disorder as possible and help a child to reach the highest level he is able to achieve. The second is that with PDD we take a multidisciplinary approach to treatment, going at the disorder with every weapon in the arsenal. When a child has PDD, careful attention must be paid to his placement in school. Some high-functioning children with PDD may be better off in a regular classroom, with normal intellectual stimulation and a garden-variety social life, than in a highly structured class filled with other children who have PDD. In all likelihood these kids will need additional attention outside of school, however. Speech therapy, language therapy, occupational therapy—any or all of these may be called for. Lower-functioning children with PDD will need the resources that special education offers, especially speech and language therapy. The primary goal of a child with autism is to learn to communicate. We try to get him to speak and use language. If he can't speak, we encourage him to write or use sign language or rely on visual cues. Communication is vital, and there's more than one way to communicate. Once a child can communicate, he's in a position to learn a variety of other skills, especially those associated with social interaction.

Behavioral therapy has been helpful in decreasing the negative behavior associated with PDD. Parents who learn behavior modification techniques can help the process along. Parent counseling is also an invaluable component of the PDD treatment package. Parents of children with PDD may benefit greatly from the company of others who are in the same predicament, who can offer information, support services, and a pat on the back when it's most needed. The Autism Society of America (see Appendix 2) provides these and other services.

Medication is nearly always recommended in the treatment of PDD and autism, not because it eliminates the core deficits that these children have but because it treats symptoms that interfere with their ability to function. Prozac, Zoloft, and Luvox increase a child's ability to relate socially, decrease repetitive thoughts, and lower aggression. One 16-year-old boy I treated for autism showed marked improvement on Luvox; he stopped banging his head against the wall of his bedroom, started participating in a day treatment program, and—perhaps most remarkably—signed a beautiful Mother's Day card for his mom.

Psychostimulants, such as Ritalin, Cylert, and Dexedrine, are used to treat the attentional problems and hyperactivity associated with PDD and autism. Once their attention span has been increased, kids with PDD are more receptive to other interventions, such as behavior modification and language therapy. These kids can be very sensitive to medication, so we start with low doses. Catapres, an antihypertensive agent, has been used to decrease irritability, hyperactivity, and impulsivity. The most common side effect of Catapres is sedation. Depakote helps the irritability, insomnia, and hyperactivity that are seen in certain children with PDD and autism. The side effects of Depakote, which are infrequent, are stomachaches, increased appetite, and drowsiness.

The child with autism may improve over time—50 percent of children who are mute in preschool eventually do speak, and some learn to play near other children—but autism cannot be cured. The best thing we can do for these kids is to help them learn how to work around these deficits and even use them to their advantage in their daily life.

One young man who was able to do just that was Bobby, 20 years old. I first saw Bobby when he was 10. He'd been in a special school program for many years, and he was doing quite well. Every day Bobby took a city bus to his school, and he never missed his stop. In fact, he had committed the entire bus system to memory. Bobby's IQ was 128 —well above average—and his grades were quite good all the way through high school. After graduation he found the perfect job: managing the flow of checks in a local bank. He had to take three buses to get to the bank—no problem whatsoever for Bobby, of course. He was absolutely terrific at his job. He never missed a day, and he never *ever* made a mistake.

PARENTING AND PDD

There was a time not long ago when parents of kids with autism had an additional burden: being blamed for their child's disease. The thinking was that mothers who were cold to their babies caused them to have autism; it was called the "refrigerator mom" theory. At least parents today don't have to suffer the agony of that guilt. Now we know that parents don't cause autism. In fact, they *can't* cause the disorder. We have seen children who have been horribly abused, neglected, mistreated, and misunderstood, and they don't develop autism any more than the general population. No matter how bad a job parents do, they can't create this disorder. Unfortunately, no matter how good a job they do, they can't cure it either.

Children with autism don't do many of the things that make babies and children lovable and emotionally rewarding. They don't coo or smile or curl up in Dad's lap. They're not affectionate; they don't cuddle or light up when they see Mom come home from work. They rarely make connections with anyone, not even their parents. It's not surprising, then, that the parents of kids with autism become very demoralized. On an intellectual level parents may understand that their child has a devastating brain disorder, but the reality that they might never be hugged or kissed by their own child is something they find much harder to accept.

Faced with the bizarre, often unpleasant behavior of a child with autism, many parents lose patience with their situation, and it's not unusual to see friction in the household. In the typical scenario the mother of a child who has autism is the "good cop"; she lets the child go through his rituals without making a fuss. Dad is usually more strict and angry—the "bad cop." For instance, one little boy I treated liked to play with the VCR, popping a video in, hitting the Eject button, then popping the video back in again. He could do this for hours. The VCR game enraged the father, and he took his anger out on Mom.

"Why do you let him do that?" he shouted.

"He's not hurting anyone, and it keeps him occupied," answers the mother, who had been following the little boy around all day. "I need a break."

Now Dad is even more frustrated and angry. "But he's acting crazy! Can't you get him to stop?"

Anger, frustration, sadness—all of these feelings are common in parents whose children have a serious brain disorder, and this is why I tell parents that it's essential to take a break now and again. Parents cannot and should not be caretakers all of the time, even when circumstances demand their constant attention. They have to take time out once in a while to be alone together as husband and wife. I highly recommend an evening out on a regular basis. If parents can spend the night away from home, so much the better. Treating PDD and autism is a marathon, not a sprint, and parents must conserve their emotional resources so that they'll be able to go the distance. That's the only way they'll be able to maintain the energy to see that a child gets the treatment he needs.

There's one final thing that a child with pervasive developmental disorder sorely needs, and that's a cheerleader, someone who will encourage him to stop thinking about what he can't do and feel good about what he can do. Jacob's mother describes what I mean.

"My main goal is to make him feel as good about himself as possible, because if he feels good, all the speech therapy and the other stuff is going to work better. He has to meet us, maybe not halfway but somewhere. I don't let him get down. I won't let him lie in bed and get depressed; I rip him out of bed and make him do something. The hardest thing for me about this whole disease is getting him to accept himself, to see that he is a good person. I want him to know that he's worth something.

"Last summer he took a giant step forward. We finally found the perfect camp for Jacob. He wasn't the highest achiever there, but he wasn't the lowest either. He was involved in all sorts of activities, and he made a lot of friends, and his letters were full of great things he was doing. He had never said those kinds of things before. When we went for Parents' Day, I could see from a distance how happy he was. He walked up to us and didn't even say hello. He just said, 'I'm coming *back* here next summer!' I think that was one of the best days of my life."

Afterword

"WORKING WITH SICK kids every day must be really sad. Doesn't it get to you?" Hardly a day goes by that I don't hear that question. I certainly understand what makes people ask it of someone in my line of work. Of course, it is sad, very sad, to see children in pain. Seeing any living thing experience distress and dysfunction—we're back to those two D's again—is upsetting. When the distress and dysfunction belong to a child and the treatments don't work, it can be heartbreaking. I'm a father as well as a doctor, so I know full well that the troubled children I treat every day could just as easily be one of my own three sons.

Nearly 20 years ago, when I decided to become a child and adolescent psychiatrist, I thought that I'd be able to help certain kids have an easier time growing up. I guess I saw myself as the Judd Hirsch character from *Ordinary People,* the wise, kindly, hip psychiatrist whose very special relationship with a teenager helped the boy get through a difficult period in his life. I didn't know then that the field I chose was about to take a giant leap forward, that I was going to do a lot more than help children and adolescents cope with their troubles. The progress that has been made in our understanding of the brain's involvement in children's psychiatric disorders and the use of medication has meant that my colleagues and I have been able to change, and sometimes even *save,* the lives of young people, just like neurosurgeons and cardiologists. I ended up getting a lot more than I bargained for.

So I tell people no, my job *isn't* sad and most times it *doesn't* get to me, because I know there's almost always something I can do to make a child's pain go away. I can relieve the suffering of his or her parents as well, first by reassuring them that what's wrong with their child is not their fault and then by telling them how we can make the child better. I hope I've gotten that message through loud and clear in these pages.

I'm in the business of helping troubled children live normal, happy, productive lives, and there's nothing sad or dispiriting about that. On the contrary: working with sick kids every day is a joy. I hope you find the same joy bringing out the best in your child.

A Definition of Terms

WHAT FOLLOWS is a list of some of the terms used frequently in *It's Nobody's Fault*. I describe them here not as they are defined in textbooks or medical dictionaries but as they apply to the field of child and adolescent psychiatry and suit the purposes of this book.

BEHAVIORAL THERAPY. A goal-oriented approach based on the principle that all behavior is learned and that undesirable behavior can be unlearned through training. The focus is on the here and now, on figuring out how to change behavior, not on finding out *why* the child feels or behaves a certain way.

BEHAVIOR MODIFICATION. The core of behavioral therapy, this is the therapeutic approach by which undesirable behavior is "unlearned" and replaced by different, more desirable behavior. Positive and negative reinforcement play an important part in behavior modification. A system of rewards and mild punishments (usually loss of privileges) can be a big help in motivating a child to change the way he reacts to a given situation. The role of parents is extremely important in behavior modification.

CAT. Computed Axial Tomography. This is an advanced form of X-ray that permits us to look at structures of the brain.

CO-MORBIDITY. A situation in which a person is diagnosed with two or more disorders at the same time. One disorder is said to be co-morbid with another. Co-morbidity is extremely common in the brain disorders of children and adolescents. Few of these disorders are completely "clean."

COGNITIVE. Having to do with thinking. Cognitive functions include remembering, understanding, judging, and reasoning. Cognitive behavioral therapy requires an ability to talk about your own thoughts and feelings, so it is more likely to be effective for older children than it is in the treatment of the very young.

CONCORDANCE. This term, which is usually used in genetics, refers to the similarity in twins with respect to the presence or absence of a disease or a trait. Higher concordance rates in identical twins than in fraternal twins indicate that there is a genetic component to that disease. Twin studies of the brain disorders in these pages all show a higher concordance rate in identical twins than in fraternal twins.

DNA. Deoxyribonucleic acid. The stuff of which genes are made. DNA is largely responsible for the transmission of inherited characteristics, including brain chemistry.

DISINHIBITION. An increase in hostility, aggressiveness, irritability, and impulsivity. This reaction can be caused by certain antianxiety agents, specifically the benzodiazepines. This side effect usually disappears when the dose is lowered and always disappears when the medicine is discontinued.

EEG. Electroencephalogram. This is a graphic depiction of the brain's electrical impulses. Since 1929 the EEG has been used to detect the presence of brain malfunctions, including the seizures associated with epilepsy.

FAMILY THERAPY. Psychotherapy in which problems are understood and treated in the family. How a child's disorder affects all the members of the family and how the family affects the child are addressed. The goal of family therapy is to bring about a change in the way family members interact. Unlike parent counseling, where a therapist advises the parents, family therapy requires the cooperation of the entire family to make changes and find solutions.

INTELLIGENCE. A person's ability to learn and to understand and process information for problem solving. An intelligence test is used to measure those aspects of mental development that are relevant for academic achievement. A person's IQ—his intelligence quotient—rates his intellectual ability, according to verbal skills and performance skills.

MRI. Magnetic resonance imaging. MRI is a neuroimaging technique that uses magnetic fields instead of radiation and allows us to examine the structure of the brain, especially the existence of tumors, vascular malfunctions, and brain deterioration.

NEUROANATOMY. The structures that compose the brain and the nervous system.

NEUROIMAGING TECHNIQUES. Techniques that provide data on brain activity and function. As far as the brain disorders of children and adolescents are concerned, these techniques are useful not for the purposes of diagnosis but for increased knowledge of how the brain functions and how it reacts to medication, among other things. Some of the most commonly used neuroimaging techniques are MRIs, PET and CAT scans, and SPECT.

PARENT COUNSELING. A therapeutic approach in which parents are educated about their child's brain disorder and given information and advice on general issues and on the specific problem they may be having with the behavior of their child.

PARENT TRAINING. This is a systematic goal-oriented process in which parents are taught, quite specifically, how to manage the behavior of their troubled child by means of positive and negative reinforcement. For instance, parents might be taught how to encourage alternatives to such negative behaviors as temper tantrums, aggressiveness, and destructiveness. This technique is used for children of all ages; but it is especially appropriate for parents of young children.

PERFORMANCE ANXIETY. The apprehension and nervousness that come before an event requiring the demonstration of a child's or adolescent's abilities—a test, piano recital, oral report, and so on. Simple performance anxiety, which is a perfectly normal response, does not negatively effect the youngster's performance. Pathological performance anxiety, which is not normal, does impair a child's ability to perform.

PET SCAN. PET stands for positron emission tomography. This neuroimaging technique produces images of the brain's activity as a patient is directed to complete specific tasks, such as reading or naming objects. Measurement of brain metabolism with the use of PET scans has been helpful in identifying differences in the brains of adults with specific brain disorders and showing us how the brain responds to various medications.

PSYCHOTHERAPY. The treatment of mental or emotional disorders by psychological means, usually involving communication between patient and therapist. Psychotherapy may involve individuals, families, or groups, and there are many different methods employed to bring about change.

PSYCHOTIC. This term describes someone whose ability to distinguish what is real from what is not real is impaired. A person who is psychotic creates his own "reality"; he may have delusions and hallucinations. Faced with concrete evidence that what he believes is true is not true, he stays with his own version. (See *reality testing*.)

REALITY TESTING. A person's ability to distinguish reality from fantasy or his inner wishes and feelings from the external world. For example, a paranoid person believes that somebody out there is trying to get him. He doesn't recognize that his fears are in his mind. When someone has hallucinations, he truly believes that the voices are real. When he's treated with medication and starts to improve, he begins to wonder if the voices are real. Once he's better, he'll say that he used to hear voices that he thought were real, but now he knows they weren't. Having good reality testing means being intact again.

SEDATION. The state of being sleepy. Sedation is a side effect of many psychiatric medications, including the antianxiety agents, some antidepressants, and certain neuroleptics.

SELF-MEDICATION. Using alcohol and illicit drugs, such as marijuana, in an effort to improve one's mood and general feeling. Untreated adolescents with brain disorders frequently turn to self-medication.

SOCIAL CUES. The facial expressions and body movements that express a person's intentions and reactions. Some kids with brain disorders are impaired in their ability to recognize and respond to social cues in their family and friends.

SPECT. Single photon emission computed tomography. This neuroimaging technique measures blood flow in the brain and the utilization of glucose, the form of sugar used by cells. It also highlights which parts of the brain are active and determines whether or not blood flow and activity are typical. SPECT is used primarily as a research tool for brain disorders in children and adolescents.

TEMPERAMENT. A set of character traits that an infant is born with. Sometimes thought of as a child's basic *disposition,* temperament is the foundation of his personality.

TITRATION. The process of determining the exact dose of medication needed for a child or an adolescent with a brain disorder by evaluating his response to the medicine. Specifically, we look for a decrease in symptoms and the presence of side effects.

TRAUMA. An event, injury, or emotional shock that has a negative effect on a person's mental or psychological state of mind.

VISUAL IMAGERY. A technique used in behavior modification in which the child or adolescent pictures himself in a certain situation and, guided by a therapist, learns how to cope with the feelings that the situation brings on. Guided visual imagery is especially useful in combating phobic reactions and anxiety.

Resources and Support Groups

THE FOLLOWING ORGANIZATIONS and other resources—categorized according to type of disorder—can be very helpful to children and adolescents with no-fault brain disorders and can offer information and support to their parents and other loved ones as well.

ANXIETY DISORDERS

Anxiety Disorders Association of America
6000 Executive Blvd, #513
Rockville, MD 20852
Phone: 301-231-9350

This group promotes the prevention and cure of anxiety disorders (generalized anxiety disorder, obsessive compulsive disorder, separation anxiety disorder, and social phobia) and works to improve the lives of people who suffer from them. Members are individuals with anxiety disorders, clinicians, researchers, and other interested individuals. A network for parent support groups is being developed. The group publishes a newsletter.

Council on Anxiety Disorders
P.O. Box 17011
Winston-Salem, NC 27116
Phone: 910-722-7760

This group promotes awareness of anxiety disorders (generalized anxiety disorder, obsessive compulsive disorder, separation anxiety disorder, and social phobia), emphasizing the impact that they have on the lives of the people who have them and the treatments that have been developed in recent years. The Council also assists patients in finding appropriate treatment and provide support groups for patients and their families.

OCD Foundation, Inc.
P.O. Box 70
Milford, CT 06460-0070
Phone: 203-878-5669

This organization is dedicated to finding a cure for obsessive compulsive disorder and improving the welfare of people with OCD. It provides education, research, and mutual support and publishes a monthly newsletter for families (*The OCD Newsletter*), a semiannual newsletter for and by kids (*Kidscope*), and a videotape called *The Touching Tree,* which describes OCD to children.

Selective Mutism Foundation, Inc.
P.O. Box 450632
Sunrise, FL 33345-0632
Phone: 305-748-7714

This organization offers support for parents of children with selective mutism. It is also open to adults who have the disorder or who have had it in the past. The group provides information and referrals as well as phone support.

ATTENTION DEFICIT HYPERACTIVITY DISORDER

Children and Adults with
Attention Deficit Disorder (CH.A.D.D.)
499 Northwest 70th Avenue
Suite 109 Plantation, FL 33317
Phone: 305-587-3700

This international organization offers information and support for families with children with ADD and ADHD and gives guidelines and assistance to parents and others interested in starting support groups. CH.A.D.D. publishes a monthly newsletter and a quarterly magazine.

AUTISM

Autism Research Institute
4182 Adams Avenue
San Diego, CA 92116

This is a network of parents and professionals concerned with autism. The group conducts and fosters scientific research designed to improve the methods of diagnosing and treating the disorder. It publishes a newsletter.

Autism Society of America
7910 Woodmont Avenue
Suite 650
Bethesda, MD 20814-3015
Phone: 1-800-3-AUTISM or 301-657-0881

This organization is dedicated to increasing public awareness about autism and the day-to-day issues faced by the patients, their families, and the professionals with whom they interact. It publishes a newsletter, holds an annual conference, and sells books related to autism.

EATING DISORDERS

Anorexia Nervosa and Related Eating Disorders, Inc.
P.O. Box 5102
Eugene, OR 97405
Phone: 503-344-1144

This organization offers free and low-cost information, distributed through booklets and a monthly newsletter, about eating and exercise disorders. It also provides speakers and programs for schools, agencies, and other groups.

American Anorexia/Bulimia Association, Inc.
293 Central Park West
Suite 1R
New York, NY 10024
Phone: 212-501-8351

This organization educates the general public about eating disorders and provides referrals for patients and their families, recommending self-help groups, treatment centers, and health care professionals specializing in this field.

National Association of
Anorexia Nervosa and Associated Disorders
Box 7
Highland Park, IL 60035
Phone: 708-831-3438

This group seeks to understand and alleviate the problems of eating disorders; to educate the general public and professionals in the health field about eating disorders and methods of treatment; and to encourage and promote research. It offers referrals to health care professionals and support groups and publishes a newsletter.

MOOD DISORDERS

National Depressive and
Manic-Depressive Association
730 N. Franklin Street
Suite 501
Chicago, IL 60610-3526
Phone: 1-800-826–3632 or 312-642-0049

This organization educates patients, families, professionals, and the public about the nature of major depressive disorder and bipolar disorder/ manic depressive illness; fosters self-help for patients and their families; works to eliminate discrimination against people with mood disorders; and improves the availability and quality of help and support. It publishes a newsletter and holds an annual conference.

National Foundation for Depressive Illness
P.O. Box 2257
New York, NY 10116
Phone: 212-268-4260

This organization provides telephone referrals of doctors and support groups for people with major depressive disorder and bipolar disorder/manic depressive illness. It publishes a monthly newsletter and conducts regular seminars and conferences.

National Alliance for Research
on Schizophrenia and Depression
60 Cutter Mill Road
Great Neck, NY 11021
Phone: 516-829-0091

This national organization raises and distributes funds for scientific research into the causes, cures, and treatment of severe mental illnesses, primarily schizophrenia and major depressive disorder. It publishes a newsletter.

Depression and Related
Affective Disorders Association
Meyer 3-181
600 North Wolfe Street
Baltimore, MD 21287-7381
Phone: 410-955-4647

This organization's mission is to alleviate the suffering arising from depression and bipolar disorder/manic depressive illness by assisting self-help groups, providing education and information, and lending support to research programs. Support services include publications and educational videotapes.

TOURETTE SYNDROME

Tourette Syndrome Association, Inc.
42-40 Bell Boulevard
Bayside, NY 11361-2820
Phone: 1-800-237-0717 or 718-224-2999

The members of this nonprofit organization include people with TS, their families and friends, and health care professionals interested in the field. The group funds research, provides services to patients and their families, and offers a variety of publications, including brochures, fact sheets, and a newsletter.

OTHER SOURCES

American Academy of
Child and Adolescent Psychiatry
3615 Wisconsin Avenue NW
Washington, DC, 20016-3007
Phone: 1-800-333-7636 or 202-966-7300

The Academy has a membership of more than 5700 child and adolescent psychiatrists who actively research, diagnose, and treat psychiatric disorders affecting children and adolescents. An excellent referral source for board-certified child and adolescent psychiatrists, the Academy publishes *Facts for Families,* a series of 53 fact sheets on topics related to child and adolescent psychiatry.

Center for Mental Health Services
5600 Fishers Lane
Rockville, MD 20857
Phone: 301-443-1333

This government organization supports the development of accessible and appropriate service delivery systems for children and adolescents with serious emotional disturbance. It offers grants to groups working in the field of children's mental health and supports their efforts to develop community-based services. It distributes several publications.

Federation of Families
for Children's Mental Health
1021 Prince Street
Alexandria, VA 22314-2971
Phone: 703-684-7710

This parent-run organization focuses on the needs of children and adolescents with emotional, behavioral, or mental disorders and the needs of their families as well. The group publishes a newsletter and holds regular conferences.

National Alliance for the Mentally Ill
200 North Glebe Road, Suite 1015
Arlington, VA 22203-3754
Phone: 1-800-950-NAMI or 703-524-7600

This grassroots support and advocacy organization, dedicated to improving the lives of people with severe mental illness and the lives of their families as well, offers education and emotional support. It publishes a newsletter.

National Institute of Mental Health
5600 Fishers Lane
Room 7C-02
Rockville, MD 20857
Phone: 301-443-4536 or 301-443-3600

This government agency, which is part of the National Institutes of Health, conducts and supports research on mental illness and mental health.

National Mental Health Association
1021 Prince Street
Alexandria, VA 22314-2971
Phone: 703-684-7722

This large nonprofit organization addresses all issues related to mental health and mental illness. It provides public education, sponsors "May Is Mental Health Month," and runs the Mental Health Information

Center, which distributes information on various mental health topics and provides referrals.

Youth Mental Health Update
P.O. Box 3926
New Hyde Park, NY 11040

This newsletter, designed for parents, educators, pediatricians, and mental health professionals (and edited by Harold S. Koplewicz, M.D. and Anita Gurian, Ph.D.), focuses on current mental health topics related to children and adolescents. There are six issues per school year; a yearly subscription is $15.

Psychopharmacology at a Glance

IN DISCUSSING the recommended treatment of no-fault brain disorders I refer often to various medications, describing how they work and their possible side effects. The charts that follow put it all together, disorder by disorder: brand name, generic name, nuisance side effects, and serious side effects.

In going through this material parents should bear in mind that the information provided is for reference only. Only a physician may prescribe medicine. Furthermore, psychiatric medication should be taken by children and adolescents *only* after a specific diagnosis has been made by a qualified child and adolescent psychiatrist and *only* when a disorder is severe enough to cause distress and dysfunction.

Parents should also be aware that many of the medications routinely prescribed for no-fault brain disorders in children and adolescents have not been approved *for that specific purpose* by the Food and Drug Administration. All of the medicines described in this book have been FDA-approved but not necessarily for the treatment of child and adolescent psychiatric disorders. (The FDA approves drugs for specific uses and age groups but only after the manufacturer of the medication *applies* to the FDA for approval for that specific purpose. Many companies choose not to go to the effort and the expense of asking the FDA for approval for many different purposes.) When it comes to prescribing any medication, a physician may and should use his or her own best judgment. He or she should also be prepared to explain to parents the rationale behind the use of any drug as well as its possible side effects.

ATTENTION DEFICIT HYPERACTIVITY DISORDER (ADHD)

MEDICATIONS			POSSIBLE SIDE EFFECTS	
Brand Name	Generic Name	Type of Medication	Nuisance	Serious
Ritalin	methylphenidate	psychostimulant	appetite reduction; delay in falling asleep; headaches; weepiness; increased heart rate	decrease in child's rate of growth with long-term use
Dexedrine	dextroamphetamine	psychostimulant	appetite reduction; delay in falling asleep; irritability; dry mouth; weepiness; increased heart rate	decrease in child's rate of growth with long-term use
Cylert	pemoline	psychostimulant	appetite reduction (very infrequent)	inflammation of the liver (reversible)
Wellbutrin	bupropion	atypical antidepressant	similar to Ritalin and Dexedrine but less frequent	at very high doses may cause seizures in adults

Continued on page 269

Continued from page 268

MEDICATIONS			POSSIBLE SIDE EFFECTS	
Brand Name	Generic Name	Type of Medication	Nuisance	Serious
Tofranil	imipramine	tricyclic antidepressant	sedation; dry mouth; blood pressure changes	cardiovascular effects; EKG changes
Norpramin	desipramine	tricyclic antidepressant	similar to Tofranil but less frequent	cardiovascular effects; EKG changes; more cardiac side effects in younger children
Pamelor	nortriptyline	tricyclic antidepressant	similar to Tofranil and Norpramin but less frequent	cardiovascular effects
Catapres	clonidine	antihypertensive	sedation; headache; nausea; dry mouth; constipation	
Tenex	guanfacine	antihypertensive	similar to Catapres but less frequent	

BIPOLAR DISORDER/MANIC DEPRESSIVE ILLNESS

	MEDICATIONS		POSSIBLE SIDE EFFECTS	
Brand Name	Generic Name	Type of Medication	Nuisance	Serious
Eskalith	lithium	cation salt	nausea; vomiting; diarrhea; mild tremor; fatigue; acne; weight gain	kidney dysfunction; hypothyroidism
Depakene Depakote	valproic acid	anticonvulsant	stomach upset; nausea; vomiting; weight gain; sedation; tremor	liver toxicity in children under two years of age
Tegretol	carbamazepine	anticonvulsant	double vision; drowsiness; poor coordination; mild nausea	reduced white blood cell count; agranulocytosis and aplastic anemia (rare, especially in children and adolescents); this sudden drop to very low white blood cell count can be life-threatening

CONDUCT DISORDER

MEDICATIONS			POSSIBLE SIDE EFFECTS	
Brand Name	Generic Name	Type of Medication	Nuisance	Serious
Ritalin	methylphenidate	psychostimulant	appetite reduction; delay in falling asleep; headaches; weepiness; increased heart rate	decrease in child's rate of growth with long-term use
Cylert	pemoline	psychostimulant	appetite reduction (very infrequent)	inflammation of the liver (reversible)
Eskalith	lithium	cation salt	nausea; vomiting; diarrhea; mild tremor; fatigue; acne; weight gain	kidney dysfunction; hypothyroidism
Depakene Depakote	valproic acid	anticonvulsant	stomach upset; nausea; vomiting; weight gain; sedation; tremor	liver toxicity in children under two years of age

EATING DISORDERS (ANOREXIA NERVOSA)

	MEDICATIONS		POSSIBLE SIDE EFFECTS	
Brand Name	Generic Name	Type of Medication	Nuisance	Serious
Periactin	cyproheptadine	antihistamine	sedation	
Prozac	fluoxetine	SSRI	nausea; diarrhea; weight loss; insomnia; stomach upset; excess sweating; jitteriness; sexual dysfunction	
Nardil	phenelzine	MAOI	lowered blood pressure; dizziness	tyramine-rich foods can cause a hypertensive (high blood pressure) reaction; over-the-counter cold medicines, such as Sudafed and Dristan, cause a similar reaction

EATING DISORDERS (BULIMIA)

| MEDICATIONS | | | POSSIBLE SIDE EFFECTS | |
Brand Name	Generic Name	Type of Medication	Nuisance	Serious
Prozac	fluoxetine	SSRI	nausea; diarrhea; weight loss; insomnia; stomach upset; excess sweating; jitteriness; sexual dysfunction	
Tofranil	imipramine	tricyclic antidepressant	dry mouth; constipation	cardiovascular effects; EKG changes

Continued on page 274

EATING DISORDERS (BULIMIA)

Continued from page 273

MEDICATIONS			POSSIBLE SIDE EFFECTS	
Brand Name	Generic Name	Type of Medication	Nuisance	Serious
Desyrel	trazadone	atypical antidepressant	sedation; dizziness; headache; nausea; vomiting	priapism (prolonged erection without sexual stimulation)
Nardil	phenelzine	MAOI	lowered blood pressure; dizziness	tyramine-rich foods can cause a hypertensive (high blood pressure) reaction; over-the-counter cold medicines, such as Sudafed and Dristan, also cause a similar reaction

ENURESIS/BEDWETTING

MEDICATIONS			POSSIBLE SIDE EFFECTS	
Brand Name	Generic Name	Type of Medication	Nuisance	Serious
DDAVP	desmopressin nasal spray	analogue of antidiuretic hormone	nasal dryness or irritation; headaches	
Tofranil	imipramine	tricyclic antidepressant	dry mouth; constipation	cardiovascular effects with higher doses than used in the treatment of enuresis
Dexedrine	dextroamphetamine	psychostimulant	appetite reduction; delay in falling asleep; irritability; dry mouth; increased heart rate	

GENERALIZED ANXIETY DISORDER (GAD)

	MEDICATIONS		POSSIBLE SIDE EFFECTS	
Brand Name	Generic Name	Type of Medication	Nuisance	Serious
Xanax	alprazolam	benzodiazepine	sedation; behavioral disinhibition	
Klonopin	clonazepam	benzodiazepine	drowsiness; irritability; oppositional behavior; behavioral disinhibition	
Valium	diazepam	benzodiazepine	sedation; behavioral disinhibition	
BuSpar	buspirone	antianxiety agent	nausea; headache	
Prozac	fluoxetine	SSRI	nausea; diarrhea; weight loss; insomnia; stomach upset; excess sweating; jitteriness; sexual dysfunction	

MAJOR DEPRESSIVE DISORDER (MDD)

MEDICATIONS			POSSIBLE SIDE EFFECTS	
Brand Name	Generic Name	Type of Medication	Nuisance	Serious
Prozac	fluoxetine	SSRI	nausea; diarrhea; weight loss; insomnia; stomach upset; excess sweating; jitteriness; sexual dysfunction	
Zoloft	sertraline	SSRI	nausea; diarrhea; weight loss; insomnia; stomach upset; excess sweating; jitteriness; sexual dysfunction	
Paxil	paroxetine	SSRI	nausea; diarrhea; weight loss; insomnia; stomach upset; excess sweating; jitteriness; sexual dysfunction	

Continued on page 278

MAJOR DEPRESSIVE DISORDER (MDD)

Continued from page 277

MEDICATIONS			POSSIBLE SIDE EFFECTS	
Brand Name	Generic Name	Type of Medication	Nuisance	Serious
Luvox	fluvoxamine	SSRI	nausea; diarrhea; insomnia; stomach upset; excess sweating; jitteriness; sexual dysfunction	
Tofranil	imipramine	tricyclic antidepressant	dry mouth; constipation	cardiovascular effects; EKG changes
Pamelor	nortriptyline	tricyclic antidepressant	sedation; dry mouth; blood pressure changes	same as Tofranil
Elavil	amitriptyline	tricyclic antidepressant	same as Tofranil but less frequent	cardiovascular effects; EKG changes

Continued on page 279

Continued from page 278

MAJOR DEPRESSIVE DISORDER (MDD)

MEDICATIONS			POSSIBLE SIDE EFFECTS	
Brand Name	Generic Name	Type of Medication	Nuisance	Serious
Nardil	phenelzine	MAOI	lowered blood pressure; dizziness	tyramine-rich foods can cause a hypertensive (high blood pressure) reaction; over-the-counter cold medicines, such as Sudafed and Dristan, cause a similar reaction
Marplan	isocarboxazid	MAOI	lowered blood pressure; dizziness	tyramine-rich foods can cause a hypertensive (high blood pressure) reaction; over-the-counter cold medicines, such as Sudafed and Dristan, cause a similar reaction

Continued on page 280

MAJOR DEPRESSIVE DISORDER (MDD)

Continued from page 279

| MEDICATIONS | | | POSSIBLE SIDE EFFECTS | |
Brand Name	Generic Name	Type of Medication	Nuisance	Serious
Parnate	tranylcypromine	MAOI	lowered blood pressure; dizziness	tyramine-rich foods can cause a hypertensive (high blood pressure) reaction; over-the-counter cold medicines, such as Sudafed and Dristan, cause a similar reaction
Meclobimide	moclobemide	reversible MAOI	lowered blood pressure; dizziness	tyramine-rich foods can cause a hypertensive (high blood pressure) reaction; over-the-counter cold medicines, such as Sudafed and Dristan, cause a similar reaction

OBSESSIVE COMPULSIVE DISORDER (OCD)

	MEDICATIONS		POSSIBLE SIDE EFFECTS	
Brand Name	Generic Name	Type of Medication	Nuisance	Serious
Prozac	fluoxetine	SSRI	nausea; diarrhea; weight loss; insomnia; stomach upset; excess sweating; jitteriness; sexual dysfunction	
Zoloft	sertraline	SSRI	nausea; diarrhea; weight loss; insomnia; stomach upset; excess sweating; jitteriness; sexual dysfunction	
Paxil	paroxetine	SSRI	nausea; diarrhea; weight loss; insomnia; stomach upset; excess sweating; jitteriness; sexual dysfunction	

Continued on page 282

OBSESSIVE COMPULSIVE DISORDER (OCD)

Continued from page 281

MEDICATIONS			POSSIBLE SIDE EFFECTS	
Brand Name	Generic Name	Type of Medication	Nuisance	Serious
Luvox	fluvoxamine	SSRI	nausea; diarrhea; insomnia; stomach upset; excess sweating; jitteriness; sexual dysfunction	
Anafranil	clomipramine	tricyclic antidepressant	sleepiness; tremor; dizziness; headache; excess sweating; dry mouth; constipation; stomach upset	cardiovascular effects; increased heart rate; blood pressure changes

PERVASIVE DEVELOPMENTAL DISORDER (PDD) AND AUTISM

MEDICATIONS			POSSIBLE SIDE EFFECTS	
Brand Name	Generic Name	Type of Medication	Nuisance	Serious
Prozac	fluoxetine	SSRI	nausea; diarrhea; weight loss; insomnia; stomach upset; excess sweating; jitteriness; sexual dysfunction	
Zoloft	sertraline	SSRI	nausea; diarrhea; weight loss; insomnia; stomach upset; excess sweating; jitteriness; sexual dysfunction	

Continued on page 284

PERVASIVE DEVELOPMENTAL DISORDER (PDD) AND AUTISM

Continued from page 283

MEDICATIONS			POSSIBLE SIDE EFFECTS	
Brand Name	Generic Name	Type of Medication	Nuisance	Serious
Ritalin	methylphenidate	psychostimulant	appetite reduction; delay in falling asleep; headaches; weepiness; increased heart rate	decrease in child's rate of growth with long-term use
Dexedrine	dextroamphetamine	psychostimulant	appetite reduction; delay in falling asleep; irritability; dry mouth; weepiness; increased heart rate	decrease in child's rate of growth with long-term use
Cylert	pemoline	psychostimulant	very infrequent appetite reduction	inflammation of the liver (reversible)

SEPARATION ANXIETY DISORDER (SAD)

MEDICATIONS			POSSIBLE SIDE EFFECTS	
Brand Name	Generic Name	Type of Medication	Nuisance	Serious
Prozac	fluoxetine	SSRI	nausea; diarrhea; weight loss; insomnia; stomach upset; excess sweating; jitteriness; sexual dysfunction	
Zoloft	sertraline	SSRI	nausea; diarrhea; weight loss; insomnia; stomach upset; excess sweating; jitteriness; sexual dysfunction	

Continued on page 286

SEPARATION ANXIETY DISORDER (SAD)

Continued from page 285

MEDICATIONS			POSSIBLE SIDE EFFECTS	
Brand Name	Generic Name	Type of Medication	Nuisance	Serious
Paxil	paroxetine	SSRI	nausea; diarrhea; weight loss; insomnia; stomach upset; excess sweating; jitteriness; sexual dysfunction	
Xanax	alprazolam	benzodiazepine	sedation; behavioral disinhibition	
Tofranil	imipramine	tricyclic antidepressant	dry mouth; constipation	cardiovascular effects; EKG changes

Continued on page 287

Continued from page 286

SEPARATION ANXIETY DISORDER (SAD)

| MEDICATIONS | | | POSSIBLE SIDE EFFECTS | |
Brand Name	Generic Name	Type of Medication	Nuisance	Serious
Nardil	phenelzine	MAOI	lowered blood pressure; dizziness	tyramine-rich foods can cause a hypertensive (high blood pressure) reaction; over-the-counter cold medicines, such as Sudafed and Dristan, cause a similar reaction
Parnate	tranylcypromine	MAOI	lowered blood pressure; dizziness	tyramine-rich foods can cause a hypertensive (high blood pressure) reaction; over-the-counter cold medicines, such as Sudafed and Dristan, cause a similar reaction

SCHIZOPHRENIA

MEDICATIONS			POSSIBLE SIDE EFFECTS	
Brand Name	Generic Name	Type of Medication	Nuisance	Serious
Haldol	haloperidol	high-potency neuroleptic	sleepiness; muscle rigidity; tremor; feelings of restlessness	acute dystonic reaction (sudden muscle cramping and pain) requires rapid treatment with an injection of Benadryl
Mellaril	thioridazine	low-potency neuroleptic	sedation; dry mouth; blurred vision; constipation; weight gain	doses above 1,000 mg may cause retina damage
Thorazine	chlorpromazine	low-potency neuroleptic	sedation; dry mouth; blurred vision; constipation; weight gain	

Continued on page 289

SCHIZOPHRENIA

Continued from page 288

MEDICATIONS			POSSIBLE SIDE EFFECTS	
Brand Name	Generic Name	Type of Medication	Nuisance	Serious
Clozaril	clozapine	atypical antipsychotic	sedation; increased saliva; dizziness; constipation; weight gain; nausea	agranulocytosis; with high doses there is an increased seizure risk; blood pressure changes; increased heart rate
Risperdal	risperidone	atypical antipsychotic	sedation; feelings of restlessness; lowered blood pressure; weight gain; decreased concentration	increased risk of seizures

SOCIAL PHOBIA/SHYNESS (GENERALIZED)

Brand Name	Generic Name	Type of Medication	Nuisance	Serious
	MEDICATIONS		POSSIBLE SIDE EFFECTS	
Prozac	fluoxetine	SSRI	nausea; diarrhea; weight loss; insomnia; stomach upset; excess sweating; jitteriness; sexual dysfunction	
Zoloft	sertraline	SSRI	nausea; diarrhea; weight loss; insomnia; stomach upset; excess sweating; jitteriness; sexual dysfunction	
Klonopin	clonazepam	benzodiazepine	drowsiness; irritability; oppositional behavior; behavioral disinhibition	
Xanax	alprazolam	benzodiazepine	sedation; behavioral disinhibition	

Continued on page 291

Continued from page 290

SOCIAL PHOBIA/SHYNESS (GENERALIZED)

	MEDICATIONS		POSSIBLE SIDE EFFECTS	
Brand Name	Generic Name	Type of Medication	Nuisance	Serious
BuSpar	buspirone	antianxiety agent	nausea; headache	
Nardil	phenelzine	MAOI	lowered blood pressure; dizziness	tyramine-rich foods can cause a hypertensive (high blood pressure) reaction; over-the-counter cold medicines, such as Sudafed and Dristan, cause a similar reaction

SOCIAL PHOBIA/SHYNESS (SPECIFIC/PATHOLOGICAL PERFORMANCE ANXIETY)

MEDICATIONS			POSSIBLE SIDE EFFECTS	
Brand Name	Generic Name	Type of Medication	Nuisance	Serious
Inderal	propranolol	beta blocker	lethargy; tingling and numbness in fingers	decreased heart rate; may be contra-indicated in children with asthma
Tenormin	atenolol	beta blocker	same as Inderal but less frequent	same as Inderal but less frequent

TOURETTE SYNDROME (TS)

	MEDICATIONS		POSSIBLE SIDE EFFECTS	
Brand Name	Generic Name	Type of Medication	Nuisance	Serious
Catapres	clonidine	antihypertensive	sedation; headache; nausea; dry mouth; constipation	
Tenex	guanfacine	antihypertensive	similar to Catapres but less frequent	
Orap	pimozide	neuroleptic	similar to Haldol but less frequent	EKG changes
Haldol	haloperidol	neuroleptic	sleepiness; muscle rigidity; tremor; feelings of restlessness	acute dystonic reaction (sudden muscle cramping and pain), which requires rapid treatment with an injection of Benadryl

Continued on page 294

Continued from page 293

TOURETTE SYNDROME (TS)

MEDICATIONS			POSSIBLE SIDE EFFECTS	
Brand Name	Generic Name	Type of Medication	Nuisance	Serious
Prolixin	fluphenazine	neuroleptic	sleepiness; muscle rigidity; tremor; feelings of restlessness	acute dystonic reaction (sudden muscle cramping and pain), which requires rapid treatment with an injection of Benadryl

Index

ADD. *See* attention deficit disorder

ADH. *See* antidiuretic hormones

ADHD. *See* attention deficit hyperactivity disorder

adopted children, 6, 131, 202–3, 216, 236, 238

Anafranil, 101, 174, 282

anhedonia, 181

anorexia nervosa, 21–22, 99, 224–28, 229, 230–31, 272

antianxiety agents, 116, 133, 149, 174, 254, 256, 276, 291. *See also specific medication*

anticipatory anxiety, 114–16, 134

anticonvulsants, 204–5, 270, 271. *See also specific medication*

antidepressants, 174, 187, 188–89, 205, 227, 230, 256, 268, 274. *See also* monoamine oxidase inhibitors (MAOIs); selective serotonin reuptake inhibitors (SSRIs); tricyclic antidepressants (TCAs); *specific medication*

antidiuretic hormone (ADH), 159, 163, 275

antihistamines, 218, 227, 272

antihypertensives, 53, 82, 173–74, 247, 269, 293. *See also specific medication*

antipsychotic agents, 53, 82, 205, 218, 289. *See also specific medication*

anxiety, 126, 142, 143, 144, 150. *See also* anxiety disorders; *specific disorder*

anxiety disorders, 117, 130, 183–84, 229, 259–60. *See also specific disorder*

attention deficit disorder (ADD), 74–75, 158, 260

attention deficit hyperactivity disorder (ADHD): and brain chemistry, 50–51, 79–80; child's perception of, 76–77; co-morbidity of, 55, 102, 111, 147, 167, 171–72, 174, 184, 201, 236, 237; diagnosis of, 76–79; and early identification/intervention, 78–79; long-term effects of, 19–20; medications for, 15–18, 57, 66, 67, 78, 79, 81–83, 174, 268–69; misconceptions about, 73–74, 80; onset of, 73, 201; and parenting, 5, 13, 17, 18, 85–90; prevalence of, 72–73; resources/support groups for, 89, 260; symptoms of, 15–17, 18, 71–76; treatment for, 15–18, 50–51, 80–86, 89–90; types of, 74–76

autism, 22, 242–43, 247, 261, 283–84. *See also* pervasive developmental disorder (PDD)

bedwetting. *See* enuresis

behavior modification, 62, 253

behavioral rebound, 83–84

behavioral therapy: and ADHD, 84–85; "booster shots" of, 102; and CD, 237; child's involvement in, 149; and coaching/rehearsal, 135–36, 137, 139; and contracts, 114–16, 117; definition of, 253; and diagnosis of brain disorders, 32; and doctor-patient-parent relationship, 32; and enuresis, 160–63, 164, 165, 166; and exposure prevention, 100; and extended exposure/flooding,

About the Author

HAROLD S. KOPLEWICZ, M.D., is one of America's foremost child and adolescent psychiatrists and an expert in pediatric psychopharmacology. He received his degrees from the University of Maryland and the Albert Einstein College of Medicine in the Bronx. Dr. Koplewicz is vice chairman of the Department of Psychiatry and director of the Division of Child and Adolescent Psychiatry at New York University Medical Center—Bellevue Hospital Center. The division was the first child and adolescent program in the United States. Currently professor of clinical psychiatry at the New York University School of Medicine, he is also founder and editor of the newsletter *Youth Mental Health Update,* a member of the National Board of Medical Examiners, and a Commissioner of the New York State Commission on Youth Crime and Violence and Reform of the Juvenile Justice System.

As a clinician Dr. Koplewicz sees more than 100 new patients a year from all over the world. A May 1996 *New York* magazine special report called "The Best Doctors in New York" featured Dr. Koplewicz, and in February 1994 he was listed as one of *Good Housekeeping*'s "327 Best Mental Health Experts." He is the 1995 recipient of the Wilfred C. Hulse Memorial Award from the New York Council on Child and Adolescent Psychiatry for his outstanding contribution to the treatment of psychiatrically ill youngsters.

Dr. Koplewicz is a well-respected teacher. He has lectured at both scientific and parent/teacher forums nationally and internationally. He has made frequent appearances on radio and television, including *Good Morning America, Donahue,* and *CBS This Morning.* Dr. Koplewicz lives in Manhattan with his wife and their three young sons.